How America Stacks Up
Economic Competitiveness and U.S. Policy

D1279595

COUNCIL*on*
FOREIGN
RELATIONS

Edward Alden and Rebecca Strauss

How America Stacks Up
Economic Competitiveness
and U.S. Policy

Contents

Introduction

American leadership in the world is built on the foundation of its economic strength. In order to preserve its own national security, to play a leading role in maintaining the global order, and to set an example of successful democratic governance that other countries will want to emulate, the United States needs a healthy, growing economy. Yet the United States today faces enormous economic competition abroad and policy challenges at home in responding to that competition. During the 2000s, U.S. manufacturing lost ground in international markets and the United States became less attractive as a location for foreign investment. The Great Recession led to a surge in both short-term and long-term unemployment from which the economy is only now recovering. With the brief exception of the late 1990s, wage growth for most workers has been weak for decades. Yet the U.S. economy also has enormous strengths, from its world-class universities to its deep venture capital markets, and it has given birth to many of the world's most dynamic and successful companies. Government policies that help build on those strengths while addressing some of the growing weaknesses are needed to ensure that the United States becomes an even more competitive economy and continues to create the prosperity at home that allows for a robust national defense and an outward-looking, engaged foreign policy.

CFR's Renewing America initiative—from which this book arose—has focused on those areas of economic policy that are the most important for reinforcing America's competitive strengths. Education, corporate tax policy, and infrastructure, for example, are issues that historically have been considered largely matters of domestic policy. Yet in a highly competitive global economy, an educated workforce, a competitive tax structure, and an efficient transportation network are all crucial to attracting investment and delivering goods and services that can succeed in global markets. The line between domestic economic policy and foreign economic policy is in many cases now almost invisible. Building a more competitive economy for the future requires that our political leaders—not just in Congress and the White House but also in state and local governments—understand how their policy choices can affect the choices of companies that can now invest almost anywhere in the world.

Getting these choices right matters for more than just U.S. living standards. The United States' ability to influence world events rests on a robust, competitive economy; if Americans lack confidence in their economic future, a less confident, more inward-looking America is likely to follow. The good news is that many of the obstacles to building a more competitive economy are well understood, and while the United States has lost ground in some areas, the measures needed to reverse those losses are not that difficult to conceive or to implement. During the 2012 U.S. presidential elections, Australia's foreign minister famously said that, given its many strengths—from increasing energy independence to its relatively young workforce—the United States "is just one budget deal away from banishing all talk of American decline." The chapters that follow suggest that, while the challenges may be somewhat larger than that, the right policy responses are certainly well within reach.

THE BUILDING BLOCKS OF A COMPETITIVE ECONOMY

Any discussion of whether the U.S. economy is competitive raises obvious questions. Competitive with whom? And in what? In its first report to President Barack Obama in 2011, the President's Jobs and Competitiveness Council, which was chaired by General Electric Chief Executive Officer (CEO) Jeffrey Immelt, wrote, "Top global business leaders continually benchmark their operations against the best in the world in order to improve. On competitiveness, the United States should benchmark its performance as well." Some high-profile efforts have been made to do just this. The World Economic Forum (WEF), which hosts the annual Davos summit, has developed its Global Competitiveness Index, which ranks countries using an elaborate formula that assesses 123 variables over twelve "pillars" such as a country's government institutions and its macroeconomic environment, as well as infrastructure, education, and technological sophistication. The good news for the United States is that, after falling as low as seventh behind such countries as Germany, Switzerland, Finland, and Singapore, it rose back to third in the most recent report, behind Switzerland and Singapore. But though the WEF report is valuable in highlighting the strengths and weaknesses of different economies, it has limited utility for policymakers. What was missing was a deeper comparative look at some of the capacities that go into making economies more or less competitive and an assessment of where the United States stands in these areas.

To help in developing such benchmarks, the Council on Foreign Relations started a new series of comparative publications called the Renewing America Progress Report and Scorecard series. Each installment took a deep dive into how the United States is measuring up against similar economies across a host of challenges pertinent to a high-functioning economy. The reports sometimes compared the United States with developing economies like China or Brazil, or with smaller economies like Denmark or Finland, but the most relevant comparisons are with other large advanced economies. Where, in other words, does U.S. performance stand alongside similar industrialized economies such as Germany, Japan, the United Kingdom (UK), France, and Canada? What can the United States learn from these countries, and they from the United States?

Many things, of course, go into making a competitive economy, from the quality of its corporate management to the smooth functioning of capital markets. The goal in this initiative was to focus on the role of government in creating the conditions for a more competitive economy. CFR therefore decided to look in detail at eight issues that are at the center of the debate over U.S. economic competitiveness.

Education. Human capital is perhaps the most important long-term driver of an economy. Smart workers are more productive and innovative. Yet the United States has fallen behind many other countries in moving its students successfully through school and college, and in particular has seen a huge achievement gap open between children from wealthier families and children from poorer families. Alone among those of other developed nations, the generation entering the U.S. labor force today is no more educated than the one that is retiring.

Transportation infrastructure. Roads, bridges, and rail lines are the arteries of an economy, allowing goods to move domestically and to international markets, and allowing people to get to and from work in an efficient manner. The current U.S. road and transportation system is only of average quality compared to those in other advanced economies.

And while the United States should be spending more to improve and expand its transportation infrastructure, it barely spends enough to maintain the existing network, even as the population continues to grow. Traffic congestion is now twice as bad as it was in the early 1980s.

International trade and investment. The United States depends far more on the global economy than it did two decades ago, and international trade and foreign investment are increasingly vital to U.S. prosperity. Yet on most measures of trade and investment performance—including the growth of exports and its ability to attract foreign investment—the United States remains in the middle of the pack among advanced economies. The good news is that the U.S. trade agenda, including the recent Trans-Pacific Partnership (TPP) agreement with Japan and ten other Pacific Rim countries, and the Transatlantic Trade and Investment Partnership (TTIP) negotiations with Europe, is the most far-reaching in two decades and could reinforce U.S. competitive advantages.

Corporate tax. Corporate tax rates play a big role in encouraging or discouraging companies from investing in the U.S. economy. The U.S. government, however, has not significantly revised its corporate tax rules since the mid-1980s. The result is that, though the United States once had among the lowest corporate tax rates in the industrialized world, it now has the highest. Most advanced countries have been lowering corporate tax rates and changing how they tax foreign profits. Worse, even with the rich world's highest corporate tax rate, the United States does not raise as much corporate tax revenue as most other rich countries. This is because U.S. tax rules perversely encourage companies to invest offshore and to move profits offshore whenever possible so that taxes payable to the U.S. government can be deferred indefinitely.

Worker retraining. The United States has long had one of the world's most dynamic and flexible job markets, with new jobs being both destroyed and created at a pace few other economies can match. But in the aftermath of the Great Recession, many more workers have faced crippling long-term unemployment. Although unemployment has fallen, the labor force participation is still the lowest in more than three decades. Ineffective worker-assistance policies slow economic recovery, leading to skills shortages for employers and hurting U.S. competitiveness. Many other advanced economies invest more in worker retraining and use more innovative programs to help workers return to the job market.

Regulation. Government regulations are increasingly costly for U.S. businesses, and especially for small businesses, even though they do not appear to pose a competitive disadvantage for U.S. companies relative to those based in other advanced economies. The American public is deeply divided over whether businesses face too many regulations, and Republicans and small-business leaders have grown more concerned over the course of the Obama presidency. Yet when asked about specific regulations, such as standards on air quality, fuel efficiency, or workplace safety, most Americans favor the status quo. Compared with some other advanced economies, however, the U.S. government does a poor job of reviewing the stock of existing regulations and altering or eliminating those that no longer make sense.

Government debt and deficits. The U.S. government faces unsustainable long-term debt, which has already crowded out investments in education, infrastructure, and scientific research that are needed to maintain U.S. economic competitiveness. And the problem will get worse. In 2000, the United States had less debt in relation to its economic output than most other advanced economies, but by 2015 it had nearly caught up to the average. The good news is that U.S. annual budget deficits have fallen from highs of nearly 10 percent of gross domestic product (GDP) in 2009–2012 as a result of the Great Recession to about 3 percent of GDP currently. But the debt burden will grow rapidly again in about a decade as entitlement spending rises with the aging population. By 2040, the U.S. debt-to-GDP ratio is projected to reach unprecedented peacetime levels, and the U.S. government has yet to take the steps needed to change that trajectory.

Innovation. The United States is well ahead of other advanced economies in technological innovation, which drives rising living standards in rich countries. Although China and some other developing countries are ramping up research and development (R&D) and graduating many more scientists and engineers than a decade ago, they remain far behind the United States in combining innovation quality and quantity. There are challenges; the United States is underinvesting in basic scientific research, and its patent and immigration systems are discouraging innovation. A successful innovation system is a complex web that requires substantial investment and brings together businesses, universities, and human capital. Few countries are seriously challenging the United States in any of those areas. U.S. government policy, though not without flaws, deserves credit for creating a nurturing innovation environment and for directly promoting innovation where the private market cannot.

WHERE DOES THE UNITED STATES STAND?

Given the broad range of policies that affect the competitiveness of the U.S. economy, the conclusions of these reports do not lead to easy judgments about whether the United States is becoming more competitive or less compared with other advanced economies. But it is still possible to draw some broad judgments about where the United States is leading and lagging, and—just as importantly—on where effective policy could make the biggest difference.

Self-inflicted wounds. The two issues on which the policy choices appear easiest, and the failure to act most puzzling, are transportation infrastructure and corporate tax reform. Congress has grappled with these issues unsuccessfully for many years. The United States has failed to maintain, let alone expand with the growing population, its network of roads, bridges, rail lines, and mass transit. Infrastructure has been woefully underfunded despite years of historically low interest rates that have made it almost cost-free to invest in long-term projects. While the new highway bill passed by Congress at the end of 2015 at least ensures stable funding for five years, it falls well short of the country's needs and relies on one-off funding gimmicks to cover the costs. Simple fixes, such as a small increase in the gas tax to finance new construction or a $10 billion seed fund to launch a National Infrastructure Bank to leverage private investments, have been beyond the reach of a divided Congress.

Corporate tax reform should not be that difficult either. The high U.S. corporate tax rate makes the United States less attractive for investment. U.S.-headquartered multinational companies have managed largely to offset the corporate tax burden by investing and holding cash offshore, and by shifting profits to lower-tax jurisdictions to avoid U.S. taxes. Many sensible proposals have been put forward that would lower the tax rate, discourage this sort of tax maneuvering, and increase incentives for companies to invest in the United States. But as with all tax reform, there will be winners and losers in the corporate sector and some will win more than others. Congress simply needs to stand up to the opposition and move forward.

Hard trade-offs. Other issues present more difficult public policy choices. Government regulation, for example, involves a genuine trade-off between health, safety, and environmental benefits, on the one hand, and costs to business, which could reduce the competitiveness of the U.S. economy, on the other. Finding the right balance is difficult. The federal deficit, which ballooned during the Great Recession before returning to more normal levels, is nonetheless on a trajectory to grow out of control as baby boomers begin retiring in large numbers. Closing that gap will require some unpleasant mixture of higher taxes and reduced benefits. The encouraging aspect of both these challenges, however, is that they are easier than they might appear. The biggest business complaint about regulations is not that they are necessarily unreasonable but that they are too numerous, overly complex, and often redundant. If the United States followed countries such as Australia, Canada, and the UK in creating a sensible regulatory management system, these complaints could be addressed. On the long-term debt picture, countries like Germany, France, and Italy face much bigger challenges than the United States: an older workforce and fewer young people entering the labor market. Yet, unlike the United States, they have been able to reduce projected spending on entitlements to levels that are likely sustainable in the long run.

Long-term challenges. Some problems are genuinely difficult, and improvements come slowly and incrementally. Such is certainly the case with education. The United States is more than two decades along in a serious experiment in educational reform driven by Washington, and encouraging signs of progress are evident. But the U.S. education system is big and complex, and control is divided among the fifty states and many private institutions. Even without the contentious debates over testing, charter schools, and student debt, progress would at best be slow, with ongoing disagreements over what is working and what is not. Retraining workers for available jobs should be easier, but here, too, understanding about what works and what does not is weak. Some of the unemployed need to develop specialized skills of the sort that can be taught in community colleges, but others need the most basic remediation in math and reading. In a rapidly changing economy, upgrading the skills of workers to match available jobs is an ongoing challenge. Here the United States has much to learn from leaders such as Germany and Denmark.

Natural advantages. Fortunately, in some areas the challenge is not to remake failing policies but to build on the advantages that the United States already enjoys. The two issues in which this is clearest are innovation and international trade. On innovation, the United States has no peer—no other country has created anything like the number and variety of highly innovative, technology-intensive firms such as Apple, Google, and Microsoft. And no other country has the rich variety of universities to drive research and the deep venture capital markets to fund new ideas. The challenge here is to keep investing and to fix problems as they arise in order to maintain U.S. advantages. On trade and investment, U.S. performance does not stand out quite so clearly, but the potential is enormous. A recent report by the Boston Consulting Group found that the United States was a better bet for investment in manufacturing than any other advanced economy in the world. If the United States can successfully conclude the TPP and the TTIP, it will be well placed to build and attract the internationally competitive industries of the future.

NEXT STEPS FORWARD

This book includes revised and updated research on each of these issues to present readers with as current a picture as possible of where the United States stands in these policy areas. The updated infographics offer a visual presentation of important conclusions on each of the challenges. They provide an easily accessible resource for anyone interested in the competitive performance of the U.S. economy, or in the particular issues raised here. Casual observers can scan the infographic images to get the highlights; others will want to delve more deeply into the details.

As the 2016 presidential election campaign heats up, this short collection can serve as a quick reference to some of the policy challenges that are likely to be front and center in the coming election-year debates. Each of these issues is about America's future: Is the United States laying the foundation to build a stronger and more productive economy that will offer better jobs and opportunities to the next generation? And is the United States nurturing the economic capabilities that have allowed the nation not only to ensure its own defense, but also to play a leading role on the global stage? The answer to both questions needs to be yes.

Remedial Education: Federal Education Policy

INTRODUCTION

The U.S. education system is not as internationally competitive as it used to be. The rest of the developed world is catching up, and some countries are surpassing the United States in high school and college completion, all while spending much less per student. The United States compares especially poorly with its low pre-kindergarten (pre-K) enrollment rate and its high college dropout rate. But the real scourge of the U.S. education system—and its greatest competitive weakness—is the deep and growing achievement gap between socioeconomic groups that begins early and lasts through a student's academic career.

Human capital is perhaps the single most important long-term driver of an economy. Smarter workers are more productive and innovative. It is an economist's rule that an increase of one year in a country's average schooling level corresponds to an increase of 3 to 4 percent in long-term economic growth.[1] Most of the value added in the modern global economy is now knowledge-based. Education, especially at the college level, will therefore likely become even more important for a nation's economy and an individual's income. And to the extent that labor markets now transcend national borders, the international competition for those high-value knowledge jobs will only grow more fierce.

The federal role in the U.S. education system, from pre-K through college, has historically been to help disadvantaged students. The tight grip of socioeconomic status has been increasingly hindering students' achievement, making the federal government's role more urgent than ever.

The Obama administration has set an ambitious education agenda. Early in his first term, President Obama pledged that by 2020 the United States "will once again have the highest proportion of college graduates in the world."[2] He has called for universal pre-K and free community college. His 2009 stimulus package tripled the Department of Education's spending in a single year, an increase larger than for any other federal agency. His education initiatives at the pre-K, kindergarten through twelfth grade (K–12), and postsecondary levels have all focused on developing and using smarter quality evaluation and accountability systems, which are intended to help the disadvantaged while trying to keep costs under control.

But more needs to be done. Expanding pre-K enrollment will cost more money. The main K–12 funding stream for low-income students, which has seen huge cuts from sequestration, should be ramped up and better targeted. Where federal education costs have gotten most out of control—student aid for postsecondary education—is also where there is the least accountability for results. And the biggest changes made to federal postsecondary policy—new debt forgiveness and tax breaks—have further tilted a playing field that already favored wealthier students, all at a steep cost to taxpayers.

WHERE THE UNITED STATES STANDS

The United States is losing its international lead in educational attainment. Among people aged fifty-five to sixty-four in Organization for Economic Cooperation and Development (OECD) countries, Americans rank first in high school completion and in postsecondary completion.[3] Among people aged twenty-five to thirty-four, Americans rank twelfth in both. Other countries are raising their high school and college attainment; the United States is not.

Younger Americans are not making significant gains on their elders. Unique among developed nations, the generation entering the U.S. labor force is not more educated than the one exiting.[4] In one respect, the entering generation may be less educated. The current high school completion rate masks a growing trend toward high school equivalency degrees (e.g., GEDs). Workers with these credentials earn incomes similar to those of high school dropouts (see figure 1).[5]

Compared internationally, the United States lags at the beginning of the educational track, in pre-K enrollment, and also at the end, in postsecondary on-time completion.

Although enrollment in pre-K programs has been expanding, nearly doubling in the past decade, it is far from universal in the United

FIGURE 1. U.S. HIGH SCHOOL AND POSTSECONDARY COMPLETION RATE,
BY AGE

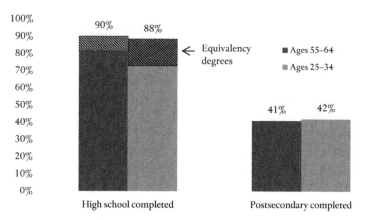

Source: OECD (2014); National Center for Education Statistics (2015).

States. In much of the rest of the developed world, universal pre-K is
the standard. Nearly all four-year-olds in the United Kingdom, France,
Germany, and Japan are enrolled in preschool.[6] Korea recently passed
legislation mandating universal preschool. Yet only 66 percent of U.S.
four-year-olds are enrolled in a preschool program.

The United States is relatively good at getting its high school graduates into postsecondary education, but not at getting them to graduate
with a postsecondary degree. Enrollment is up. In 1980, only 50 percent of high school graduates went on to some postsecondary institution within two years.[7] Now close to 70 percent do. But the likelihood
that an enrolled college student will graduate on time is down. Nearly
half of students who enroll have not graduated six years later—a worse
on-time graduation rate than in 1980.[8] The United States has an above-
average postsecondary enrollment rate, but it also has the highest dropout rate in the developed world.[9]

TEST SCORES: SMALL GAINS DOMESTICALLY,
BUT MEDIOCRE WHEN COMPARED INTERNATIONALLY

Measured by test scores, U.S. student achievement has been mediocre. National Assessment of Education Progress (NAEP) scores—the

standard for measuring U.S. student achievement over time—are higher than ever. The gains, however, have been small and concentrated at the elementary level and mostly in math, and in 2015, for the first time in decades, elementary math scores slipped.[10] On international tests in core subject areas, U.S. K–12 students consistently score on or slightly below average compared with their developed-world peers. But U.S. students score well in confidence surveys—a trait that has downsides, but also one that correlates strongly with entrepreneurship.

EXPENDITURES: ADEQUATE TOTAL SPENDING, WITH FLAT OR DECLINING PUBLIC SPENDING MORE RECENTLY

The United States spends plenty of money on its education system, which includes public and private expenditures. Given its relative wealth, U.S. per-pupil spending on K–12 education is roughly on track with the rest of the OECD.[11] On postsecondary education, however, the United States spends lavishly: two-thirds more than the OECD average.

U.S. education money is spent differently as well. Compared with other developed countries, it spends less on direct instructional expenses and more on school buildings and grounds, extracurricular activities, and student career and counseling services.

Like most service industries, the U.S. education system has historically suffered from low productivity. One symptom of this is cost growth without matched improvement in quality. Until the recent recession, public K–12 per-pupil spending had been on a steady increase, having nearly doubled in real terms since 1980.[12] Budget cuts have struck public colleges harder: state per-pupil spending has fallen by nearly one-third since 2000 and is now lower than it was in the 1980s.[13] More of the cost burden is being shifted to individual students in the form of sharply rising tuition (see figure 2).

U.S. students pay the highest tuition in the world.[14] Adjusted for inflation, average tuition and fees charged to students at public four-year colleges has increased 231 percent since 1984, with the steepest increase in the past five years.[15] The increase in student debt has been just as steep. Total student debt now constitutes more than $1 trillion, recently surpassing total U.S. credit card debt. It is a debt burden the equally college-educated cohort aged fifty-five to sixty-four never faced.

FIGURE 2. STATE APPROPRIATIONS PER FULL-TIME STUDENT VERSUS
TUITION AND FEES AT FOUR-YEAR PUBLIC COLLEGES

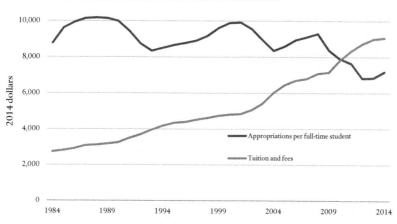

Source: College Board (2015).

THE BIGGEST PROBLEM IN THE U.S. EDUCATION SYSTEM:
INEQUALITY IN SPENDING AND OUTCOMES

This is the U.S. education story told only with national averages. Parse the averages, and a new, compelling story emerges that gets to the heart of the real crisis of U.S. education: stratification in spending and achievement by race and especially income.

There are areas of excellence in U.S. education. If ranked internationally as nations, Massachusetts and Minnesota would be among the top six performers in fourth-grade math and science.[16] Among fifteen-year-olds, Asian Americans are the world's best readers and white Americans are third only to Finns and New Zealanders.[17] A higher share of U.S. students takes more demanding math and science courses now than in 1990.[18] The U.S. postsecondary system includes eight of the world's top ten universities.[19] The most selective colleges have seen their dropout rates fall to record lows. U.S. dominance in Nobel Prize winners is unrivaled. In a Harvard Business School alumni survey, high-quality universities were rated the country's chief competitive advantage.[20]

The problem is that such excellence is not extended to huge swaths of U.S. society. Everyone—black, white, rich, and poor—is testing better and gaining greater access to college than the previous generation.[21] But rich students are making bigger gains than everyone else. The achievement gap on standardized tests between high- and low-income students is 75 percent wider today than when baby boomers were in school.[22] Strikingly, these gaps exist when children first begin elementary school, are locked in place all the way through high school, and are carried over to the postsecondary level.[23] The influence of parental wealth on student achievement is stronger in the United States than anywhere else in the developed world.[24]

In the fierce competition to attend high-quality colleges, wealthy Americans have an advantage during the admissions process. They are becoming more concentrated in the best schools. Students from families in the highest income quintile are eight times more likely to enroll in a highly selective college than students in the bottom quintile, a gap that has widened over time.[25] Even though all income levels are increasingly more likely to graduate with a bachelor's degree, the rich have a growing lead.[26]

Race is not the barrier to academic success that it used to be. Indeed, wealthy black students with strong academic backgrounds are actually *more* likely to go to an elite college than equally wealthy and qualified white students.[27] In reality, however, this is a rare occurrence, given that wealth correlates so strongly with race. As a whole, blacks are less likely to go to highly selective colleges now than in the 1980s.[28] Low-income students, and therefore also disadvantaged minorities, are more and more concentrated in community colleges and lower-tier schools.

Unequal investments are part of the reason for unequal outcomes. This inequality begins in one's childhood: wealthy and better-educated parents invest more time and money in their children's early development—more even than in past generations, since the research has grown more definitive about the importance of pre-K cognitive enrichment.

Unequal investment continues at the K–12 level. The United States has wide funding disparities in large part because most revenues to pay for K–12 public schools are raised by local property taxes. For the majority of OECD countries, more resources are invested per pupil in lower-income districts than in higher-income districts. The reverse is true in the United States.[29]

Unequal investments also exist at the college level. Since the 1960s, annual per-pupil spending at the most selective public and private colleges has increased at twice the rate as at the least selective colleges.[30] In 1967, the difference in real annual per-pupil spending between the most and least selective colleges was $13,500. In 2006, it was $80,000. Money also makes a difference for postsecondary quality and student outcomes. For equally qualified students, the most selective colleges have higher on-time completion rates, and their graduates earn more and are more likely to progress toward an advanced degree.[31]

Community colleges account for most of the nation's decline in postsecondary on-time completion rates. According to one estimate, inadequate resources are to blame for up to two-thirds of that decline.[32] Ranked by the share of its population with bachelor's degrees, the United States is close to the top. Where the United States lags against its competitors is in the sub-bachelor's, or middle-skill, degree fields (e.g., certificates, vocational degrees, or associate's degrees).[33] This is despite the fact that U.S. job growth is projected to be stronger for middle-skill degrees than for high- or low-skill degrees.[34] The postsecondary dropout rate increases with every step down the postsecondary degree ladder. Whereas 59 percent of bachelor's students finish on time, only 29 percent of sub-bachelor's students do so.[35] Every step down the degree ladder, the proportion of the student body that is low-income increases (see figure 3).[36]

Completing college is more crucial than ever for landing a well-paying job. Going back to the 1970s, all net job growth has been in jobs that require at least a postsecondary degree. Postsecondary graduates, whether they hold a vocational certificate or a bachelor's degree, earn more on average and are also less likely to be unemployed than college dropouts and high school graduates.

FIGURE 3. ON-TIME COMPLETION RATE AND PERCENT OF LOW-INCOME STUDENTS BY POSTSECONDARY DEGREE

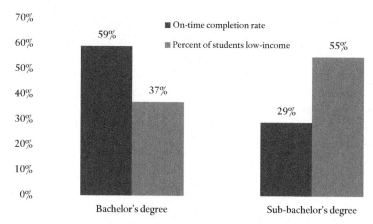

Source: NCES (2015); College Board (2012).

Americans are aware of these opposing trends. Over the 2000s, an increasing share of Americans believed a college degree was necessary for a person to be successful in today's world, and a decreasing share believed that qualified and motivated students had the opportunity to obtain a college degree.[37] In a 2014 survey, 96 percent said it was somewhat or very important to have a degree beyond high school, but only 21 percent thought getting one was affordable.[38]

The challenge for the U.S. education system is to weaken the link between income and achievement and push more low-income and disadvantaged minority students through high school and on to postsecondary completion—all while keeping already high education costs and postsecondary tuition under control.

THE PRE-K SYSTEM

Enrollment in pre-K education in the United States is low by international standards but climbing quickly. The biggest change has been in the growth of state-run pre-K programs, most of which are means-tested. Since 1980, the number of states offering such programs rose from eight to forty-one, and today one-third of the nation's four-year-olds are in enrolled in state programs.[39] Roughly one-quarter of four-year-olds are enrolled in no program.[40]

THE BENEFITS OF PRE-K

High-quality preschool programs raise achievement for all students.[41] The effect is largest on the most disadvantaged. In model preschool programs using intensive instruction techniques, at-risk students were less likely to repeat a grade and more likely to graduate high school, go on to postsecondary education, and, later in life, commit fewer crimes, earn higher wages, and have more stable living arrangements.[42] A conservative estimate for the return on these model programs is three dollars in benefits for every dollar invested.[43]

FEDERAL ROLE IN PRE-K

The federal government's role in pre-K varies. It directly pays for and regulates a preschool program for low-income children called Head

Start. It also gives subsidies to states and low-income parents to help pay for child care and also gives families of all incomes a tax credit for child-care expenses.

Head Start for low-income children. The federal government's largest and best-known early childhood program, Head Start, is targeted at low-income children. Launched in 1965 as part of President Lyndon B. Johnson's Great Society reforms, Head Start was the first public pre-K program in the country. Initially, it was a summer catch-up program run by local agencies to prepare four-year-olds at or below the poverty line for kindergarten. Over time, Head Start expanded dramatically—incorporating three-year-olds, adding full-year and full-day programs, easing income eligibility requirements, and offering more wraparound health and social services. Head Start now serves close to one million children, or 10 percent of all four-year-olds.

Assessments of Head Start have been mixed. A 2010 federal study found that immediate cognitive or IQ gains were small and had faded by the end of first grade.[44] It may be too early to come to definitive conclusions. The first randomized Head Start trial survey only began in 2002, so it is too soon to capture longer-term achievement, social, and behavioral effects that have been linked to Head Start in other analyses.[45] But there is a consensus that there is too much variation in quality among Head Start programs. With an annual federal cost of roughly $8 billion, it is also expensive. Although no other program is directly comparable, some state pre-K programs (e.g., Oklahoma's) have shown more substantial immediate cognitive gains for a wider population and a comparable price.[46] Access could be better as well; nearly half of Head Start's targeted population is not being served by any pre-K program.[47]

Child-care subsidies for low-income families. The main federal child-care subsidy for low-income families, the Child Care and Development Fund, gives block grants to states that can then be spent on child-care centers and programs for low-income families or turned into vouchers for those families to seek out child-care programs.

The problem is that the kind of child care low-income parents buy with their subsidies is generally of questionable quality, often more akin to babysitting in a safe environment than a cognitively enriching experience. On average, children gain more from Head Start and other public pre-K programs.[48] But quality could soon improve because of tightening federal regulations. Beginning in 2016, programs accepting subsidies will have to meet some licensing, health, and safety requirements, and states will have to spend more money on monitoring the programs' quality.

Child-care tax credits for all families. Federal child-care tax credits are available to all families. The principal tax credit is the Child and Dependent Care Tax Credit. But credits can be claimed only if an individual owes taxes, and poor Americans generally do not. Only if a tax benefit is refundable—meaning it can be paid out to a recipient with or without a tax payment to the Internal Revenue Service (IRS)—do the poor reap any gain. The child-care tax credit is nonrefundable, so more than 60 percent of child-care tax credits go to the richest 40 percent of families.[49]

OBAMA'S PRE-K AGENDA: FOCUSING ON QUALITY

Under the Obama administration, federal reforms are trying to leverage more quality out of the country's pre-K system without increasing baseline funding or expanding Head Start access. Real, baseline pre-K funding, including tax credits, has essentially remained unchanged, with a modest onetime boost from the stimulus. Compared with other discretionary spending priorities under sequestration, pre-K has fared reasonably well.

Reforms are in the works to improve Head Start. Studies are not conclusive about what makes pre-K programs effective, but teacher quality is believed to be essential. Model programs generally use well-trained and well-compensated staff in intensive educational instruction with small student-teacher ratios. By 2014, half of all Head Start teachers were required to hold bachelor's degrees. The lowest-performing Head Start programs have been forced to "recompete" for funding, using a new teacher evaluation based on in-class observations.

The stimulus package created a new competitive grant program for states called the Race to the Top Early Learning Challenge.[50] Proposals were judged based on whether they would expand access to high-quality pre-K programs for low-income children, integrate public and private programs into a cohesive system, and build robust program evaluation systems for better quality control. The program was especially good at pushing more states to adopt the Quality Rating and Improve-ment System, which evaluates and publishes assessments of child-care centers for parents. Many states have also been developing their own evaluation systems to make themselves more competitive in the grant-application process.

ASSESSING FEDERAL PRE-K POLICIES

Focusing attention and resources on pre-K quality—and systems for monitoring that quality— could do much for low- and middle-income children, whose parents cannot hope to afford private programs. Given that the nation's pre-K system is still in its infancy, at least compared with the K–12 and postsecondary systems, there is much less regulation and information for consumers about what kind of care they are buying.

Ultimately, the end goal for federal—as well as state and local—policy should be universal pre-K, with checks in place to ensure some level of standards across the country. Most developed countries either have or are on their way to having universal pre-K. For the United States, it might make the most sense to fold pre-K, including Head Start, into the existing K–12 public school system, as kindergarten was in the 1970s.

The politics have never looked brighter for universal pre-K. Demo-cratic and Republican state governors are embracing it in principle. In his 2013 State of the Union address, President Obama called for high-quality pre-K for all four-year-olds, and his budget proposals call for a funding boost for Head Start. But thus far, little has changed to expand access to pre-K, perhaps because universal pre-K would cost more. And for all the supportive rhetoric coming from state politicians, states are backtracking on their pre-K spending; per-pupil expenditures have been declining since 2002.[51]

In the short term, the focus should be on getting low-income chil-dren into the best possible child-care and pre-K programs, whether that means expanding Head Start or helping parents spend their federal child-care subsidies on better programs. Low-income children have the most to gain from pre-K. It is where, if programs are well designed for cognitive enrichment, the education buck garners the biggest bang, and it is indispensable for narrowing the chasm in academic achievement that currently exists from day one of kindergarten and follows students for a lifetime.

Remedial Education
Federal Education Policy

Weak Report Card

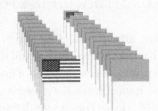

High School	College

1ST   **12**TH   **1**ST   **12**TH

Ages 55-64   Ages 25-34   Ages 55-64   Ages 25-34

U.S. ranking, worldwide, educational attainment

The United States used to lead the world in educational
attainment, but has fallen behind.

Preschool enrollment rate   College dropout rate

66% 83%   **47% 32%**

United States versus the developed world

Compared to the rest of the developed world, the United
States has a low preschool enrollment rate and a high
college dropout rate.

THE K–12 SYSTEM

Unlike pre-K and postsecondary education, public K–12 education is free and available to all students, with taxpayers footing the entire bill. Enrollment in K–12 is mandatory and therefore generally universal. The vast majority (89 percent) of school-age students are enrolled in public schools, with the rest mostly in private schools.[52]

FEDERAL ROLE IN K–12: TITLE I AND IDEA FUNDING TO SUPPORT DISADVANTAGED STUDENTS

The federal government is legally forbidden from forcing schools to adopt specific curricula, standards, or tests. Such matters are constitutionally delegated to states and local school districts.

Historically, the federal government's role in K–12 education has been to expand access and funding support for disadvantaged children. That role began in earnest in the 1960s with legislation and court cases mandating that public schools serve all races, and then in the 1970s that they serve all special-needs children. Federal funding streams were created to help local school districts fulfill these duties— Title I for low-income students and Individuals with Disabilities Education Act (IDEA) grants for special-needs students. These funds are distributed to school districts based on the number of disadvantaged students they serve. The reach and scale of both funding streams have expanded over time. The terms of eligibility for Title I grants have also been gradually ratcheted down so that nearly all school districts receive some amount. The federal government now shoulders about 12 percent of national K–12 funding, most of it through Title I and IDEA grants.[53]

BUSH-ERA NO CHILD LEFT BEHIND: PUSHING FOR ACCOUNTABILITY

It was not until the 2001 No Child Left Behind (NCLB) Act that the federal government used Title I to shape the direction of education policy beyond expanding access for all. With NCLB, Title I money became contingent on student achievement. NCLB continued the longstanding federal role of helping the disadvantaged, but it came with unprecedented funding penalties—the loss of Title I money—if schools failed to eliminate achievement gaps among the disadvantaged. NCLB also cast the accountability net wider to include all students, regardless of income or disability status.

It was a tidal shift in federal education policy, passing with overwhelming bipartisan support in Congress. The broadly shared sense was that increased K–12 education costs had not significantly improved achievement. Accountability for results, it was believed, would force schools into action and raise achievement.

According to the new law, all students had to be "proficient" in reading and math within twelve years. States defined their own proficiency levels and designed accompanying standardized tests that were administered annually for grades three through eight. School scores were reported by subgroup (e.g., race, income, disability status) and measured against an Annual Yearly Progress (AYP) metric, which indicated whether a school was on schedule for making the 100 percent proficiency target by 2014. For each successive year a school failed to make AYP, it faced increasingly severe consequences. After four years, corrective action would be taken against the school, which could mean dismissal of staff, closure, or reconstitution as a charter school.

A decade later, both political parties were equally disappointed with NCLB. The accountability system was poorly constructed and hardly affected achievement. The absolute definition of failure (i.e., making or not making AYP) lumped together schools that had made some progress on test scores with schools that had made no progress at all. An entire school would fail if any subgroup missed the mark. The proficiency goals and timeframe were unrealistic, and even some of the nation's highest-achieving schools in wealthy districts were failing to make AYP. No states were on track to meet their proficiency goals. A National Academy of Sciences report concluded that NCLB's test-based accountability may have led to tiny gains in achievement, but nothing transformative as the law's architects had hoped.[54] In instances where a school did make remarkable progress, far too often cheating and score manipulation were later uncovered.

After years of gridlock, Congress finally replaced NLCB in late 2015 with the Every Student Succeeds Act (ESSA). It softens the hard edges of NCLB. States will still have to test and monitor their students and also have some kind of accountability system—but each state will be free to decide what that accountability system looks like, with no federally imposed automatic penalty triggers.

OBAMA-ERA NO CHILD LEFT BEHIND:
WAIVERS FOR CONFORMING TO THE OBAMA AGENDA

Before the passage of ESSA, President Obama allowed states to set new proficiency goals and apply for waivers from the strictest provisions of NCLB, including meeting AYP requirements—but only if states adopted Obama's policy guidelines in their waivers, which most did. Under the waivers, some Bush-era hallmarks remained, including accountability through standardized testing and charter schools as a corrective-action option. But in a change of course, teachers, rather than schools, were held accountable for student test scores, and reform efforts shifted to focus on only the worst-performing schools.

THE OBAMA EDUCATION AGENDA: BETTER-CALIBRATED
ACCOUNTABILITY AND INNOVATING FOR QUALITY

The Obama administration continued the Bush administration's broad commitment to accountability as a way to ensure some basic level of quality while controlling costs. The administration has been creating a more workable K–12 education accountability system, which better measures education quality and more efficiently focuses resources on the worst-performing schools while also nurturing promising innovations that improve education quality. These efforts were centered on four pillars: improving teacher evaluation and effectiveness; expanding high-quality charter schools; encouraging states to adopt common, college-ready standards; and developing data systems to track student performance. This agenda was largely set by the 2009 stimulus package and its two signature competitive grant programs, Race to the Top (RTTT) and Investing in Innovation (i3).[55]

RACE TO THE TOP AND INVESTING IN INNOVATION

The RTTT program was created by the stimulus bill and funded three rounds of competition. Nearly every state applied. Eighteen won and split more than $4 billion in awarded grants. States had a better chance of winning money if their applications promised to innovate in the four pillars. With so many states in fiscal distress, the prospect of winning relatively small amounts of money led to sweeping changes in state education policies, even in states that did not win grants. Most states enacted reforms to make themselves more competitive for RTTT, from removing caps on the number of charter schools to instituting new teacher evaluation systems.

The stimulus bill also created a much smaller competitive grant program, i3, for research-based innovations that closed achievement gaps. It offered three different-sized grants—large awards for scaling up proven, effective innovations, and smaller grants for testing new ideas. Unlike the state-based RTTT program, the i3 competition required a private funding match and was open to nonprofits that partner with schools.

Innovation pillar: improving teacher evaluation and quality. Outside the home, teacher quality makes the biggest difference in a child's education. Just as in any profession, there should be a way of separating who is doing a good job from who is not.

Headway is being made in designing better teacher performance metrics. Subjective assessments by principals used to be the most common way to evaluate teachers, but principals generally are easy graders; one study found that principals rated only 1 percent of their teachers as "unsatisfactory."[56] Value-added evaluations, which measure student test score gains over the course of a year, have been shown to be a good marker for teacher effectiveness.[57] Such systems, however, are not perfect and are seldom used as the sole factor for high-stakes job decisions. In practice, value-added evaluations are usually combined with assessments by colleagues and principals, allowing for a well-rounded evaluation and helping catch statistical errors or outliers. Encouraged by federal programs and money, more states are experimenting with and adopting value-added evaluations. But using student test scores to grade teachers is not without controversy, and teachers unions are pushing back.

Less headway is being made in figuring out how to improve teacher quality, an undertaking more complex than simply recruiting new teachers with better academic credentials or offering higher salaries. In high-achieving countries, such as Finland, Singapore, and South Korea, teachers come from the top of their high school graduating classes, teaching schools have a high bar for acceptance, and teachers' salaries are competitive with those of lawyers and scientists. It is generally the opposite in the United States.

Grading on a Curve

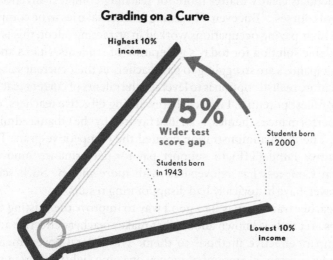

Highest 10%
income

75%
Wider test
score gap

Students born
in 2000

Students born
in 1943

Lowest 10%
income

The test score achievement gap between low- and
high-income students has increased.

Enrolled in College	Completed on Time
29% Lowest income	**9%** Lowest income
10 20 30 40 50 60 70 80 90 100	10 20 30 40 50 60 70 80 90 100
●●●○○○○○○○	●○○○○○○○○○
80% Highest income	**54%** Highest income
10 20 30 40 50 60 70 80 90 100	10 20 30 40 50 60 70 80 90 100
●●●●●●●●○○	●●●●●◐○○○○

30 to 34 year olds

And parental income is strongly correlated with
student achievement.

It is unclear, however, whether more academically talented adults necessarily make better teachers. In the United States, teachers with better academic credentials (e.g., higher SAT scores or holding an advanced degree) on average do not have an edge in raising student test scores.[58] Credentials clearly matter more for teaching complex, advanced high school courses.[59] But even if boosting teacher salaries to be competitive with high-paying occupations worked in attracting talent, this is hardly a scalable solution for today's generation of students. States and local municipalities are struggling to pay teachers at their current salaries.

A more realistic option is to leverage the talents of current teachers to their fullest potential. Financially rewarding effective teachers, or pay-for-performance schemes, is an idea favored by the Obama administration. The Bush administration created the competitive-grant Teacher Incentive Fund (TIF) to support pay-for-performance innovations, which Congress has rejuvenated with more money. Such schemes, however, have historically had disappointing results.[60]

Teacher training may be a good way to improve the existing teacher corps. Yet little is known about what makes teachers effective and how to impart effective methods to them. The federal government does spend a substantial amount of money on some eighty different teacher programs. Most of the money goes to the formula-based Improving Teacher Quality State Grants program (known as Title II) for low-income schools. The program has changed little since the 1960s, and states and local districts spend most of their Title II funds on class-size reduction or anything that falls under the broad rubric of professional development activities.

Several new federal teacher training programs have been launched. Teacher Quality Partnership competitive grants, created in 2008, support innovation in research-based teacher training models and teacher residency programs in which successful, experienced teachers coach novice ones. Top-performing countries tend to use similar peer-to-peer and hands-on training.[61] In 2011, the Department of Education rolled out the Our Future, Our Teachers program to help states and localities evaluate the performance of their teacher training programs.

Innovation pillar: high-quality charter schools. Charter schools are publicly funded but independently managed. They have more flexibility to innovate with management, staffing, curriculum, and teaching techniques. Although their number has exploded in recent years, charter schools are still relatively rare outside cities. Just 4 percent of U.S. K–12 students are enrolled in one, compared to nearly half in Washington, DC, and two-thirds in New Orleans.[62]

On average, charter schools do not outperform public schools nationally.[63] But certain charter models, such as Knowledge Is Power Program (KIPP) schools, with their "no excuses" discipline and longer school days and academic year, have significantly improved test scores for at-risk students in struggling urban school districts.[64] Charter school regulations, which vary from state to state, also appear to make a difference. For example, Massachusetts is known for stringent charter oversight, with authorities quickly stepping in when charters veer off course. Charter schools in Massachusetts tend to be higher quality.[65]

One risk with charter schools is that they take only the most motivated students, leaving the most vulnerable behind and making the local public schools even worse. Charter schools, then, might exacerbate inequality. But high-quality charter schools still have a better track record of improving achievement for at-risk youth than the other major education choice option, vouchers, which allow students to use public money to attend private schools.[66]

Innovation pillar: common college-ready standards. States, with federal support, are leading an effort to develop and use common national standards for English and math—the first time in U.S. history that learning expectations could be the same across the country. These Common Core standards, which are more rigorous than most existing state standards, are designed to prepare students for college, and some states began using them in the 2013–2014 school year. The federal government is doing its part, providing money to the consortia designing the Common Core assessments and favoring state grant applications that promise to adopt them. Initially, the standards were widely popular, and forty-five states and the District of Columbia signed on to use them, though several states have since taken steps to delay implementation or have withdrawn to write their own standards.

The Common Core should bring big efficiency gains. States will no longer waste resources reinventing the curriculum wheel, and scaling up education reforms and innovations will be easier. Such standards, however, are unlikely to lift achievement on their own. High- and low-achieving countries alike use national standards, and the rigor of state standards has historically had little impact on student achievement.[67]

But common standards could form a better basis on which to compare education quality across the country.

Innovation pillar: data systems. Data systems at the state and local levels are essential for measuring and improving education quality. Data-informed classrooms lead to better teaching. Longitudinal data systems that track the same students over their entire academic careers give educators a sense of where most tend to fall behind. Data can also help evaluate teachers, charter schools, and other innovative pedagogical or organizational methods more reliably. Linked up with the Common Core Standards, data systems can show how different parts of the country are performing on a common scale over time, down to neighborhood and subgroup.

ASSESSING FEDERAL K–12 INITIATIVES

Under the Obama administration, federal policy has been retooled to chip away at the achievement gap between low- and high-income students. Low-income schools would be the main beneficiary of policies the administration has advocated, including charter schools and teacher effectiveness, given that low-income districts have difficulty attracting and retaining teacher talent. Other changes still need to be made, notably in modernizing Title II, the biggest federal teacher training program and funding stream.

More could also be done with Title I money, the main federal funding stream for helping low-income students. Little has been done to make the baseline Title I program better funded, targeted, or effectively spent. Most new baseline K–12 federal funding during the Obama administration has been concentrated in comparatively small competitive grant programs, which altogether amounts to less than $2 billion a year. Title I is gargantuan by comparison, funded at $14 billion a year. If federal money is to make any dent in unequal spending in education, it will be from Title I. Yet baseline funding has not been boosted. The stimulus package temporarily doubled Title I and IDEA spending in 2009, but sequestration and budget caps decreased each program's annual baseline funding by nearly 7 percent between 2011 and 2015.[68] Existing Title I regulations could also be streamlined to get rid of loopholes that in many cases make local funding inequalities worse.[69] Moreover, little is known about how Title I money is spent in individual schools, which is where the money has a direct impact on low-income students.

Although states have been given more power and flexibility under recent legislation, the federal government has been pushing for workable accountability systems: trusted and accurate teacher evaluations, common standards for comparison, and data systems holding everything in place. This would help the country come to a better understanding about what value looks like in K–12 education, which is all the more important when fewer resources are available to go around.

THE POSTSECONDARY SYSTEM

Most U.S. postsecondary education also takes place in public institutions, where roughly three-quarters of all undergraduate students are enrolled.[70] Two-year community colleges serve more students (40 percent of undergraduates) than four-year public colleges (36 percent). State and local tax revenues cover the majority of these public institutions' costs, but all still charge tuition. After tremendous growth since 2000, today 8 percent of postsecondary students are enrolled in for-profit institutions. The remaining 16 percent are in private, not-for-profit colleges.

THE FEDERAL ROLE IN POSTSECONDARY EDUCATION: HELPING STUDENTS PAY FOR COLLEGE

The federal government helps students and families cover college costs through long-standing programs such as means-tested grants and subsidized student loans and, more recently, through tax breaks. Nearly all federal postsecondary aid is given to students and their families to purchase services from providers. This contrasts with federal pre-K and K–12 funding support, which is given to education service providers or to states to distribute. Close to half of all full-time undergraduate students receive federal loans or grants.[71] All students and their families can claim tax benefits.

The federal cost of postsecondary student aid and tax expenditures has risen dramatically over the last decade and is roughly twice what the federal government spends on K–12 education.[72] Yet the federal government exerts virtually no control over how students spend their federal financial aid beyond requiring that it be used at accredited institutions.

Remedial Education
Federal Education Policy

Difficult Arithmetic

College   K through 12

U.S. ranking, worldwide, per-student education spending

The United States spends more money than
most countries on its education system.

$13,500

1967

$80,000

2006

Real per-student spending gap between the least
and most selective colleges

But the gap in spending between the least and most
selective colleges has increased.

Pell Grants for low-income students. The Pell Grant program for low-income students evolved in the same era—the mid-1960s—as the other big low-income education programs, Head Start for pre-K and Title I for K–12. With total funding of $31 billion in 2015, Pell Grants are by far the largest federal student grant program and the single largest component of the Department of Education's budget.[73] Students qualify if their family income is under $60,000. Award size varies based on income and tuition costs, but the maximum is $5,775 for 2015–2016. About eight million students received Pell Grants in 2015.

Student loans for all students. Also since the 1960s, the federal government has provided loans at below-market interest rates to all undergraduate and graduate students who may have insufficient collateral, credit, or employment history to qualify for private loans. Stafford loans constitute the vast majority of all federal loans and have an interest rate roughly half of a comparable private loan, and are variable, or pegged to market interest rates.[74] Means-tested subsidized Stafford loans come with a lower interest rate and more flexible repayment terms. Roughly 40 percent of all undergraduate students take out federal loans.[75] In 2015, outstanding federal student loans (both undergraduate and graduate) totaled about $1.1 trillion, with about $100 billion of new federal loans taken out every year.[76] Although graduate students constitute less than 20 percent of all postsecondary enrollment, they shoulder 40 percent of all federal student loan debt.[77] The cost of the federal student loan program fluctuates year to year depending on changes in market interest rates, but the program usually breaks even or earns a profit.

Postsecondary tax benefits for all families. The federal tax code also gives students and their families big tax breaks, which mostly operate on sliding income scales. There is a tuition-and-fees deduction that reduces taxable income. Parents can open a college savings account that appreciates tax-free. The main higher education tax credit program, the American Opportunity Tax Credit (AOTC), was created with the 2009 stimulus to replace a less-generous program and extended benefits to upper middle–income families. In 2015, postsecondary tax benefits cost the federal government $32 billion.[78]

PRESIDENT OBAMA'S POSTSECONDARY AGENDA

Over President Obama's first term, federal student aid increased, and the expansion has benefited higher-income students the most. Costs have risen a great deal; total federal baseline spending on postsecondary education, including appropriations and tax expenditures, has more than doubled since he first entered office. This is the reverse for pre-K, which has remained mostly flat, and for K–12, which saw big cuts from sequestration.

At the same time, the Obama administration is spearheading the first serious attempt at making the postsecondary schools that are most dependent on federal aid, and that are most likely to serve low-income students, more accountable for education quality and value. In so doing, the federal government has for the first time defined *good value*, measuring the cost of a program against how well a program's graduates fare in the labor market. In addition, President Obama has championed community colleges.

More federal student aid, especially for higher-income students. Since 2008, the number of Pell Grant recipients has increased by one-third, driven mostly by a weakened economy. More students qualified because their incomes fell, and more students were pushed out of the labor market and into college. The maximum grant amount has been raised. The costs of the program have therefore risen sharply, with annual baseline funding nearly twice the amount it was a decade ago.[79]

In response to skyrocketing costs, Pell availability has been cut. Early on in the Obama administration, Congress loosened income eligibility and introduced a summer and full-year Pell Grant program. Since 2010, as a cost-saving measure, the expansions were rolled back and a new cap on lifetime eligibility has been put in place, disproportionately affecting nontraditional students. Even with the recent award increase, Pell Grants cover a smaller share of a student's college expenses than they did in the 1970s.

Where student aid policy has become more generous—such as debt repayment and forgiveness—the benefits will overwhelmingly go to higher-income students. For students enrolled in the Income-Based Repayment Plan, Congress lowered the monthly cap on student loan payments from 15 to 10 percent of discretionary income and reduced the amount of time after which loans could be forgiven from twenty-five to twenty years. Borrowers with the largest debts—who tend to be graduate or professional students and who also tend to have higher incomes and more earning potential—will reap nearly all the benefits, and those benefits are enormous.[80] A person earning $70,000 a year with an advanced degree could have $100,000 of federal debt forgiven under this alteration. This federal subsidy is four times larger than the maximum provided to low-income students through Pell Grants ($23,100) to obtain a college degree in four years. Enrollment in the Income-Based Repayment Plan has risen fast, doubling between 2013 and 2015, so that 25 percent of those eligible are now participating. The current annual cost to taxpayers is huge, about $11 billion a year.[81] The costs will be many times greater if all graduate students enroll.

Postsecondary tax breaks have also gone up—again, mostly benefiting the better-off. The biggest change in federal postsecondary policy in the past two decades has been the growth in tax incentives. As recently as the early 1990s, these incentives (e.g., credits and deductions) totaled just a few billion dollars, adjusted for inflation.[82] Now they total more than $34 billion.

The 2009 stimulus bill's American Opportunity Tax Credit accounted for most of the recent increase. The AOTC is a version of its precursor, the Clinton-era Hope credit, sweetened by an increase in the annual credit maximum and the number of years it can be claimed, inclusion of nontuition expenses in the coverage, and broadened eligibility to include families earning between $120,000 and $180,000. Part of the credit was also made refundable for low-income Americans who have no tax liability. Nevertheless, wealthier families earning more than $120,000—who received nothing under the previous credit—captured most of the gains from AOTC.[83] And there is little evidence that tax breaks make any difference in a student's decision to go to college.[84]

Ramping up federal student aid and debt forgiveness gives colleges every incentive to continue raising tuition. These increases result in greater demands for student aid. Although federal student aid could be more efficiently targeted toward needier students, cutting back on all forms of aid seems an unfair bargain for students, who are more dependent than ever on federal aid. Twenty years ago, half as many college students took out federal student loans.[85] State financial aid has fallen off, making students more reliant on federal dollars.[86] This is even truer for low-income students, given that the aid that states offer is increasingly merit-based instead of need-based.[87]

The federal government cannot afford, however, to continue subsidizing spiraling tuition costs for low-income students. If the maximum Pell Grant covered the same percentage of college expenses today that it did in the late 1970s, the program's annual bill would be more than twice as high, or close to $80 billion.[88] Yet the Pell Grant program has historically struggled to meet its obligations, surviving year to year on emergency stopgap measures. A rare surplus in recent years means the program will be funded through 2017, but in 2018 new funding solutions will have to be found.

The shift in responsibility for higher education costs from state to federal taxpayers has not been an equal bargain either. Because state governments set tuition levels for their own public higher education institutions, federal taxpayers are paying more—with almost no control over how the money is spent.

The best long-term solution is to rein in tuition costs and ensure federal dollars are better spent educating students in line with the needs of the economy. The Obama administration has been trying to push in this direction, leading the first serious effort to increase accountability in postsecondary education.

Initial push for accountability: transparency and the gainful employment rule. Transparency has been the federal government's main tuition cost–control strategy. Going back to 1965, colleges have had to report basic institution-wide figures—tuition, expenditures, graduation rates, and student aid—to the federal government to receive accreditation. Now efforts are under way to make these reported figures more transparent and accessible to students. All accredited institutions were required by 2011 to display a net price calculator for prospective students, showing the cost of attendance minus any grant or scholarship aid. President Obama had pledged to rank colleges based in part on whether students do well in the labor market, or instead borrow heavily to land low-paying jobs. But after fierce resistance from colleges, the administration backtracked on the rankings and instead rolled out a website in 2015 as a tool for students to judge institutions on their own. The hope is that students, empowered with this information, will be more careful consumers of postsecondary education, keeping tuition costs down and services more aligned with the economy's needs.

But critics argue that these transparency initiatives are not enough. Because so much federal taxpayer money at stake, critics insist, the

Remedial Education
Federal Education Policy

Final Grade

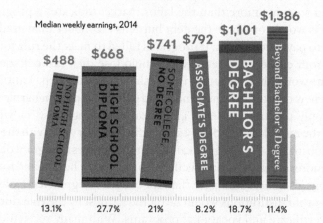

Median weekly earnings, 2014

$488 — NO HIGH SCHOOL DIPLOMA

$668 — HIGH SCHOOL DIPLOMA

$741 — SOME COLLEGE, NO DEGREE

$792 — ASSOCIATE'S DEGREE

$1,101 — BACHELOR'S DEGREE

$1,386 — Beyond Bachelor's Degree

| 13.1% | 27.7% | 21% | 8.2% | 18.7% | 11.4% |

Percentage of all adults over 25

More education leads to higher incomes.

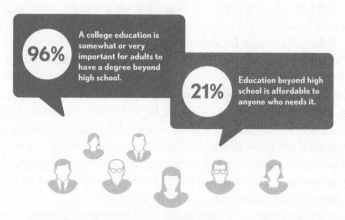

96% — A college education is somewhat or very important for adults to have a degree beyond high school.

21% — Education beyond high school is affordable to anyone who needs it.

The vast majority of Americans see the value of a college education, but a minority think students can afford one.

federal government should be pressuring colleges to offer better value for their services or to better prepare students for jobs.

In a big shift, the U.S. government is set to begin holding a small number of postsecondary institutions more accountable through the gainful employment rule put into place in 2015. For the first time, the federal government will impose consequences on institutions that charged students more than the labor market indicates a program or degree is worth, or where the debt burdens are higher than graduates' ability to pay off that debt. If programs failed to meet the rule for three out of four consecutive years, they would lose their accreditation and students would then be barred from using federal aid to pay tuition.

The new disclosure requirement and gainful employment rule would only apply to career colleges and vocational programs, for which it makes the most sense to closely align education services with the needs of the job market. The wage advantage of the degrees they grant depends much more on getting a job specific to the degree. The demand for these positions also fluctuates more than for bachelor degree–level jobs.

For-profit institutions would be hit the hardest by the rule since they favor certificate and vocational programs. With many receiving more than 80 percent of their revenue from federal student aid, for-profits also rely more heavily on public funds than other postsecondary education institutions.[89] They serve more low-income and minority students who tend to be less ready for college, but simple arithmetic suggests they could be offering better value to their students and taxpayers. For-profit colleges account for one-twelfth of the nation's postsecondary enrollment and a quarter of federal student aid, but nearly half of student loan defaults.

The other Obama administration proposals to push back against rising higher education costs would be voluntary. President Obama pitched a $10 billion fund to reward schools for lowering their tuition, but that idea has gone nowhere in Congress, and neither has his proposal for a Race to the Top competitive-grant program for postsecondary institutions.[90] For now, hopes for cost control will have to rest on transparency and the shoulders of student consumers.

State governments are taking the lead in applying accountability pressures to their vocational and community colleges. Six states now include student labor market outcomes in their funding formulas, and several formulas also reward completion rather than enrollment.

Some advocates for cheaper postsecondary education hope that online education will shake up the higher education market and deflate the tuition bubble. Institutions like the University of Phoenix have been offering discount online courses and degrees for about a decade, although with no appreciable effect on college tuition. In 2011, private companies like Udacity and Coursera began offering a new type of online learning program: the Massive Open Online Course (MOOC). The courses are often taught in research-based, fresh, and innovative styles—and they are open to anyone and charge no fee. In 2013, elite institutions including Harvard University, the Massachusetts Institute of Technology (MIT), and the University of California, Berkeley, entered the MOOC market.

But MOOCs are unlikely to do much to improve higher education outcomes. The students who need the most help also tend to have the least motivation. Remote or online learning in community colleges without a teacher checking in has been ineffective.[91] And available evidence suggests it could make the college dropout crisis worse. Only one in ten students enrolled in the typical Udacity course completes it. Other studies found that community college students were less likely to graduate if they enrolled in online courses.[92] Moreover, ensuring the integrity of MOOC test systems is a significant hurdle.

Community colleges: high on rhetoric, low on funding, but with more support for private partnerships. The Obama administration has placed community colleges higher on the federal agenda than any of his predecessors did, even calling for nationwide free community college education. Obama's positive spin on community colleges from the bully pulpit may be one reason why public opinion now gives community colleges high marks in value for cost.[93] Community colleges serve the most postsecondary students and have absorbed a disproportionate share of the historic college enrollment increase among black, Hispanic, and low-income students. They also have high dropout rates. If the United States becomes a world leader in college degrees by 2020, it will be in large part because more students are finishing community college and similar vocational programs.

But federal appropriations for community colleges have been modest. President Obama proposed $5 billion for community colleges in his Jumpstart Our Business Startups (JOBS) Act, $12 billion for the American Graduation Initiative, and, most recently, $8 billion for the Community

College to Career Fund. None passed in Congress. The 2009 stimulus package initially pledged $12 billion for community colleges. Only $2 billion was eventually appropriated for a new competitive grant program.[94]

The U.S. government is trying to make community colleges more effective without appropriating much money. Federal initiatives are encouraging community colleges to collaborate more directly with private-sector employers, a model that has been proven to place students in jobs after graduation. The new competitive grant program requires community colleges to partner with at least one employer as well as use evidence-based methods to carefully measure and track the success of participants. In a separate program, the Skills for America's Future initiative, the federal government is facilitating industry-funded partnerships with community colleges. United Technology Corp, Accenture, and the Gap, among others, are directly funding programs for community college students whom they have committed to employ.[95]

ASSESSING FEDERAL POSTSECONDARY INITIATIVES

The Obama-era federal government has improved the situation for low-income postsecondary students in several ways—raising the Pell Grant maximum and securing more Pell funding, making the AOTC tax credit refundable, developing accountability measures for vocational and technical programs, and shifting national attention to community colleges and other institutions that grant middle-skill degrees.

For too long, helping disadvantaged students meant giving a small portion more access to selective and well-funded colleges. Broader assistance to low-income students can only be achieved by making the institutions most likely to serve low-income students—community colleges—better funded, more affordable, and more effective. The Obama administration deserves credit for recasting community colleges as the primary agents for addressing lower-income underachievement.

However, no concrete changes have been made to reward students or institutions for on-time degree completion or to lower dropout rates that disproportionately afflict low-income students and the less selective institutions they attend. Without such changes, President Obama's pledge to make the United States the world leader in postsecondary attainment by 2020 is unlikely to be fulfilled. Lack of funding and resource support for community colleges is part of the problem, but so is federal student aid, which is distributed based on enrollment instead of completion.

As policymakers strengthen accountability, they should guard against the danger that it could lead to restricted access for disadvantaged students. With more pressure to keep costs down and completion rates and job placements up, schools might start to limit the number of students they admit who cannot afford full tuition or need more academic remediation. Postsecondary accountability measures should reward access in addition to completion and affordability.

The concrete changes that have been made to federal postsecondary policy—new debt forgiveness and tax breaks—have tilted a playing field that was already in favor of wealthier students even more so, all at a cost to taxpayers. Evidence suggests that well-designed, need-based aid does induce more students to go to college and reduces the likelihood they will drop out.[96] This is much less the case with tax incentives, which are poorly targeted at low-income students, given that they tend to have no or little tax liability.[97] A more cost-effective way to expand college access and completion would be to undo the regressive changes made to the student debt repayment plan and tuition tax credits, funnel the savings into the fiscally distressed Pell Grant program, and expand Pell generosity and eligibility.[98]

FUTURE PROSPECTS

Congressional Republicans and Democrats have been in remarkable agreement on the substance of education policy. The biggest differences are that Republicans tend to favor more market-oriented approaches, such as vouchers and accountability through transparency, and would rather leave more decision-making to states.

More than ideology, fiscal austerity will likely be the principal roadblock for federal education policy. Linking funding to quality is more important than ever, both to improve efficiency and to protect students from any negative blow from budget cuts. President Obama's push for more cost and quality accountability, especially for education providers who cater to low-income children and students, will likely continue.

But much more can be done for poor students who are falling behind the wealthy. More low-income children should have access to high-quality public preschool programs to narrow achievement gaps early on. Title I funding for low-income K–12 schools should be better targeted and designed. Regressive changes to postsecondary student aid should be reversed, support for community colleges ramped up, and aid formulas redone to reward degree completion.

Road to Nowhere:
Federal Transportation Policy

INTRODUCTION

The United States has a transportation infrastructure funding problem. The way the federal government raises money to pay for highways and transit no longer works, leading to budget shortfalls and underinvestment in infrastructure. Drivers pay a federal gas tax, with those revenues placed in trust funds dedicated solely to pay for highway, roads, and transit. But the gas tax is not producing as much revenue as it did in the past, and Congress has struggled to find a solution for plugging the gap. Congress has either resorted to multimonth patches or used funding gimmicks to try to close the shortfalls. Since 2002, highway and transit funding has been declining in real terms for all levels of government, and the biggest drop-off is at the federal level.

The United States should be spending more to improve and expand its transportation infrastructure, but instead barely spends enough to maintain the existing network. According to surveys, the quality of U.S. roads and transit is mediocre compared with other peer countries in the Group of Seven (G7). Although road and bridge conditions have actually been improving over time, capacity has not expanded as fast as population growth or miles driven. Congestion is now twice as bad as it was in the early 1980s.

In the face of federal inaction, states and localities have raised their own gas and sales taxes to pay for transportation investments. Politicians from across the political spectrum have supported using more public-private partnerships (P3s) to take some of the burden off the public sector. But private financing only works for a limited number of projects that have a high enough rate of return. Transportation infrastructure is a public good, and public dollars should make up the lion's share of the investment gap. Ultimately, the American people will have to spend more to pay for their infrastructure.

Other peer countries are doing a better job at securing funding to pay for multiyear investment plans. Even conservative governments in the UK and Canada have pushed through big long-term funding increases. And whereas the federal government hands out the vast majority of transportation dollars via formula without any accountability for how they are spent, other countries make more needs-based and strategic investment decisions—which is especially important when budgets are lean.

TRANSPORTATION INFRASTRUCTURE AND THE ECONOMY

Moving people and goods efficiently matters for the U.S. economy. Workers need to get to and from their jobs with ease and without wasting time sitting in traffic. Faster and more reliable on-time deliveries mean supply chains can be more dispersed and with less inventory standing time. All this energizes the economy. Infrastructure projects can also directly create jobs, especially for construction workers. With interest rates remaining at historic lows, an opportunity exists to marry short-term job creation with investments that will pay long-term benefits to U.S. economic competitiveness.

Compared with other kinds of public spending, infrastructure investment tends to have a larger stimulating effect on the economy, called a multiplier effect, and the effect is largest during a recession.[1] According to the Congressional Budget Office (CBO), of all the spending and tax relief components to the 2009 stimulus package, the infrastructure component delivered among the greatest boost.[2] One stimulus dollar spent on infrastructure was estimated to boost the economy by as much as just over two dollars.

WHERE THE UNITED STATES STANDS

QUALITY: AVERAGE AMONG PEERS

U.S. transportation infrastructure is mediocre compared with its peer competitors in the G7. For overall infrastructure quality, the United States used to rank fifth in the world; now it ranks sixteenth. Japan,

Road to Nowhere

Failing U.S. Transportation Infrastructure

Falling Behind

2015 ranking of U.S. infrastructure quality, worldwide

The United States lapped by eleven countries in the last decade:
UAE, Finland, Netherlands, Austria, Iceland, Japan, France, Portugal, Spain, Luxembourg, and Denmark

2002 ranking of U.S. infrastructure quality, worldwide

The United States has fallen in international rankings
of infrastructure quality.

Highway miles traveled by U.S. drivers:
UP 96%

New highway miles to travel on:
UP 9%

1980
— TO —
2013

New highway construction has not kept pace
with highway use.

Germany, and France consistently rank higher than the United States in
road and rail quality—at least according to surveys of their citizens who
use them day to day.[3] Only for airports does the United States come out
on top among G7 countries. International comparisons are difficult and
perhaps not totally fair; the United States has a much larger geographic
area to cover and lower population densities to serve than most other
advanced countries. Globally, it has the most paved roads, rail tracks,
and airports.[4]

For surface transportation like roads, highways, and transit—where
roughly 90 percent of all American travel-miles occur and where 85
percent of federal transportation funding is spent—government moni-
tors suggest conditions are not getting worse.[5] Between 2000 and 2010,
average pavement conditions actually improved and driving fatality
rates declined. The number of deficient bridges has been decreasing
since the 1970s, though future repairs may not go as smoothly as in
the past. The easy fixes have been crossed off the list, but several tricky,
giant, and expensive bridges—like the Tappan Zee Bridge near New
York City and the Columbia River Bridge near Portland, Oregon—are
in urgent need of repairs.

Even if maintenance is up to date, capacity is not expanding as quickly
as it should. Since 1980, the U.S. population has grown four times faster
and vehicle miles traveled have grown ten times faster than new lane
construction.[6] The average American is driving slightly less than ten
years ago. But total miles driven in the country, which had gone down
during the recession, hit record highs once again in 2015.[7]

Roads have become more congested. Compared with twenty years
ago, the average American spends twice as much time, or forty-two
hours a year, stuck in traffic (see figure 1).[8] In the major metropolitan
areas that fuel the nation's economy, traffic is far worse. In Washington,
DC, each driver loses eighty-two hours a year in traffic. The annual cost
to the economy in fuel, wear, and wasted worker time tallies to $160 bil-
lion nationwide.

Some wild cards could see future capacity needs veer from the historical trend. The number of cars on the road could decrease if car-sharing
services take off. Driverless or automated cars loaded with sensors may
need less distance from other cars, squeezing more use out of existing
capacity. Traffic sensors could relay information to these cars to send
them along the most efficient route.

FIGURE 1. HOURS SPENT IN TRAFFIC PER COMMUTER PER YEAR
AND ECONOMIC COST OF CONGESTION

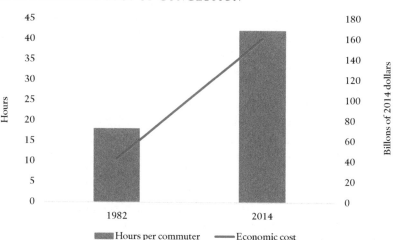

Source: Texas A&M Transportation Institute and INRIX (2015).

Congestion and infrastructure wear are unlikely to ease up any time soon, however. Smart-growth proponents argue the solution to easing congestion is to change infrastructure planning and spending priorities; instead of paving more highways and roads, the government should encourage Americans to live in denser communities and use more public transit or ride-sharing schemes. The share of commuters using transit is the highest in fifty years. Most major U.S. cities, including notoriously car-dependent Los Angeles, are making massive new investments in public transit. But the reality is that expanding transit alone cannot be a solution. Transit remains a tiny fraction (roughly 1.5 percent) of all travel miles. Yet the U.S. population is expected to expand steadily for decades to come, most of it in the suburbs rather than urban cores. In the era of home shopping and Amazon Prime, trucking miles are projected to increase at twice the rate of passenger car miles, and multiton trucks do more damage to roads.[9] Just to keep congestion at its current level, overall capacity in road and transit miles will have to be expanded at a faster pace than it is today.

SPENDING: SHOULD BE HIGHER

The United States should be spending more on its transportation infrastructure. Although internationally comparable data is poor, the best available evidence suggests that for the last twenty years the United States consistently spent less of its GDP on transportation infrastructure than its peers.[10]

No hard-and-fast rule applies to how much a county should apportion to infrastructure. Developing countries, such as China, which are building their initial transportation network, usually spend more than developed countries that have established networks. The U.S. federal government went on a spending blitz in the 1950s and 1960s, when the interstate highway system was first being built.

But government projections suggest current national spending levels are not enough to improve or expand the country's highways, bridges, and transit systems. Making all the investments that pass a cost-benefit analysis would require at least an additional 46 percent of spending.[11]

Yet highway and transit spending trends have been going in the opposite direction, declining in real terms since 2002 for all levels of government (see figure 2).[12] The biggest drop-off has been at the federal level, by 15 percent. A substantial one-time boost in 2009 is attributable to

FIGURE 2. FEDERAL, STATE, AND LOCAL GOVERNMENT HIGHWAY AND TRANSIT SPENDING

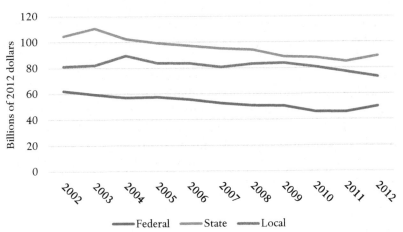

Source: Pew Charitable Trusts (2014).

the federal stimulus package, but that was an exception to the underlying downward trend. Although the federal government only shoulders about 25 percent of highway and transit spending, it plays an outsize role for capital investment, which is usually for new construction—exactly the kind of construction most projections say the country needs and the kind of investments that have fallen off the most.[13]

FINDING THE MONEY

The way the federal government raises money to pay for surface transportation no longer works, leading to budget shortfalls. Drivers pay a federal gas tax, and those revenues are placed in trust funds dedicated solely to pay for highways, roads, and transit. But the gas tax is not producing as much revenue as it did in the past, and Congress has struggled to find a solution for plugging the gap.

Federal gas tax revenues have not been going up with infrastructure costs. The tax is set at an absolute level (18.4 cents per gallon) and is not indexed to inflation, so the real value has eroded over time. The only way to increase its value is if Congress votes to raise it—a rare and difficult feat. The last time Congress increased the gas tax was in 1993, and the real value of the gas tax has since fallen by 39 percent.[14] Improved car and truck fuel efficiency, though better for the environment and energy security, also means lower gas tax revenues. Some cars do not use gas at all. Gas tax expenditures now routinely exceed revenues, and Congress has had to transfer money from general funds since 2009 to fill the gap. In 2015, highway and transit trust fund outlays exceeded gas tax revenues by 24 percent, amounting to a $15 billion deficit.[15]

Congress for many years was unable to pass long-term funding bills. The federal government has traditionally set highway and transit policies and budgets through authorization laws that last four to six years. This helps local and state transportation officials plan for larger multi-year construction projects. Between 2009 and 2013, however, Congress resorted to more than thirty short-term patches that extended the existing spending level, ranging from one week to several months. State and local governments slowed up their capital project pipeline because of the funding uncertainty.[16] A five-year bill was passed in late 2015, but Congress kept funding levels mostly flat and resorted to one-off budget gimmicks to plug the trust fund shortfall.

MOVE AWAY FROM THE GAS TAX?

The gas tax is unlikely to be raised any time soon. To cover its payments, the tax would have to nearly double, to about 30 cents per gallon.[17] Gas prices in late 2015 were just over half of what they were in 2012, which could offer an opportunity either to raise the tax or to index it inversely with the direction of gas prices to limit the impact on consumer budgets.[18] Yet few elected policymakers in Washington support a gas tax hike.

The federal government could move away from a user-fee revenue system and pay for transportation infrastructure through the general fund. Although every other rich country has gas taxes, rarely do they dedicate those revenues just to transportation spending.[19] Most U.S. states supplement their gas tax revenue with sales tax or general revenues.[20] Nor do gas taxes conform well to the user-pay principle, which was a major reason the gas tax was established. Electric-powered cars wear on roads as much as gas-powered cars do. And trucks wear far more on roads than what they pay in gas costs.[21] Drawing on the general fund could be justified from a user standpoint; nondrivers and drivers alike benefit from consumer goods trucked in on highways and on the broader economic gains from high-quality infrastructure.

Instead of a gas tax user fee, the country could transition to more accurate user fees—the vehicle miles traveled (VMT) tax or tolls. For a VMT system, drivers would install a mileage counter and pay a tax per mile driven. VMT pilot programs with several thousand volunteer drivers are under way in Oregon and Washington. Some Americans, however, may not feel comfortable with electronic devices in their cars reporting their driving stats to the government. Tolling has become more common. Since 2011, toll roads have expanded twice as fast as regular roads.[22] Modern tolling is all electronic and without traffic-clogging toll booth plazas. Polls suggest Americans prefer tolls when given the choice alongside increasing gas or sales taxes, and tolling is more common in peer countries.[23] Yet still only 5 percent of total national transportation revenues come from tolls, and if tolls are steadily expanded, public opinion might shift.[24] Transitioning to a VMT or tolls as a major funding stream would take at least a generation. There needs to be a more intermediate financing fix.

Road to Nowhere

Failing U.S. Transportation Infrastructure

Running Low

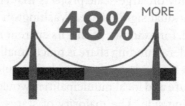

48% MORE

United States vs. G7

The rest of the G7 spends more of its GDP on transportation
infrastructure than the United States.

 **$103**

2012 actual capital spending, in billions

$85–$109

Recommended spending, maintenance

$151–$177

Recommended spending, improvement

To improve and expand its infrastructure, the United
States should be spending more.

SPEND ONLY AS MUCH AS GAS TAXES RAISE IN REVENUE?

The federal government could only spend as much as it collects in gas tax revenue, which would cause federal funding of highways to fall by one-third and transit by two-thirds. With less funding, the federal government would have a smaller role in transportation policy, focusing only on large-scale projects that cross state boundaries or projects of national significance. Washington's role in surface transportation could, for example, mimic its current role in aviation—where the overall federal funding share is much smaller and responsibilities more narrowly focused on safety regulations and air traffic control coordination.

State and local municipalities would have to take up the slack on the funding side. The majority of states have already responded, raising their gas taxes or finding other revenue streams to pay for transportation projects. But these revenue hikes are unlikely to fill the entire gap and extremely unlikely to raise overall national spending to improve and expand capacity. According to one analysis, even with recent state revenue increases, if the federal government cut spending to the level of gas tax revenues, states would only be able to cover 60 percent of those cuts from their own resources.[25] The adjustment may be easier in states that rely less on federal funding. For states such as Virginia, South Carolina, and Rhode Island that get more than 80 percent of their funding from the federal government, the cuts could be devastating. The federal government could help by bringing back tax subsidy programs on municipal debt, like the Build America Bonds program, which lasted only from 2009 to 2010 but helped raise $181 billion and gave states and local municipalities a generous 35 percent subsidy on interest payments. But state and local tax relief is not a costless solution for federal taxpayers, because federal tax revenue would drop.

A LARGER PRIVATE ROLE?

If the public sector is taking a step back, a larger role could be given to the private sector. Politicians across the political spectrum have endorsed using more public-private partnerships to finance and manage infrastructure projects. P3s are still rare in the overall context of U.S. infrastructure investment. In the past decade, though, they have become more common, and most large-scale new capital construction, such as the I-70 East highway in Colorado or the LBJ expressway in Texas, involves P3s. States have been tweaking their laws so that now a majority of states allow P3 contracts for public infrastructure.

P3 projects tend to be expensive and complex—when private expertise can come in handy—and have an immediate revenue stream, either from user tolls or government payments. The contracts themselves, stipulating the private party's role, can take a variety of forms. Some, such as the Indiana Toll Road or Chicago Skyway, are "concession" agreements where the state sold ownership for a lump-sum payment. Others, such as the I-595 repairs in Florida, have "availability payment" agreements under which a private developer finances the capital and operating costs of the facility but the government retains ownership and pays the developer an annual fee. Analysis of the relatively small number of completed P3 projects suggests that they are completed slightly more on budget and on time compared with those carried out exclusively by the public sector.[26]

The federal government has long been trying to encourage P3s. Loan programs and tax relief programs, many of which were created under the Bill Clinton and George W. Bush administrations, have been expanded and the terms made more generous. The largest loan program, the Transportation Infrastructure Finance and Innovation Act (TIFIA), provides federal credit assistance (e.g., direct loans, loan guarantees, flexible terms, low interest rates) to leverage private capital and finance large-scale P3 surface transportation projects. The program has been largely successful. Only two of forty TIFIA loans initiated so far have defaulted. The loans are being paid back, meaning that the program has not actually cost the government or taxpayers much money. Qualified Private Activity Bonds have existed for transportation projects since 2005, enabling state and local governments to take out tax-exempt bonds for P3 projects. Federal restrictions on the tolling of interstate highways have been scaled back. Additionally, a new office within the Department of Transportation was created in 2014 to help states and local governments, which often have no P3 expertise, write P3 laws and navigate P3 contracts.

President Obama and some Democratic members of Congress have favored creating an "infrastructure bank." Like TIFIA, it would supply federal credit assistance and loan guarantees to finance large-scale, interstate, and multimodal projects with leveraged private capital. An initial federal infusion of $10 billion could raise $100 billion to $200 billion from capital markets. Unlike TIFIA, the bank would finance all

Road to Nowhere

Failing U.S. Transportation Infrastructure

Out of Gas

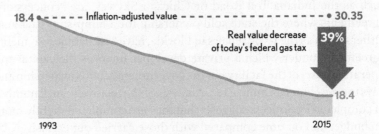

The real value of today's federal gas tax is far below
what it was twenty years ago.

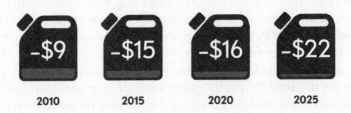

Annual deficit in the highway and transit trust fund, in billions

The trust fund deficit is getting worse.

infrastructure projects, from transportation to water, energy, and technology. It would also make it easier to compare the benefits and costs of projects in a competitive selection process. The bank would be an independent entity with an independent board, free from the political grip of Congress and the Department of Transportation.

The idea has not gained political traction, however. Skeptics question whether the solution to the country's infrastructure woes is yet another government institution. It could take years to organize and get it up and running, and finding an extra $10 billion in the federal budget would require difficult negotiations. If the bank were a purely lending institution, they argue, why not instead expand existing federal lending programs like TIFIA? Or the federal government could provide more support for the thirty-two states that already have state infrastructure banks.

THE LIMITS OF PRIVATE FINANCE

Private finance is unlikely to be a substantial source of new transportation funding, however. P3 projects in the United States have so far brought small sums of money to the table; over the past twenty-five years, private finance has accounted for $24 billion, or roughly 0.5 percent of the $4 trillion total the country spent on highways.[27] Most P3 contracts are for managing and operating infrastructure, not financing it. And most private partners are paid by state and local governments from general funds.

To be sure, private dollars for infrastructure projects are trending up. Two-thirds of that private money has come in just over the last five years. Infrastructure could be a smart investment for pension or sovereign wealth funds that are looking for relatively safe assets that provide long-term steady returns. In the last ten years, global infrastructure investment funds have raised roughly $300 billion for projects.[28] Although one-third of that money came from the United States, nearly all of it was invested in Europe, Canada, or Australia.[29] New financing tools are being proposed in Washington. President Obama has pledged to create a new kind of tax-exempt loan for P3 infrastructure projects—called Qualified Public Infrastructure Bonds (QPIBs)—where the private partner would pay the same low interest rate that a public entity would. Another idea from Senators Ron Wyden (D-OR) and John Hoeven (R-ND), called Move America Bonds, would go further, allowing private entities to claim a tax credit for work on property that is not government owned.

But taxpayers may not actually save much money with P3s, aside from small efficiency gains in project delivery. Financiers get involved to make money, in the form of either user tolls or tax revenue. The TIFIA loan portfolio is entirely made up of tolled facilities to repay the loan. Yet widespread toll use may hit up against public opinion. Public opposition to tolling nearly killed the Colorado I-70 East expansion. Texas embraced tolls with a zeal in the 2000s, but now Republican lawmakers are pulling back because of a grassroots campaign against tolls.[30] The trucking industry is lobbying hard against more tolls. Private money can be useful for getting an alternative initial capital source if, for example, federal dollars are delayed. Eventually, though, Americans will have to pay it back. And when all relevant costs are taken into account, private finance is no less costly for the taxpayer than public finance.[31]

Private financing only works for projects that have a high enough rate of return on investment. Congestion-relief projects, which offer a steady flow of traffic, are ideal. Private finance is a big player in high occupancy/toll lanes that are either in operation or being planned in most major metropolitan areas. The vast majority of road or highway projects cannot deliver as a high a rate of return. Even in Canada, which has been engaging with P3s for decades and has the expertise to execute, P3s still make up no more than 10 percent of all projects.[32] TIFIA actually has more for loans available than there are viable P3 projects that have a high enough rate of return or an immediate revenue source like tolls. In 2014, 64 percent of the $1 billion apportioned to TIFIA went untaken.[33]

Transportation infrastructure is a public good, and public dollars need to make up the lion's share of the investment gap. Ultimately, the American public will simply have to spend more to pay for infrastructure.

PUBLIC OPINION: WILLING TO PAY MORE WHEN FRAMED IN SPECIFICS

When asked in broad terms, Americans favor increasing national infrastructure investment. When given a list of federal budget priorities, roads and infrastructure follow closely behind education and entitlements.[34] A majority say reducing traffic and maintaining roads should be a "high priority," and two-thirds say funding infrastructure is either extremely or very important.[35] Yet, when asked in broad terms, Americans, in similar margins, reject raising the gas tax, installing more tolls, or using a miles-driven tax.[36]

Americans appear to be more willing to pay, however, when they know their money is going to be spent on a specific project or closer to home.[37] In recent years, state and local ballot initiatives support-ing increased investment have had a stellar success rate, many of them asking voters to increase their own gas and sales taxes.[38] More transpar-ency in how federal money is spent locally might help generate wider support for increasing federal revenues for transportation.[39] Getting rid of old funding formulas in favor of a more competitive process could help as well.

MAKING MORE STRATEGIC INVESTMENTS

If the federal government invests less in infrastructure in the next few decades, at least it could be more efficient and strategic about where it invests, targeting scarce money where the needs are greatest.[40] Roughly 90 percent of federal highway and transit funding is distributed based on a formula that is partly the result of political negotiation and partly based on the amount of gas tax receipts from each state. How the money is spent is almost entirely up to the political bodies in state and local governments, and does not necessarily require a careful and transpar-ent cost-benefit analysis by an independent body. Rarely does a federal follow-up assessment evaluate how the formula-based money was spent. Because the federal government is the source for nearly half of state and local capital spending, it could use the money to hold those governments accountable for their investment decisions.

The federal government has taken a few initial steps in the right direction. The stimulus package created a competitive grant program that forced states to compete for funding, requiring states to defend their project submissions and to rank priorities. The 2012 highway bill, called MAP-21, consolidated highway programs and sped up the project planning process by allowing agencies to conduct regulatory reviews concurrently. It also directed federal bureaucrats to design highway performance metrics that could be used for performance-based spend-ing. Also, for the first time, MAP-21 asked states and metropolitan areas to set highway conditions and performance targets, though the targets are not yet linked to actual funding allocations.[41]

Road to Nowhere
Failing U.S. Transportation Infrastructure

Catching Up

31%	71%	59%
Support 10 cent gas tax increase	Support 10 cent gas tax increase, if used for maintaining roads and highways	Support 10 cent gas tax increase, if it adds modern, technologically advanced systems

In national public opinion polls, Americans are most
likely to support a gas tax hike if they know the revenues
are going toward a specific goal.

75%
of recent state and local transportation
spending ballot initiatives have passed.

Voters tend to support transportation taxing
and spending hikes within their own state and
local communities.

OTHER COUNTRIES ARE BETTER
AT INFRASTRUCTURE FINANCING

Other peer countries are doing a better job at securing funding to pay for multiyear investment plans. In 2013, Canada authorized a giant funding increase in a ten-year infrastructure investment plan, the longest in Canadian history. A similar plan was put in place in the UK in 2010. In both cases, fiscally conservative governments initiated the funding push, even at a time of austerity. Australia and Japan have made some spending cuts in recent years and spending has been flat in Germany, but all make those commitments in multiyear—often five-year—plans.

Others also make more needs-based and strategic investment decisions. The UK, Australia, and Germany all have independent bodies to conduct cost-benefit analysis and rank national priorities for large-scale infrastructure projects. Although the Canadian federal government does distribute most transportation money via a population-based formula, the provinces need to report back how the funded projects delivered national benefits.

Most P3 innovation has been occurring elsewhere as well, with the United States playing catch-up. P3s are far more common in countries such as Australia, Canada, Spain, and France. The UK and Canada have government institutions, such as Infrastructure UK and PPP Canada, to help P3 projects along—institutions that served as the model for a similar office called the Build America Transportation Investment Center in the U.S. Department of Transportation.

FUTURE PROSPECTS

Prospects appear dim for a long-term funding solution that would significantly increase investments in transportation infrastructure. President Obama's budget proposals have consistently called for an increase in transportation funding, most recently by one-third, but Congress has resisted.[42]

Obama started his presidency championing transportation, yet many of his initiatives have since fallen flat. Infrastructure spending was among the biggest components of the 2009 stimulus package, receiving close to $100 billion, half of which went to transportation. There was also a new push for high-speed rail that included hefty funding to back it up. But the idea turned out not to be so practical in a country that has does not have Europe's or Japan's density or China's willingness to stomach huge system costs.[43] Congress has since zeroed out funding for the high-speed rail program. And in spite of Obama's attempts to get the country on track to consistently spend more on its transportation system, a flat or downward trajectory is more likely for the next few years.

States and localities can try to levy more taxes, expand public-private partnerships, or seek voter approval for specific projects. Without more transportation dollars available, though, the governments will struggle to deliver a better transportation system.

Trading Up: U.S. Trade and Investment Policy

INTRODUCTION

The United States depends far more on the global economy than it did two decades ago, and international trade and foreign investment are increasingly vital to U.S. prosperity. Yet on most measures of trade and investment performance, the United States remains in the middle of the pack among advanced economies, though with some recent signs of progress.

The United States is among the more open economies in the world, the world's biggest importer of foreign goods, and the largest overseas investor. But the United States still does not export as much as would be expected, given the size of its economy and the mix of goods and services it produces. Its share of global exports has fallen more sharply than that of most other advanced countries over the past decade in the face of competition from emerging markets such as China. The United States is in the middle of advanced economies in attracting foreign investment as a percentage of gross domestic product, and has also lost ground in this area over the past decade. Where it is most competitive—in services—is also where trade obstacles are largest.

The Obama administration has explicitly tried to tackle some of these shortfalls and challenges, but has had only mixed results to date. The National Export Initiative (NEI), launched in 2010, for the first time set a target for export growth, calling for doubling U.S. exports from 2009 to the end of 2014. After strong gains in the first two years, exports have grown much more slowly in the past three years, largely due to weaker economic growth overseas and a rising dollar, and the NEI has fallen far short of its target. President Obama has made attracting foreign investment a bigger priority than it was for previous administrations, overhauling the Commerce Department's investment promotion arm with the creation of SelectUSA and engaging business leaders on strategies for increasing investment. Foreign investment flows to the United States have generally been strong coming out of the recession, though the U.S. share of global investment has fallen significantly over the past decade. The Obama administration has also followed the Bill Clinton and George W. Bush administrations by embracing an increasingly ambitious set of international trade negotiations to reduce nontraditional and services barriers and to open new market opportunities around the world. These include the Trans-Pacific Partnership agreement with eleven Asia-Pacific countries, the Transatlantic Trade and Investment Partnership negotiations with Europe, and a renewed effort to liberalize service sector trade and expand coverage for information technology through the World Trade Organization (WTO).

These initiatives should open more opportunities for the United States in global markets. But the country needs to do more to take full economic advantage of those openings.

WHERE THE UNITED STATES STANDS

Over the past half century, the United States has gone from being a fairly self-sufficient economy to one far more integrated into the world economy. In 1960, exports and imports were equivalent to less than 10 percent of U.S. GDP; by 1990, that had risen to 20 percent; and today the figure is more than 30 percent.[1] U.S. investment abroad and foreign investment into the United States have increased enormously as well.

Indeed, the same could be said of the world. Practically every country is importing and exporting more and receiving and sending more investment. Global trade has historically expanded faster than global output. Except for dips in the business cycle, including the most recent steep drop-off following the 2008 financial collapse, global trade and investment have been on a historically upward trend since World War II.

The big trade story, beginning in the early 1990s, has been the rise of the developing world, especially China. The developing world's share of international trade has increased from 33 percent in 2000 to 48 percent in 2012, with China accounting for almost all of that increase.[2] Global investment flows to the developing world are now larger than those going to the advanced economies.

There is no simple measure of success in trade and investment policies. China is the world's largest exporter; the United States is the

Trading Up
💾 U.S. Trade and Investment Policy

Integrating into the World Economy

IMPORTS:
10.3%

IMPORTS:
16.4%

EXPORTS:
9.0%

1990

2014

EXPORTS:
13.5%

International trade is growing as a share of gross domestic product.

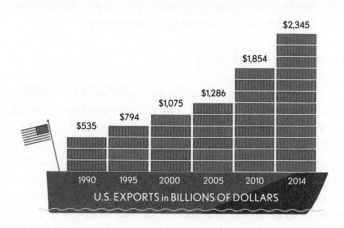

$2,345

$1,854

$1,286

$1,075

$794

$535

| 1990 | 1995 | 2000 | 2005 | 2010 | 2014 |

U.S. EXPORTS in BILLIONS OF DOLLARS

U.S. exports are at record levels.

second. The United States is also the world's largest importer, but its market is not as open to imports as some other advanced economies, including the United Kingdom, Germany, France, and Australia. Germany runs the largest trade surplus in the world; the United States runs the largest trade deficit. The United States is also the largest source of outbound foreign direct investment (FDI) and attracts more inward FDI than any other country; however, relative to the size of its economy, many other countries attract more investment. Jobs in internationally competitive sectors in the United States pay more than jobs in other sectors, but rising productivity means that exports must grow rapidly to support additional job growth.

A full range of measures can be used to assess how the United States is doing in international economic participation. These include openness to imports, success at exporting goods and services, the U.S. ability to attract direct investment on its own soil, and overseas direct investment by U.S. companies. The picture is a mixed one: areas of progress are interspersed with big economic challenges and future economic opportunities. Some other advanced countries have been more strategic than the United States in identifying and responding to those opportunities, but the United States is narrowing the policy gap.

IMPORTS AND EXPORTS

Over the past two decades, nearly all countries in the world have been removing barriers to imports. The reasons are many. The end of the Cold War created huge new consumer markets and brought hundreds of millions of new workers into the global economy, growth of container shipping dramatically reduced the costs of sending goods overseas, new communications technologies have permitted companies to build elaborate global supply chains and take advantage of the most competitive business locations, and successive rounds of global trade negotiations and regional pacts have sharply lowered tariffs and other barriers to trade. The *Wall Street Journal*/Heritage Foundation index of trade freedom shows that trade barriers fell steadily from 1995 to 2010—even through two recessions.[3]

The United States is a reasonably open economy, and U.S. import growth has remained strong over the past two decades. Openness to imports has helped keep prices of intermediates and consumer goods low, which improves the ability of U.S. companies to produce goods at competitive prices. Two decades ago, the domestic content share in U.S. exports was close to 90 percent; today it is about 77 percent, meaning that nearly a quarter of the content of U.S. exports comes from imported intermediate goods.[4] Imports also lower costs to American consumers; one estimate suggests that import competition led to the equivalent of a 5.4 percent drop in consumer merchandise prices between 1992 and 2005.[5]

Every administration since the end of World War II has favored policies that continue to reduce import protection at home while also pushing for the removal of tariffs and other barriers in foreign markets. The United States has moved faster than some countries and more slowly than others to reduce import tariffs. The simple average tariff on goods in the United States has fallen from 5.2 percent in 1990 to 2.8 percent in 2012, which is about the same as Canada and slightly higher than the European Union (EU) and Japan.[6]

Some sectors continue to enjoy high levels of protection, however, which limits benefits to U.S. consumers. The U.S. sugar program, for instance, restricts sugar imports through tariffs and quotas and has kept U.S. sugar prices at roughly twice the world price for decades, though the gap has narrowed significantly in recent years due to record domestic production and duty-free imports from Mexico permitted under the North American Free Trade Agreement (NAFTA).[7] The International Trade Commission estimates that the higher retail prices for sugar and sugar-containing products caused by these tariffs and quotas have added $277 million in extra costs, though other estimates are as high as $3.5 billion per year.[8] U.S. farm subsidies also effectively restrict imports of many agricultural goods. The U.S. government recently paid $300 million to Brazilian cotton growers as compensation for the U.S. refusal to eliminate cotton subsidies, following a ruling by the WTO that those subsidies violate international trade rules.[9] And though U.S. tariffs are generally low, they remain high for certain essential consumer products like clothing, shoes, and bedding, imposing the heaviest burden on poorer Americans. These tariffs persist even though domestic production of these goods has all but disappeared. Of the roughly $26 billion that the United States collects annually in tariffs, more than half is for such necessary items as clothing, shoes, towels, bed sheets, and tableware. Tariffs are especially onerous on the least-expensive goods— polyester men's shirts face a 32 percent tariff, for example, but silk shirts only 0.9 percent. Trade analyst Edward Gresser has estimated that these tariffs cost low-income American families some $2 billion each year.[10]

Although the United States is still the world's largest importer, other countries are catching up. In 2000, the United States accounted for more than 18 percent of global imports of goods and services.[11] In that same year, Germany had the next largest share, at just below 8 percent, and China accounted for around 3 percent. By 2013, the U.S. share had dropped to 12 percent and China, at nearly 10 percent, had become the second-largest importer.

Export growth also matters. Sales abroad of U.S. goods and services boost overall GDP and create jobs, and those jobs generally pay higher wages than in companies that do not export.[12] The good news is that U.S. exports of goods and services grew rapidly coming out of the recession, and are now at record dollar levels, despite the recent slowdown in growth in big export markets like China. The bad news is that the United States is still underperforming against some peer economies in global market share and is struggling to improve its export performance, given the recent strength of the dollar. Although the United States was once the world's leading exporter of goods and services, it has lost significant ground over the last decade, particularly to rising economies such as China. As recently as 2000, the United States held the largest share of global exports, nearly 14 percent.[13] That share has since dropped, to under 10 percent in 2013. Other developed economies, with the exception of Germany, have seen similar relative declines. China's share, on the other hand, has grown rapidly. Accounting for only 3.5 percent of the world total in 2000, China's export share grew to more than 10 percent in 2013, surpassing the United States.

Although the rise of China and other developing economies has reduced export shares for almost all the advanced economies, the United States has lost relatively more ground. Given its historical mix of products and relative currency values, it exports less with respect to the size of its economy than other peer countries, though its level of imports is similar.[14] Much of the difference is likely due to the large and prosperous U.S. domestic market; most small- and medium-sized U.S. companies succeed simply by producing for the domestic market. That large domestic market has likely discouraged some U.S. companies from pursuing new market opportunities abroad. But even though the United States is the world's single-largest consumer market, an estimated three-quarters of world purchasing power is outside U.S. borders.[15] The fastest U.S. export growth has been to developing economies such as China and Mexico rather than to traditional markets such as Canada and the European Union; from 2004 to 2014, the share of U.S. exports going to emerging economies rose from 35 percent to 47 percent.[16] The global middle class is expanding at an unprecedented rate, particularly in emerging markets, and future U.S. growth will depend heavily on capturing a share of those markets.

The United States also has one of the most competitive service industries in the world, and it is one of the bright spots for U.S. trade performance. The United States consistently runs a trade deficit in goods and a surplus in services (see figure 1).[17] The United States has a highly skilled workforce, and most tradable services—such as engineering, architectural design, financial consulting, and legal services—are skill intensive. There is also plenty more export potential for U.S. services. Only 5 percent of U.S. business services firms export, versus 25 percent of manufacturers.[18]

The business services sector has also been a solid job creator and now accounts for 25 percent of employment in the United States, more than double the manufacturing sector.[19] From 1997 to 2007, employment in the business services sector increased nearly 30 percent as manufacturing employment fell by 20 percent. It is a common misconception that most services-sector jobs are low wage. In 2007, the business services sector, which made up 25 percent of U.S. employment, paid an average of $56,000 per year.[20]

FIGURE 1. U.S. TRADE BALANCE, BY GOODS OR SERVICES

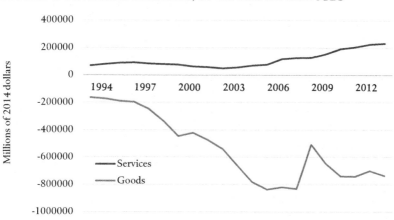

Source: U.S. Census Bureau.

Overall, the steadily high level of imports and the comparatively weaker U.S. export performance has led the United States to run large trade deficits since the mid-1970s. Trade deficits alone are not a good measure of the U.S. competitive position because they are influenced by the comparative growth rates of different economies, the relative value of currencies, and the levels of national savings. U.S. trade deficits tend to rise when the economy is strong and fall when it is weak, so that a rising trade deficit normally signals U.S. economic strength rather than weakness. That said, the sharp rise in the U.S. trade deficit as a percentage of GDP from about 1 percent of the economy in the early and mid-1990s to more than 5 percent by the mid-2000s was clearly a sign of competitive weakness. After falling sharply during the recession in 2009, the U.S. trade deficit has remained at a lower level—less than 3 percent of GDP—even as the economy has recovered. But the United States continues to run large trade deficits with export-oriented economies such as China, Korea, and Japan.

FOREIGN DIRECT INVESTMENT

One of the clearest signs of a competitive economy is that foreign companies want to invest there. When companies buy assets or establish businesses through direct investment, they are expressing confidence in that country as a place to make money. The United States is the largest recipient of FDI in the world, and foreign investment has grown rapidly in recent decades; the stock of FDI in the United States grew from $83 billion in 1980 to nearly $2.8 trillion in 2013, and the United States was the largest recipient of FDI flows, totaling $236 billion in new investments in 2013.[21] The European Union, Canada, and Japan remain the largest sources of investment in the United States.[22] FDI from countries like China has also been growing strongly, though from a small base. Chinese FDI in the United States has soared over the past five years from almost nothing to a cumulative value of nearly $50 billion.[23] Huge opportunities will exist in the coming years to court foreign investors from advanced and developing economies. One estimate suggested that China alone is expected to make more than $1 trillion in foreign investments by 2020.[24]

Although the United States remains a strong magnet for investment, its performance relative to other countries has been mediocre. It has slipped against its competitors in terms of its global share of

FDI; the U.S. share of total world stock of FDI fell from 37 percent in 2000 to 19 percent in 2013.[25] Much of the relative decline reflects the rise of developing countries like China, India, and Brazil as investment targets, but FDI shares have remained more stable and growth has been stronger in most other advanced countries. The stock of FDI in the European Union, for instance, rose from 31 percent of the world share in 2000 to 34 percent in 2013, though inflows have been weaker to Europe since 2007.[26]

In international surveys, U.S. performance as a destination for foreign investment has been varied. The Conference Board of Canada has developed a barometer that compares the relative success of advanced economies in attracting FDI. In 2011, the United States ranked tenth of sixteen peer countries, behind the United Kingdom, Canada, Sweden, Australia, and Ireland, but slightly ahead of France and Germany and well ahead of Japan.[27] In a 2012 OECD study on openness to foreign investment, the United States placed thirty-fourth of fifty-five countries, behind such countries as Brazil, South Africa, and Argentina.[28] Again, however, some encouraging signs of progress are evident—over the past two years the A. T. Kearney annual survey of global executives has listed the United States as the most desirable location for foreign investment, and investor sentiment has turned strongly positive.[29] Falling energy costs have contributed to this shift, as new drilling technologies have made huge shale gas and oil deposits in the United States accessible and caused U.S. energy production to surge. This has reduced the price of natural gas in the United States to one-third or less of European prices and has been a major factor in the global oil price plunge. These changes have encouraged expanded investment in energy-intensive sectors such as chemicals and steel. Rising wage costs in China, flat wages for Americans, and the growing use of advanced manufacturing techniques that require higher skills have also boosted the attractiveness of the United States for investors.[30]

Outward foreign investment by U.S. companies has been comparatively stronger. The United States is the world's largest foreign investor and accounted for about 25 percent of global FDI outflows in 2013.[31] Investment abroad by U.S. companies has also been growing strongly, and in most years over the past decade, direct investment abroad by U.S. companies has been larger than foreign investment in the United States. With economic growth in developing countries far outpacing U.S. growth, successful U.S. companies have expanded overseas investments to take

Losing Ground

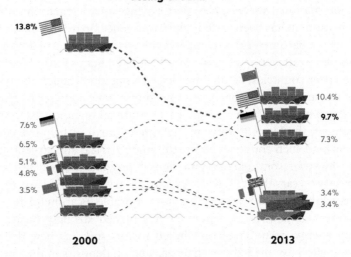

2000   **2013**

The U.S. share of global exports is down.

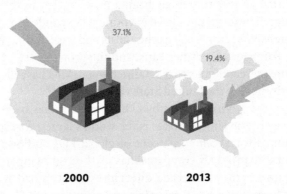

2000   **2013**

The share of global foreign direct investment into
the United States is down.

advantage of those opportunities. From 1999 to 2009, profits at foreign affiliates of U.S. companies grew much faster than in their U.S. headquarters, by an average of 7 percent versus just 1.7 percent for the U.S. parent companies.[32] Ninety percent of overseas production by these companies was sold abroad rather than being imported back to the United States.

The overall U.S. record on trade and investment flows is mixed—the United States has seen strong growth in both imports and exports and in both inward and outward direct investment. But relative to many other advanced economies, the United States continues to underperform in exports and has fallen behind in attracting foreign investment. The policy challenge facing the U.S. government is to continue to address those areas of weakness so that greater economic benefits will flow from increasing U.S. integration into the global economy.

WHAT HAS BEEN DONE SO FAR

The Obama administration has embraced an active trade and investment policy, though it took several years to develop. President Obama was elected in 2008 after a campaign in which he expressed considerable skepticism about the benefits of continued trade opening. His administration waited nearly three years before sending to Congress three bilateral trade agreements—with South Korea, Colombia, and Panama—that the George W. Bush administration had negotiated. Since then, however, Obama has embraced what has become the most ambitious trade agenda in nearly two decades. The turnaround is not entirely surprising. Since the end of World War II, U.S. presidents have consistently favored policies that have accelerated U.S. integration into the global economy.

THE RISE OF THE REST: A STALLED WTO AND THE GROWING PROBLEM OF NONTARIFF/SERVICE BARRIERS

The United States has long been a leader in negotiations under the General Agreement on Tariffs and Trade, now a part of the World Trade Organization, and in a series of bilateral and regional trade negotiations, which have brought the average tariff on goods in most advanced nations down to well under 5 percent.[33] Agreements in the 1990s on financial services and telecommunications also helped set some basic rules for services trade, as did the accession agreements for new WTO members like China and Russia. Until recently, global rounds of trade negotiations were dominated by the advanced economies, particularly the United States and the European Union, and their interests largely dictated the final terms of the agreements.

But the rise of wealthier and more influential developing countries—such as China, India, Brazil, and South Africa—has made global trade negotiations far more complex and difficult to conclude. The most recent round of WTO negotiations, the Doha Development Round, which began in 2001, has stalled. An important agreement to improve trade facilitation was reached in 2013 and finalized in 2014, though it has yet to be ratified by a sufficient number of countries to enter into force. Although average tariff levels on goods in emerging markets are much lower than in the past, they continue to be two to three times higher than in the developed world, ranging from 9 to 15 percent.[34]

As conventional tariffs have become less of a problem, however, nontariff barriers have become a larger one, especially in emerging markets. These protective measures favor domestic industries at the expense of foreign competition. In multiple surveys since 2012 by the U.S.-China Business Council, for example, tariffs and quotas did not rank in the top ten problems for U.S. companies in doing business with China.[35] Instead, business leaders cited things like licensing approvals, intellectual property theft, foreign investment restrictions, competition with state-owned enterprises, and unfair regulatory standards. According to the WTO, the percentage of global trade affected by these nontariff barriers grew from less than 30 percent in the mid-1990s to more than half in the 2000s (see figure 2).[36] Although methodologies differ for estimating the effects of these various nontariff measures on trade, they are thought to impose costs at least twice as large as those added by tariffs and possibly much larger.[37]

These kinds of barriers are especially problematic for services trade, where the United States is most competitive. The European Commission (EC) has developed estimates of the tariff equivalent of various protective measures around the world. In developing countries, the EC estimates that the telecommunications sector enjoys the equivalent of a 50 percent tariff but that exporters of construction services face an 80 percent hurdle.[38] Again, the problem is worse in emerging markets. Whereas average tariff-equivalent barriers on services are generally below 15 percent in advanced economies, they are many times higher in the major emerging markets, from 45 to 70 percent.[39] The United

FIGURE 2. SHARE OF GLOBAL TRADE VALUE COVERED
BY NONTARIFF BARRIERS

Source: World Trade Organization (2012).

States, with a share of global services trade more than twice its nearest competitor, the United Kingdom, has the most to gain from removing such barriers.

Existing WTO negotiations have so far been inadequate for dealing with nontariff and services barriers. Many of these restrictions pose challenges for trade negotiators because the use of certain nontariff measures are allowed under WTO rules, and it is often difficult to distinguish between legitimate measures to safeguard consumers or the environment and measures intended to circumvent the rules in favor of domestic industries at the expense of foreign competition. In the service sector, the Uruguay Round's General Agreement on Trade in Services resulted in only modest commitments by member states to remove obstacles for foreign services providers, and little progress has been made in the Doha round negotiations.

FAVORING FREE TRADE AGREEMENTS
AND PROTECTING INVESTMENT

Although the United States remains committed to multilateral trade liberalization, it has—like other countries—pursued bilateral and regional free trade agreements (FTAs) as a second-best alternative, given the stalemate in WTO negotiations. FTAs also tend to be more comprehensive, eliminating tariffs and reducing nontariff and services barriers. FTAs have an added political and strategic advantage in that they signal a specific U.S. commitment to a country or region.

To date, the United States has entered into FTAs with twenty countries that account for about 40 percent of total U.S. trade, though two countries—Mexico and Canada—make up most of that share.[40] No FTAs have been reached with some of the largest emerging markets, including China, India, and Brazil.

The first FTA was signed with Israel in 1985. NAFTA, which was signed in 1994, created a trading bloc among the United States, Mexico, and Canada, and eliminated virtually all tariffs and most nontariff barriers on goods traded in the region within fifteen years. Many FTAs with smaller economies were negotiated under the George W. Bush administration, including the U.S.-South Korea FTA and the Central American FTA.

It is unclear what effect FTAs are having on overall U.S. trade levels. To some extent, FTAs divert U.S. trade from other countries as companies shift production to take advantage of tariff preferences, so it is difficult to assess whether overall trade is growing more rapidly than it would have in the absence of FTAs. Coming out of the recession since 2009, however, both U.S. exports and imports have grown more strongly with FTA partners than with countries that are not part of the preference arrangements. From 2009 to 2014, U.S. exports to FTA partners grew by 64 percent (versus 45.5 percent for non-FTA partners), and imports grew by 57 percent (versus 47 percent from the rest of the world).[41]

The United States has also sought to expand protection for its companies that are investing around the world, largely through the negotiation of bilateral investment treaties (BITs). BITs establish predictable rules for foreign investors, and in particular protect companies against arbitrary government expropriation of their assets. The United States has long favored provisions in these agreements, and in free trade agreements, that permit neutral arbitration in such disputes, commonly known as Investor-State Dispute Settlement (ISDS). The Obama administration recently reiterated its support for ISDS in the face of growing criticisms that the provision may weaken domestic laws.[42] The TPP agreement, however, includes some changes to the ISDS procedures, and excludes tobacco companies from using private dispute settlement. The EU is seeking broader changes, including the creation of an appeal mechanism, in the TTIP talks. Since 2013, the United States has been in BIT negotiations with China, which may address long-standing U.S. concerns over the treatment of investors in China and may also help facilitate Chinese investment in the United States. If successful, it would be the most important trade-related agreement between the United States and China since China's entry into the WTO in 2001.

PUBLIC OPINION: EMBRACING TRADE, WORRIED ABOUT UNEQUAL BENEFITS

Though U.S. public opinion on trade has long been divided, in recent years Americans appear to be more persuaded that the potential gains outweigh the costs. Since 1992, Gallup has asked Americans whether they see foreign trade as primarily "an opportunity for economic growth through increased U.S. exports" or as "a threat to the economy from foreign imports." Although public support for trade declined during the recession, over the past three years the poll has shown a comfortable majority of Americans view trade positively. In 2015, 58 percent of those surveyed responded that foreign trade is an "opportunity for growth," an all-time high, and 33 percent saw it as a "threat to the economy," an all-time low.[43] The last time the American public was this positive about trade was in 2000, which came at the end of nearly a decade of strong economic growth.[44]

Americans are concerned, however, about what they perceive as unequal benefits from growing international trade. A 2012 Harris poll that looked at growing American concerns over economic inequality found that 81 percent of Americans believed that the loss of manufacturing jobs to China, India, and other low-cost countries has been a source of rising inequality. That was greater than the numbers pointing to any other cause, including education, the tax system, and the influence of big business and the wealthy.[45]

This concern—that the benefits of trade are not being spread widely enough—has driven many of the recent Obama administration initiatives. Administration policies have focused particularly on boosting exports and attracting investment, with the explicit goal of creating more and better-paying jobs for Americans.

High Hurdles

2014

Services
$231,792 million
(trade surplus)

Goods
-$736,839 million
(trade deficit)

The United States is most competitive in exporting services.

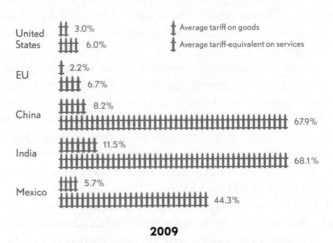

2009

But barriers are much higher for services than for goods.

OBAMA ADMINISTRATION INITIATIVES

The Obama administration is pursuing an ambitious trade agenda that has renewed efforts to open foreign markets through trade negotiations and increased federal government support and advocacy for U.S. exports and FDI into the United States. Current trade negotiations with the Asia-Pacific and the European Union could lead to a significant expansion in U.S. trade opportunities, though the overall economic effects on the United States will likely be modest.

EXPORT PROMOTION: NATIONAL EXPORT INITIATIVE

The administration's first major trade initiative was aimed explicitly at turning around the historical U.S. underperformance in exports. In his 2010 State of the Union address, President Obama launched the National Export Initiative, promising that "we will double our exports over the next five years, an increase that will support two million jobs in America."

Under the NEI, the United States followed countries like France, Germany, and Canada in advocating more aggressively for its own exports. Advocacy efforts have involved a range of measures in which Commerce and State Department officials helped to find overseas buyers for U.S. goods and open doors in foreign markets. The U.S. Export-Import Bank's support for financing and insuring foreign purchases of U.S. products rose sharply during the recession and its aftermath, when private sources of financing were less available. Since then, lending has returned to historic norms. U.S. Export-Import Bank authorizations more than doubled from fiscal year (FY) 2008 to FY 2012, reaching a record $35.8 billion, but in FY 2014, that number fell to $20.5 billion.[46] These figures, however, remain small compared to authorizations made by other competitors.[47] The administration has also taken steps to boost tourism in the United States, which is the largest source of services exports, by speeding up consular processing of tourist visas and by concluding a 2014 deal with China to mutually extend the validity of tourist and business visas from one year to ten, so that Chinese who travel frequently to the United States will no longer have to renew their visas each year.

Although difficult to measure, given the larger macroeconomic factors that chiefly determine trade flows, the NEI has likely had a positive effect. The number of U.S. firms exporting topped three hundred thousand in 2012, a new record, and is up more than 10 percent from 2009, despite a slight dip in 2013. Exports reached an all-time high of over $2.3 trillion in 2014. In comparison with other countries, however, the rate of U.S. export growth coming out of the recession was roughly on par with the global trend.[48]

The NEI fell well short of the president's goal of doubling exports by the end of 2014. From 2009 to 2012, exports grew by 40 percent, but growth has slowed dramatically since then. Since 2012, exports have grown by less than 3 percent per year, which is less than half of the historical average since 1990. The NEI also fell short of its job goals, though rising exports have supported a growing number of jobs. According to Commerce Department preliminary estimates, exports supported 11.7 million U.S. jobs in 2014, an increase of 1.8 million jobs since 2009.[49]

In 2013, the NEI transitioned into a new phase called NEI/NEXT, which shifted the focus away from broad numeric goals in favor of specific policies that create a favorable export climate. Government agencies will continue to provide firm-level assistance like export financing and guidance from government staff, as well as complete larger projects like implementing a digital "single window" portal for trade documents.

INVESTMENT PROMOTION: SELECTUSA

Investment promotion has also been a high priority for the administration, though the effort remains a fledgling one. The administration launched its new SelectUSA initiative in June 2011. The program works at the federal level to coordinate FDI promotion efforts, reach out to foreign governments and investors, support investment promotion at the state level, and address investor concerns about the U.S. business climate. Since 2013, the Commerce Department has hosted an annual SelectUSA Investment Summit aimed at connecting international businesses that are looking for investment opportunities with U.S. economic development organizations at the state, regional, and local levels that are looking to attract foreign investment. FDI flows are volatile; foreign investment in the United States was $236 billion in 2013, the third-highest level over the past decade, but then fell to just $98 billion in 2014, the lowest in more than a decade.

SelectUSA remains a small operation, however, and most efforts to attract foreign investment are led by individual states. President Obama has asked Congress for $20 million for the program in his FY 2014 and FY 2015 budgets, but Congress has only authorized a fraction of that amount. In comparison, competitor economies such as France, Germany, Canada, and the United Kingdom each spend an average of nearly $60 million each year on investment promotion.[50] Congress has also considered, but failed to pass, legislation that would require the administration to develop new strategies for boosting foreign investment.

TRADE NEGOTIATIONS: TPP, TTIP, AND TACKLING TECHNOLOGY AND SERVICES BARRIERS

In October 2015, the United States reached an agreement in the TPP talks with its eleven negotiating partners—Australia, Brunei, Canada, Chile, Malaysia, Mexico, New Zealand, Peru, Singapore, Japan, and Vietnam. The Obama administration played a crucial role in bringing Japan into the talks, and Japan formally joined the negotiations in July 2013. South Korea has announced its desire to join the TPP as well, and other countries including Indonesia and the Philippines have expressed interest. The Obama administration has called TPP a "twenty-first century agreement" that goes beyond previous pacts in removing trade barriers and raising standards in areas such as environmental protection, workers' rights, and intellectual property rights. The agreement, if successfully ratified, will include an accession clause, and participants hope that other countries, especially China, will sign on to the high-standard, comprehensive agreement after it is formed. In addition to lowering or eliminating traditional trade barriers like tariffs and quotas on agricultural and industrial goods, the TPP is aimed at reducing regulatory barriers that hinder the performance of U.S. companies, especially in services sectors, ensuring the free flow of data and reducing subsidies and other government support to state-owned enterprises.

In June 2013, the United States and the European Union launched the Transatlantic Trade and Investment Partnership negotiations, aimed at creating what would be the world's largest trading pact, encompassing nearly half of global economic output. The most difficult issues concern

Looking Ahead

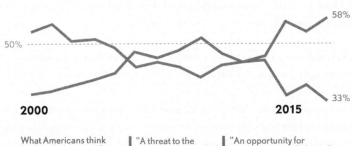

2000

2015

58%

33%

| What Americans think foreign trade means for the United States: | "A threat to the economy from foreign imports" | "An opportunity for economic growth through increased exports" |

Americans are again positive about trade.

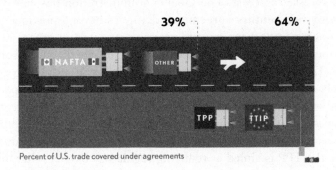

39%

64%

Percent of U.S. trade covered under agreements

U.S. government trade talks with Asia (TPP) and Europe (TTIP) could deliver the biggest market opportunities in a generation.

ways to mesh U.S. and EU regulations. The Centre for Economic Policy Research in the United Kingdom has estimated that 80 percent of the potential economic gains from the TTIP will come from reducing conflicts and duplication between U.S. and EU rules on regulatory issues ranging from food safety to automobile parts.[51]

Neither of these agreements promises enormous short-term economic gains. The TPP is estimated to add 0.4 percent annually to U.S. GDP by 2025, while the TTIP will similarly boost U.S. growth by about 0.4 percent of GDP after ten years.[52] But both agreements could have significant longer-term benefits. The TTIP, by increasing cooperation on regulatory standards in the world's two biggest consumer markets, could increase investment in the United States by ensuring that goods made to U.S. standards can be sold freely in Europe, and vice versa. Other countries will face increased pressure to adopt similar regulatory standards. By setting new trade rules for much of the Asia-Pacific, the TPP will likely encourage large developing countries such as China and India to either seek membership or harmonize their trading practices with the TPP rules.[53]

The Obama administration is also taking on nontariff and services trade barriers in other negotiations. The United States, the European Union, Japan, and twenty other WTO economies began talks on a "plurilateral" services agreement in March 2013, aimed at further liberalizing trade in services industries. The big developing economies, including China, Brazil, and India, are not participating, though China has indicated some interest in joining. The demand for services will likely expand in the coming years with the growth of middle-class populations around the world and further advances in Internet and communications technology. Thirty-three WTO members, including the United States, also recently reached an accord to further liberalize trade in high-technology products, updating the 1996 Information Technology Agreement. And in 2014, forty-three WTO members finalized revisions to the Government Procurement Agreement, which opens government purchases to foreign providers. This agreement also has twenty-eight observer members, of which ten—including China—are currently working to become full members. Efforts are being made bilaterally as well. For example, the U.S.-China Strategic and Economic Dialogue and the U.S.-China Joint Commission on Commerce and Trade are attempting to address a range of regulatory, licensing, and standards barriers.

Besides negotiating new trade agreements, the administration has also emphasized enforcement of existing trade agreements. It created a new Interagency Trade Enforcement Center in 2012 to better coordinate U.S. government actions to prevent violations of trade agreements and to challenge violations through the WTO and other mechanisms. The United States has won several big WTO disputes with China, including China's restrictions on electronic payment services, its subsidies for auto and auto-parts exports, and its export restraints on certain raw materials. These cases have been aimed at opening the Chinese market to exports of U.S. goods rather than at protecting the U.S. market from Chinese imports.

FUTURE PROSPECTS

If the United States completes and ratifies the various trade negotiations currently under way, it will mark the biggest expansion of trade liberalization since the conclusion of NAFTA and the Uruguay Round in the early 1990s. The TPP and TTIP would increase the share of U.S. trade covered under FTAs from 39 to 64 percent. In addition, the negotiations on services and high-technology goods promise additional market opening in sectors where the United States is highly competitive. The result will be not only future opportunities for exports and investment, but also an increasingly competitive landscape to which U.S. companies and governments will need to respond. Although U.S. performance has been improving, the United States is still far from realizing the potential to strengthen its economy through trade and foreign investment.

The Obama administration also faces challenges in winning congressional approval for its trade agenda. Despite broad agreement between most Democrats and Republicans on the value of increasing trade, deals with developing regions such as Mexico and Central America have been more controversial than those with more advanced economies because of concerns over competition from low-wage countries. The TPP includes both developing countries, such as Vietnam, and more advanced ones, such as Japan, that have traditionally run large trade surpluses with the United States.

If these agreements are concluded successfully and ratified by Congress, challenges will still remain in exploiting these new market opportunities in ways that bring broad benefits to U.S. workers and consumers. The Obama administration's initiatives on exports and foreign investment have targeted the right problems, but the results are still modest to date. Future progress will require concerted focus by governments to make the United States a more attractive place for companies to invest in, produce, and export goods and services.

Standard Deductions:
U.S. Corporate Tax Policy

INTRODUCTION

The way the United States taxes its corporations is outdated. The statutory U.S. corporate tax rate, which is the official rate before any tax breaks are applied, is the highest in the developed world and has remained largely unchanged for three decades. Unlike most other developed countries, the United States has a worldwide tax system, through which it taxes foreign profits. Yet the tax code allows corporations to defer these taxes if foreign profits stay abroad. Congress has also approved a number of tax breaks to encourage capital investment or research and development. Over the past three decades, these breaks have grown more generous and the share of profits earned abroad has increased so that the effective tax rate U.S. corporations actually pay has been steadily declining.

One consequence is that, even with the rich world's highest corporate tax rate, the United States does not raise as much corporate tax revenue as most other rich countries. And while U.S. corporate profits have reached record highs, the share of federal tax revenues coming from corporate taxes remains at historic lows. The high tax rate at home, combined with the deferral for overseas profits, also encourages corporations to hold profits abroad in lower-tax countries rather than return the money to the United States for investment or distribution to shareholders. Some corporations are also able to shift profits so they appear to have been earned in offshore tax havens. Finally, individual corporations pay highly uneven tax rates depending on whether they qualify for these tax breaks, with research-intensive multinational companies paying much lower rates, for example, than domestic retailers.

Long-term government inaction is mostly to blame. The way the United States taxes foreign profits was established in the 1960s. The last major tax overhaul was in the mid-1980s. While the U.S. government has stood still on corporate tax reform, most advanced countries have been lowering corporate tax rates, reducing tax breaks, and changing how they tax foreign profits.

Both political parties and President Obama agree on the general contours of a likely reform that would move the tax system in the right direction: cutting the corporate rate, broadening the base, and taxing foreign profits differently. The main difference is that Democrats would cut rates by less than what Republicans are seeking, and President Obama would strengthen the worldwide system instead of shifting toward a more territorial system. But a strong bipartisan consensus exists to rein in profit shifting. Paying for tax cuts is politically difficult, however, since the obvious way is to scale back tax breaks that corporations rely on and many Americans support. But, with Americans increasingly supporting a tax overhaul, there may be growing political payoffs for politicians who can deliver tax reform.

WHERE THE UNITED STATES STANDS

An ideal corporate tax system strikes the right balance among seemingly competing objectives. Policymakers who are concerned about competitiveness usually favor lower corporate taxes. Taxes slice into profits that could otherwise go toward productive investments, shareholder dividends, or employee wages. Corporations work to minimize their tax burden to maximize their profit margins and outcompete rivals. Countries want their corporations to be as competitive as possible; if a country's corporate taxes are high by international standards, their corporations are at a disadvantage. Countries also want to make sure they remain attractive destinations for corporations to locate, invest, and employ workers, and high taxes can affect those corporate decisions. But corporate taxes also pay for services—infrastructure, an educated workforce, stable rule of law—that corporations need to flourish. At the same time, under the current system, some types of companies pay high federal taxes but others pay scarcely any at all.

HIGH STATUTORY TAX RATE, BUT AVERAGE EFFECTIVE TAX RATE AND BELOW-AVERAGE REVENUES

Within the rich world, the United States has the highest statutory corporate tax rate. The federal rate is 35 percent and the average state rate is 4 percent, adding to a 39 percent total tax rate. The United States had one of the lower statutory corporate tax rates in the world the last time the rate was significantly cut in 1986. But while the U.S. rate has remained flat, other countries have been lowering their statutory rates over time (see figure 1). Some, like in the United Kingdom and Ireland, have carved out special low tax rates for patent-related income, called patent boxes, that are often half the statutory rate.

U.S. corporations, however, seldom pay the full statutory rate. Corporations can claim tax breaks that lower the effective tax rate, which is the rate they actually pay. When comparing effective tax rates, U.S. corporations on average pay closer to 27 percent, which is roughly on par with what other corporations pay in similarly advanced economies.[1]

Yet the United States collects relatively little corporate tax revenue. Statutory rates are lower in the rest of the OECD, yet those countries raise more corporate tax revenue—3 percent of GDP on average in 2013 against the United States' 2 percent.[2]

CORPORATE TAX BURDEN IS FLAT, BUT PROFITS ARE UP

The share of all federal tax revenues coming from corporate taxes has remained steady since the 1980s, at about 11 percent.[3] The relative tax

FIGURE 1. U.S. STATUTORY CORPORATE TAX RATE VERSUS REST OF THE OECD, WEIGHTED

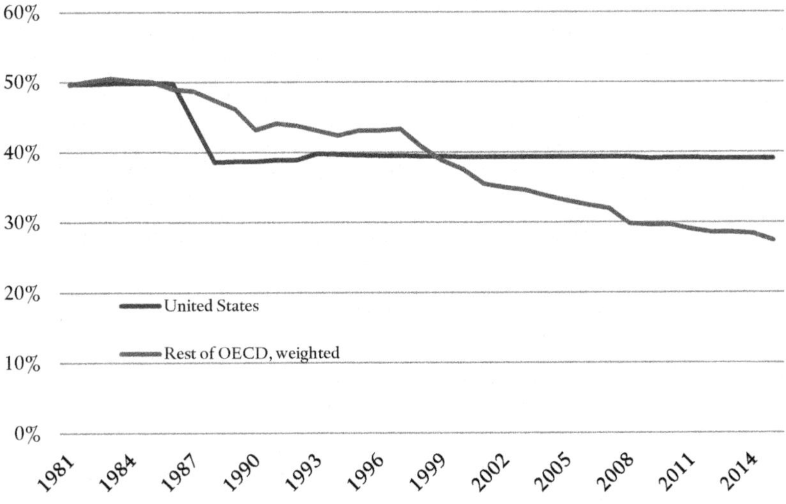

Source: OECD.

burden levied on individual taxpayers has also been flat. Yet the ability of corporations and individuals to pay taxes has moved in opposite directions. Corporate profits as a percentage of GDP are at record levels and, except for normal business cycle fluctuations, have been increasing since the 1980s. Wages as a share of GDP have been falling.

LOW TAX RATE ON RISING FOREIGN PROFITS

The United States stands apart most from other developed countries in the way it handles foreign profits. All corporations have to pay the local corporate tax rate in the countries in which they are doing business. For U.S. corporations, those same foreign profits are, at least in theory, subject to U.S. federal taxation. Taxing foreign profits is usually referred to as a worldwide tax system. The majority of rich countries are moving toward more territorial tax systems under which they exempt most foreign profits from taxation. Many U.S. corporations claim this creates an unfair playing field abroad, given that foreign competitors, in theory, face a lower overall tax burden.

Yet, in practice, U.S. corporations rarely pay much in U.S. taxes on foreign profits because they receive a credit for taxes paid abroad and are allowed to defer tax payments as long as those profits are retained abroad. The U.S. tax is only levied if and when profits are repatriated to the United States. As a consequence, U.S. corporations keep most of their foreign profits abroad—as much as $2 trillion is currently retained offshore.[4]

Even including taxes paid to foreign governments, U.S. corporations face a lower overall tax burden on foreign profits than they do on domestic profits (see table 1). The best available estimate suggests that

TABLE 1. U.S. CORPORATE TAX RATES COMPARED

Statutory tax rate*	39.1%
Average effective tax rate (i.e., what U.S. corporations actually pay)	
... on *all* profits**	27.1%
... on *foreign* profits, including foreign and U.S. taxes***	15.7%
... on *foreign* profits, only U.S. taxes***	3.3%

Sources: *OECD 2013, **Gravelle 2012, ***Gravelle 2011.

U.S. corporations face an effective tax rate (including all foreign and U.S. taxes) of just 15.7 percent on their foreign profits.[5] The U.S. government collects only 3.3 percent in taxes on those profits.[6]

Foreign profits have been steadily increasing so that in the 2000s they constituted close to 20 percent of all U.S. corporate profits, double their share in the 1970s. Primarily because of this, the average effective corporate tax rate paid by U.S. corporations has been *steadily declining*—even though the U.S. statutory rate has remained essentially unchanged for three decades.[7]

HUGE VARIATION IN TAX RATES
FOR INDIVIDUAL CORPORATIONS

But, like the statutory tax rate, the average effective tax rate is a misleading indicator because it hides the tremendous variation in what individual U.S. corporations actually pay after tax breaks. In the United States, the largest tax break is the deferral on foreign profits, followed by accelerated capital depreciation, the domestic production credit, and the R&D credit. The share of corporate profits coming from abroad has grown steadily, making the deferral tax break more substantial now than in the past. The remaining three big-ticket credits have also grown more generous in the 2000s.[8] Taken together, these credits benefit, for example, manufacturing, technology, or exporting companies more than retail companies. Thus, in 2014, General Electric, which has large capital and R&D investments and earns large foreign profits, self-reported having paid just 9.7 percent, while Target, whose sales are heavily retail and domestic, paid 36.5 percent in taxes.[9] A generation ago, the gap in effective tax rates was narrower.

Different tax rates for different types of corporations are not always a bad thing. Some tax breaks correct for market failures. Many economists argue, for example, that businesses involved in R&D generate more benefits for society than retail businesses. And because R&D is highly speculative, or carries substantial costs and risks for businesses, these businesses would underspend on R&D if it were not for government subsidies like the R&D credit. The tricky part is finding the right subsidy level and keeping it well targeted. The R&D credit could be better targeted.[10] More corporations (and small businesses) are claiming the credit and reaping larger breaks. Yet too many normal business expenses are leaking into R&D credit claims that should only include truly scientific and technological research. The merit of specific tax breaks aside, the larger question is whether society is benefiting enough to justify the hugely uneven tax rates that exist between corporations like General Electric and Target.

MORE NONCORPORATE PROFITS

A growing number of firms do not pay the corporate tax, which has become essentially a tax on big business. Less than 10 percent of U.S. businesses file as corporations, and among these, a tiny proportion pays the lion's share. In 2008, approximately 83 percent of all corporate taxes came from the 0.1 percent of corporations that earned more than $250 million in profits.[11] Conventional corporations (called C corporations for tax purposes) still make up the majority of the country's business receipts. But their share is down from what it was in 1980, and an increasing share is made up of businesses whose profits can "pass through" to lower individual tax rates (see figure 2).

The problem is that many of these pass-through businesses closely resemble C corporations that are subject to the corporate tax. Policy changes, mostly to help small businesses, have made it easier for firms to enjoy all the benefits of corporate status, like limited-liability protection, without paying corporate taxes. But today some of these firms are not so small when it comes to profits, particularly S corporations. These

FIGURE 2. SHARE OF TOTAL U.S. BUSINESS RECEIPTS, CORPORATIONS VERSUS PASS-THROUGH BUSINESSES

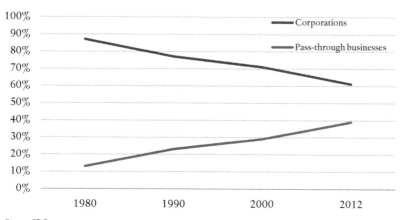

Source: IRS.

corporations, which cannot have more than one hundred shareholders, account for most of the business growth in pass-through firms. S corporations with annual earnings over $50 million account for roughly 30 percent of all S-type corporate revenue.[12] According to one analysis, these firms pay an average tax rate that is 6 percentage points lower than a firm that is subject to the corporate tax.[13] The Congressional Budget Office estimates that if all S corporations and limited-liability businesses were taxed at the corporate rate, federal corporate tax revenues in 2007 would have been 22 percent higher.[14] It is not uncommon for other developed countries to have similar rules allowing tax pass-throughs for businesses, but those businesses tend to have much smaller profits and play a smaller role in their economies than in the United States.[15] The difference between their corporate and pass-through tax rates also tends to be narrower, so taxes play a smaller role in how firms decide to organize themselves.[16]

MORE PROFIT SHIFTING TO TAX HAVENS

Deliberate tax avoidance by holding profits in tax havens is also eroding the corporate tax base. Corporations can alter profits made in high-tax countries so they appear to have been earned in low-tax countries, a tactic called profit shifting. Most large countries have statutory corporate tax rates above 20 percent. Tax haven countries tend to be small and have rates far below that. Ireland, for example, has a 12.5 percent corporate tax rate, and Bermuda has no corporate tax at all. A U.S. corporation can start a foreign subsidiary in a tax haven for allocating profits, lending money, or housing intangible assets like patents and trademarks. This is especially useful for technology companies such as Apple or pharmaceutical companies such as Pfizer that rely heavily on intangible income. Corporations can move intangible assets abroad for reasons other than taxes—for example, to align the location of such assets with the markets in which they will be used. But most profit shifting (in dollar volume) occurs through the manipulation of intangible assets.

Profit shifting also contributes to uneven effective tax rates on foreign profits. Corporations relying on intangible assets can drive their overall tax burden on foreign profits down to zero if they are smart about parking those assets in tax havens. But corporations relying on immovable tangible assets, such as oil or mining operations, cannot shift profits to tax havens, and face steep local taxes that are often higher than the U.S. statutory rate.[17]

Such tax avoidance is widespread. The five most popular tax havens account for 1 percent of the global economy, but 24 percent of reported foreign profits by U.S. multinational corporations.[18] The problem is getting worse; the gap has grown over time between the location of U.S. corporate investments and the location of their reported profits.[19] According to a Congressional Research Service report, profit-shifting tax avoidance is estimated to cost the federal government upward of $100 billion annually in lost revenue.[20]

This problem is not exclusive to the United States. All major developed countries are facing eroding corporate tax bases because of profit shifting. Although firm statistics are hard to come by, anecdotally at least, U.S. corporations such as Apple and Google appear to benefit the most from these tactics.[21] U.S. laws are also more lax when it comes to profit shifting.

OTHER COUNTRIES ARE DOING MORE
TO PREVENT PROFIT SHIFTING

Countries that have been moving toward territorial tax systems and cutting rates have also been tightening anti-avoidance laws. The UK and Australia recently created a penalty, dubbed a Google Tax, under which any company caught profit shifting would have to pay an elevated tax on those profits.[22] If the German government sees that the location of investments and sales is out of balance with reported profits, tax authorities can quickly move to tax the profits in question. Japan recently began taxing profits reported in countries with corporate tax rates below a certain threshold. In Italy, profits are taxed if reported in blacklist tax havens. The European Union is going after member states, such as Ireland, Luxembourg, and the Netherlands, that have signed preferential tax agreements with individual companies on the grounds that such agreements violate internal EU competition fairness laws.[23]

Although it is difficult to know how effective these new anti-avoidance measures are in practice, such policy changes imply that other advanced countries are more serious than the United States about combating profit shifting. In the 1990s and through 2004, the United States

Standard Deductions
U.S. Corporate Tax Policy

Uneven Rates

39.1%   **27.4%**

Statutory tax
rates, 2015

United States   Rest of OECD

The United States has the highest corporate tax rate in the developed world before tax breaks are taken into account.

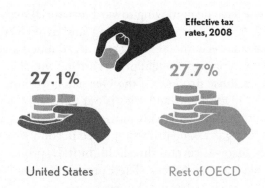

Effective tax
rates, 2008

27.1%   **27.7%**

United States   Rest of OECD

But because of tax breaks approved by Congress, U.S. corporations pay an effective tax rate similar to what their international competitors pay.

actually loosened its foreign profit anti-avoidance rules and has taken few major steps to reverse course to date.[24]

INTERNATIONAL COOPERATION
TO COMBAT TAX AVOIDANCE

Some tax scholars are skeptical that any anti-avoidance provisions or rate reductions will make a real dent in profit shifting. Corporations with armies of highly paid tax lawyers will find ways to exploit tax rate and policy differences among countries. Even if Congress found a revenue-neutral way to lower the federal rate to 25 percent, the U.S. national rate would still be more than twice the Irish rate, for example. And if the United States lowers rates, other countries may respond by lowering their rates further, as they did the last time the U.S. federal government cut corporate rates in 1986.

But no large advanced country wants a race to the bottom in corporate tax rates. One response has been new efforts by countries to cooperate through tax information exchanges and transparency. Tax transparency will help policymakers keep closer tabs on where and how corporations are reporting their profits. More visibility will also give policymakers more political leverage to strengthen anti-avoidance provisions. Tax auditors would have the public backing to be more aggressive. And image-conscious corporations might be compelled to change their ways.

This is similar to what happened with Starbucks in the United Kingdom. The company had not paid any taxes in the United Kingdom for five years until its tax-avoidance strategies made front-page news and sparked a consumer boycott. To console consumers, Starbucks announced in 2013 that it would pay British taxes.[25] Amid the public furor, conservative Prime Minister David Cameron promised to crack down on such avoidance.[26]

The U.S. system could benefit from more transparency. The U.S. Internal Revenue Service already has reams of data that could shed light on U.S. corporate profit shifting. But the information is not systematically analyzed or made publicly available. Just this past year, the European Union passed legislation requiring public disclosure of corporations' country-by-country profit and tax information.

The OECD has been leading the charge on tax transparency for some time. In the 1990s, it began identifying and exposing harmful tax practices. In 2009, it expanded its efforts to include a review of each country's tax system to evaluate the legal and regulatory framework, including transparency of tax calculations and payment information. One hundred and twenty countries are now participating in the review process. Under international pressure, all major tax havens have agreed to share tax information with higher-tax countries. The number of bilateral tax information–exchange agreements signed has soared, which allow countries to request information to verify their corporations' business dealings abroad, including bank statements, interest payments, and employee wages.[27] As recently as 2006, only a handful of these agreements were signed per year. By 2010, that rate reached hundreds per year.

In 2015, the OECD went further than promoting transparency, writing a new set of legal standards that member states can use to combat profit shifting. The project's leading architect claimed the golden era of international corporate tax avoidance was coming to a close.[28] That may be wishful thinking, but governments are getting more serious about profit shifting, and companies are taking note, adjusting their behavior. In the summer of 2015, for example, Amazon began reporting revenue where purchases had been made in the UK and France rather than in low-tax Luxembourg, where it had been reporting revenue in the past.[29]

COMPETITIVENESS IS NOT THE MAIN PROBLEM

In the popular press and within the business community, the U.S. corporate tax system is often accused of weakening U.S. economic competitiveness. Indeed, in a World Economic Forum survey of executives, U.S. respondents ranked taxes as the most problematic factor for doing business in the United States.[30] And according to the WEF's competitiveness index, besides government debt, U.S. performance is ranked poorest on taxes.[31] In a 2015 Harvard Business School survey of ten thousand alumni working in senior business positions, the U.S. tax code was the most-cited weakness for U.S. competitiveness compared to other advanced economies.[32]

But other evidence suggests competitiveness is not the main problem with the current corporate tax system. U.S. companies that do much of

Standard Deductions
U.S. Corporate Tax Policy

Tax Breaks

Foreign profits as percentage of total corporate profits, before taxes

The biggest tax break is for foreign profits, which have been increasing steadily as a share of corporate profits.

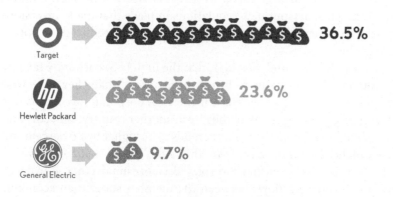

Target — 36.5%

Hewlett Packard — 23.6%

General Electric — 9.7%

Company annual effective tax rates, 2014

As a result of these rules, some companies with high foreign profits pay a low tax rate.

their business overseas normally pay much less in taxes than corporations that do most of their business within the United States. With such a low effective rate on foreign profits, it is not clear that U.S. corporations operating abroad are facing significant disadvantages compared with competitors based in other countries with territorial tax systems. According to one study that calculated the global tax burden of the largest two hundred Europe- and U.S.-based multinational corporations, U.S. corporations were no worse off and perhaps even better off than their European counterparts.[33]

In theory, U.S.-headquartered corporations could reduce their tax burden by reincorporating in a country with a territorial tax system, and this has happened in a few cases.[34] But evidence is scant that this is occurring on a large scale, perhaps given the many avenues already available for reducing tax liabilities.[35] Nor is there any trend toward new companies incorporating abroad. Other factors like lower wages, proximity to fast-growing markets, and government investment incentives are usually larger inducements for U.S. corporations to invest overseas than tax rates.

A few high-profile inversions in 2014 saw much smaller foreign companies in lower-tax countries buying giant U.S. corporations— deals motivated in large part to avoid tax bills.[36] Within a few months, the U.S. Treasury put new regulations in place that made inversions harder to achieve from a technical standpoint and reduced the potential tax benefits.[37]

Research has found, however, that the high U.S. corporate tax rate encourages corporations to invest more abroad than they otherwise would. According to one study, if the U.S. corporate tax rate is one percentage point higher than the rate in another country, U.S. corporations' employment in that country tends to be higher by 1.6 percent and sales higher by 2.9 percent.[38] Another study found that corporate tax rates within the European Union played a more important role in determining investment flows between EU member states than economic fundamentals.[39]

But the corporate tax may not have a large influence on overall economic output. Two authoritative studies have projected that lowering the U.S. corporate tax rate closer to rates in the rest of the developed world would raise U.S. output by two-tenths to four-tenths of 1 percent of GDP.[40]

THE REFORM DEBATE

The golden rule of tax reform is to lower rates and broaden the base. The two usually go together because of revenue constraints; the lower rates lead to less revenue, and eliminating tax breaks is the most common and politically palatable way to offset the lost revenue. The tax overhaul of 1986 attempted to do just that, and most serious corporate tax reform proposals today take the same approach.

Consensus is growing among economists that, compared with a personal income or consumption tax, the corporate tax is most harmful to investment—and therefore to productivity and economic growth.[41] Critics of the corporate tax argue that it is effectively a double tax, in that corporate profits are taxed again when they are paid out as dividends. Ideally, taxes would only be applied once to the same income. Many economists would like to do away with the corporate tax altogether and to have all income taxed as individual income or to tax consumption instead of income.

Differences in how conservatives and liberals have viewed corporate tax reform are significant. Conservatives tend to want to keep the corporate tax burden low and also worry about how the corporate tax may distort business behavior. Liberals have historically been more comfortable using the corporate tax system to encourage certain economic and business outcomes. Tackling climate change may mean giving a tax break to green energy companies, for example, and tax policy could be used to discourage companies from outsourcing jobs.

CURRENT PROPOSALS

Most of the problems facing the corporate tax system have accumulated from years of inaction on tax policy. The economy has changed, but lawmakers have failed to update the corporate tax system with it. To be sure, lawmakers have contributed to the growing unevenness in tax rates over time by sweetening some big corporate tax breaks for specific industries. But the U.S. corporate tax system has remained largely frozen since the last major overhaul in 1986. The rules that govern how to tax foreign profits were written in the 1960s, long before U.S. corporations became true multinational entities and earned large foreign profits, and long before they began shifting intangible assets abroad to tax havens.

Standard Deductions
U.S. Corporate Tax Policy

Eroding Base

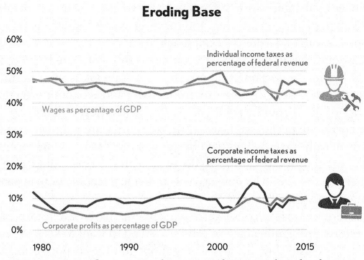

Corporate profits are up and wages are down, yet there has been
little change in tax burden.

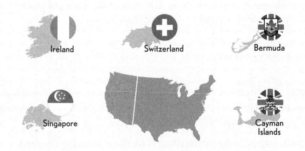

Tax havens make up   **...but shelter**

1%   # 24%

of the world economy...   of U.S. corporate foreign profits

Encouraged by U.S. tax law, U.S. corporations are moving profits
to tax havens.

The good news is that in theory both Republicans and Democrats favor reforms that would modernize the U.S. corporate tax system by lowering rates, broadening the base, and changing how foreign profits are taxed. This would make the system more coherent and effective rates more even, as well as bring the United States closer in line with other rich countries. And policymakers from both sides of the aisle want to curtail profit shifting, so that corporations would not be able to shift as much money to tax havens. Stronger anti-avoidance rules, for example, could place a minimum tax on foreign intangible (i.e., patent or trademark) income and limit the amount of money that could be borrowed on behalf of a foreign subsidiary. One bipartisan Senate proposal in 2015 called for a U.S. patent box similar to ones in the UK and Ireland to boost innovation and to encourage such income to be reported in the United States.[42] Some bipartisan discussion has focused on subjecting repatriated foreign profits to a one-time toll tax at a lower rate than the statutory level and using the new revenue to pay for highway maintenance and construction.[43]

Where Democrats and Republicans tend to disagree most is how far tax rates should be cut and how to reform the tax on foreign profits. Obama's budget proposals would lower the federal statutory corporate rate to 28 percent, which would still leave the U.S. rate the third-highest in the OECD, behind Japan and France. Most congressional Republican plans would lower the rate to 25 percent, putting the U.S. rate closer to the OECD average. Obama's plan would strengthen the worldwide system, tweaking accounting metrics so that the share of foreign profits that cannot be deferred—and therefore would be subject to U.S. taxation—would increase. Republicans would rather transition toward a more territorial system.

The bad news is that for now there is little political will to push through a tax overhaul that would require harsh trade-offs in repealing coveted tax breaks to pay for rate cuts. The politics are understandably hard. Rate cuts may be a relatively easy sell, but rolling back major tax breaks to pay for them is not. Take manufacturing. Across the political spectrum, policymakers champion the cause of U.S. manufacturing. But because manufacturing has been a winner with the current tax breaks, any reform of the corporate tax system would likely hurt that sector. And because manufacturing is the sector of the economy most subject to international competition, it would be difficult to sell a tax increase on manufacturers as somehow "pro-competitive." The R&D

credit is also popular with the public, and economists generally believe it generates substantial spillover benefits for the U.S. economy. The depreciation tax credit offers huge benefits, too. A 2007 Treasury report argued its repeal may actually harm investment in the long run and would offset any advantages of lowering the statutory rate.[44] Domestic investment in the United States has been weak over the past decade, which would argue for continuing to encourage investment through the tax system.[45]

The difficult arithmetic and politics make tax reform a delicate dance. Case in point is the less-than-warm reception of former House Ways and Means Committee Chairman Representative David Camp's (R-MI) 2014 tax overhaul proposal, the most ambitious and realistic plan written in decades. It would have rolled back nearly all the big-ticket tax breaks to offset the reduced 25 percent rate. Congressional leadership quickly shelved the proposal, however, in the face of business opposition, and Camp left office later that year. Without repealing the tax breaks, using base-broadening to pay for rate cuts is all but impossible. Repealing them, however, would touch off an epic battle with certain corporate interests. Few options to broaden the tax base are politically easy.

OTHER POLICY IDEAS

Tax holiday. Corporations have pushed for a tax holiday that would allow them to voluntarily repatriate foreign profits housed abroad. This is different from the congressional and presidential proposals, which would set a mandatory tax on all unrepatriated profits. Policymakers temporarily lowered the tax rate on foreign profits to 5.25 percent in 2004 with the expectation that corporations would use the repatriated money for new domestic investment and job creation. Instead, firms mostly used the tax holiday to increase dividends for shareholders.[46] The companies that benefited the most actually cut their employment rolls the following year. There are also concerns that another holiday could set a dangerous precedent by which corporations would park more profits abroad awaiting the next repatriation holiday.

Formula apportionment. Another policy option is to tax profits based on a formula indicating where corporate spending takes place instead of where profits are reported. To give a rough example, if 20 percent of a corporation's payroll expenses and investments are located in the

Standard Deductions
U.S. Corporate Tax Policy

Future Opportunities

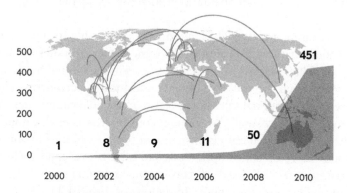

Number of tax information sharing agreements signed annually

Through tax agreements, the developed world is trying to crack down on tax avoidance.

The public is increasingly in favor of a tax code overhaul.

United States, the U.S. government would tax 20 percent of its global profits. Although no federal policymaker has endorsed the method, several U.S. states use formula apportionment to calculate corporate taxes for business activity within their borders. The European Union has been taking steps to adopt formula apportionment for internal business activity as well. A different possibility is to tax foreign profits only in countries with tax rates below a certain level, as Japan is doing.

National consumption tax. The United States is the only advanced country without a national consumption tax, the most common form being a sales or value-added tax (VAT). Sales taxes in the United States have historically been the preserve of state and local governments, which have resisted a national sales tax in fear that it would cannibalize their tax revenues. Many small-government conservatives are also opposed to creating a new federal tax instrument. Other advanced countries rely much more on consumption taxes to raise tax revenue. Including all excise and state and local sales taxes, consumption taxes raise just 15 percent of all U.S. tax revenue.[47] In the rest of the OECD, the share is twice that. Under world trade rules, VATs could also be rebated when a company exports from the United States, offsetting any competitive disadvantage from the additional tax burden. One of the biggest challenges with corporate tax reform is finding enough revenue to offset rate cuts, and a VAT could help make up the difference.

FUTURE PROSPECTS

Congress may be shelving tax reform for now, but political payoffs may be growing for politicians who can deliver it. Corporate tax avoidance has attracted more media attention, most notably after Apple CEO Tim Cook testified in front of a Senate panel trying to defend the highly successful U.S. company against accusations of "tax gimmickry."[48] Although few Americans understand the complexities of corporate tax rules, 72 percent say the nation's tax system needs major changes or should be entirely reconstructed, a substantially higher share than the 46 percent who said so in 2005. It is an opinion equally shared among Republicans, Democrats, and all demographic groups.[49]

While working together on the congressional supercommittee in 2011, the two heads of the major tax-writing authorities in the House and Senate said the greatest common ground on major tax code revisions was on corporate taxes. The contours of a likely reform have been drawn—cutting corporate rates, evening out effective rates, and taxing foreign profits differently. But difficult political compromises are still ahead before the United States can move forward on corporate tax reform.

No Helping Hand:
Federal Worker-Retraining Policy

by Robert Maxim, former Research Associate for
Competitiveness and Foreign Policy, Council on Foreign Relations

INTRODUCTION

During the Great Recession, the United States experienced one of
the largest increases in long-term unemployment in the industrialized
world. When people remain out of the workforce for extended periods,
they often have difficulty getting rehired. Many stop looking for work
altogether, and those who are lucky enough to find new positions are
usually rehired at lower wages. As a result, long-term unemployment
can strain a country's public assistance programs and permanently
damage its workforce.

Today, though U.S. job growth has been fairly strong, many companies
are still reluctant to hire because of growing international and domestic
competitive pressures. This forces many unemployed workers to leave the
industries in which they have spent their entire careers. The U.S. federal
worker-assistance system—the collection of federal programs designed
to help job seekers—does not adequately address this new kind of unemployment. It was particularly unable to cope with the massive spike in
long-term unemployment brought on by the Great Recession. The U.S.
system is also fragmented, consisting of several large programs accessible to any American and many smaller programs that provide services to
narrow groups. A 2011 Government Accountability Office (GAO) report
identified forty-seven employment and training programs spread across
nine federal agencies.[1] But these programs often lack sufficient resources
to help qualified workers. Additionally, some programs—such as assistance for workers displaced by increased foreign trade—offer greater
income support and easier access to training than others, resulting in
resource inequality among the unemployed.

Ineffective worker-assistance policies undermine economic recovery, lead to skills shortages for employers, and hurt U.S. competitiveness. Other advanced economies invest more in worker assistance and

use innovative programs to minimize unemployment. Apprenticeships, which play a large role in some countries, have helped reduce long-term unemployment among younger workers. These countries successfully mitigated some of the worst consequences of the Great Recession through effective worker-assistance policies.

In recent years, the Obama administration and Congress have taken steps to streamline U.S. worker-assistance programs, culminating in modest bipartisan reform via the Workforce Innovation and Opportunity Act (WIOA). However, more ambitious changes were scrapped in the face of partisan disagreement, and additional reforms are still needed. Congress should increase funding for worker-assistance programs to ensure access to necessary services for every worker, increase benefits for workers who lose their jobs for reasons other than foreign trade, and buffer funding for worker-assistance programs from the annual appropriations process to prevent partisan interference.

In the absence of federal support, some state and municipal governments, as well as nonprofit organizations, have taken steps on their own to help workers. These include expanding apprenticeship programs to develop the skills of younger workers and experimenting with new forms of training to better connect the unemployed with jobs. Although these programs are helping fill the gap in services, the federal government should also act to bolster assistance programs for all U.S. workers.

ACTIVATING UNDEREMPLOYED WORKERS

The Great Recession caused a huge increase in long-term unemployment in the United States. Long-term unemployment, which is generally classified as unemployment that lasts for more than six months, hurts both individual workers and the economy as a whole. When workers are out of a job for an extended period, the skills they have developed during their careers begin to atrophy. Long-term unemployment typically occurs when jobs are permanently lost, notably when a firm relocates abroad or technological advances make a job obsolete. Workers who lose their jobs to foreign trade or technological change often have to find a job in a new industry, which requires the development of a completely new set of skills.

Worker-assistance policies are generally divided into two broad categories. Under *active* labor-market policies, the government directly helps people find work. Examples of active labor-market policies include job-search assistance, worker training, employment incentives, and direct job creation. *Passive* policies, like unemployment insurance, replace income lost during times of unemployment but do not directly help workers find new jobs.

There is evidence that active labor-market policies can help funnel workers into jobs, which helps reduce unemployment even during downturns. An analysis by economists at the Federal Reserve Bank of Kansas City showed that a 1 percent increase in spending on active labor-market policies typically reduces the unemployment rate by 0.11 percent.[2] Among the different active labor-market policies, job-search assistance and job training have demonstrated the largest positive effect on helping workers find employment. Active labor-market policies can also increase workers' earnings. Another study indicates that job-search assistance is likely to boost pay in the short run, and vocational training, which is targeted at specific occupations, produces increased earnings in the longer term.[3]

Active labor-market policies are more effective for some groups than others. Young people entering the labor force for the first time can benefit from programs that combine classroom and vocational instruction, as well as programs that offer on-the-job training. However, youth training programs in the United States vary in design, which leads to discrepancies in their effectiveness.[4] Meanwhile, the evidence is mixed on whether programs to retrain displaced older workers help them find employment or secure higher wages. A recent study showed that displaced workers fare the best when they receive a degree or certificate and find employment in their field of retraining.[5]

Economic downturns can limit the immediate benefits of active labor-market policies. When labor markets are "loose," meaning the demand for jobs exceeds the supply of available positions, resources such as job-search assistance and job training may not be sufficient to reduce unemployment in the short run. Also, because many skilled workers lose their jobs in times of weak economic growth, additional training may not help them find employment more quickly.

Despite these limitations, active labor-market policies actually become more important during a downturn. When job growth is weak, these policies help prevent unemployed workers' skills from atrophying. Worker retraining also keeps the unemployed connected to the labor market, which is particularly helpful for the long-term unemployed,

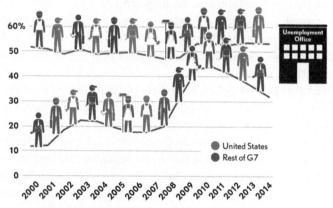

Percentage of unemployed workers out of work for more than six months

The United States used to have much lower levels of long-term unemployment than other rich countries. That advantage has shrunk since the Great Recession.

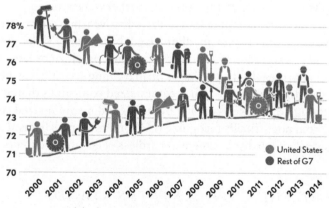

Labor-force participation rate, ages fifteen to sixty-four

U.S labor-force participation is falling, hurting long-term economic growth prospects.

who are the most likely to be discouraged, suffer from waning skills, and be seen as a risk by employers. Active labor-market policies can also help prepare the workforce as a whole for the next period of strong economic growth.

Moreover, many job vacancies remain difficult to fill, even when unemployment is high. Throughout the downturn in 2009 there were still more than two million job openings, and by mid-2015 that number had risen to above 5.4 million. Many of these vacancies are for skilled positions that require specific training or certifications to obtain. Active labor-market policies can help unemployed workers gain the skills they need to fill these positions.

Active labor-market policies also help older displaced workers, who have the most difficulty finding work again. These workers have often spent their entire careers developing skills for one type of job; if that job is permanently lost to international competition or new technologies, then they need to develop a new skill or face a significant loss of income. Although older workers are less likely to be laid off than younger workers, they are significantly less likely to be rehired.[6] Yet impact assessments do not show significant increases in income for these workers after completing retraining programs. This is because many of these workers were at the height of their experience and lifetime earnings before losing their jobs and are unlikely to see higher wages in any new career. Nonetheless, active labor-market policies can help these workers identify new positions and prevent further wage erosion.[7]

Active labor-market policies are also effective when directed toward employees of small- and medium-sized businesses. Skills development and worker training are most commonly provided by large firms. According to the OECD, participation in training activities can be up to 50 percent lower in small- and medium-sized companies than in large ones (though on-the-job training by small- and medium-sized companies is often not formally recognized).[8] Workers at small firms also face a higher risk of job displacement, regardless of economic conditions.

WHERE THE UNITED STATES STANDS

Until the Great Recession, the United States had one of the most dynamic labor markets in the developed world. Because workers were hired and fired with relative ease, job turnover was more frequent than in other countries, but the average length of unemployment was also shorter. During the downturn, however, the United States suffered a significant increase in long-term unemployment. In 2000, the United States had the lowest share of long-term unemployed among G7 nations, but by 2012 that rate had greatly increased, becoming closer to the G7 average. Although the U.S. rate has come down more recently, it is still historically high. This long-term unemployment increases the risk of workers losing their skills and facing permanent unemployment or underemployment, even after the economy recovers.

The recession also accelerated the decline in U.S. labor force participation, or the percentage of the working-age population that is either employed or looking for work. Low labor force participation can hinder long-term growth and strain government finances, because fewer people work and pay taxes, and more people use public services. Throughout the 1980s and 1990s, the United States was a global leader in labor force participation among all age groups. By 2012, that advantage had largely disappeared, except among adults over the age of sixty.[9] Even after the recession, U.S. labor force participation continued to fall. Meanwhile, Social Security disability claims have exploded, suggesting that many people have left the workforce and will not return.[10] When long-term unemployed workers run out of unemployment benefits, the Social Security disability benefit is one of the few government programs that provide a permanent paycheck, provided the worker can demonstrate some sort of physical or mental disability.

The United States spends far less on active labor-market policies than other developed countries. Historically, American workers who lost their jobs could expect to find a job in the same industry in a reasonable amount of time. Therefore, American workforce policy traditionally put the onus on individuals to secure new jobs, with only limited government assistance. Other developed nations, particularly in Europe, have a longer history of long-term unemployment. As a result, the governments of those countries have taken a more proactive role in training their workforce and matching workers with jobs. Among all OECD countries, only Mexico and Chile spend less on active labor-market policies as a percentage of gross domestic product than the United States does.[11]

As a percentage of the economy, the United States spends less money than it used to on active labor-market policies. During the twenty years prior to the Great Recession, spending on active labor-market policies declined from 0.24 percent of GDP to 0.13 percent.[12] During downturns, governments typically increase spending as the number of unemployed soars and more people use job-search and training services. Most other G7 countries increased active labor-market spending between 2007 and 2010, but U.S. expenditures were essentially flat during this period, even as U.S. unemployment increased at a faster rate than in other countries.

Employer-based training programs have been on the decline as well. One area where this is particularly noticeable has been apprenticeships in the United States, which decreased by 40 percent from 2003 to 2013. The downturn particularly hit industries such as manufacturing and construction that traditionally supported the majority of apprenticeships. Apprenticeships are also poorly understood by the general public. Many Americans are skeptical of vocational education, which they view as second tier to a university degree.[13] The perception is widespread that apprenticeships are exclusive to manufacturing or construction.[14] However, according to the Department of Labor, more than one thousand career areas, including white-collar professions, have registered apprenticeship programs.[15] Nonetheless, only about 0.2 percent of American workers—approximately 358,000 people—are in an apprenticeship program.[16] In comparison, over 60 percent of German high school students—roughly 1.8 million people—go through some kind of apprenticeship, and apprenticeship is widely seen as an acceptable path to a fulfilling career.[17] The drop in U.S. apprenticeships has been exacerbated by the decline in unionization in the United States, because unions have traditionally sponsored and organized apprenticeship programs.[18]

FEDERAL WORKER-ASSISTANCE POLICY: INSUFFICIENT AND UNEQUAL

The U.S. federal worker-assistance system fails to provide adequate assistance for eligible Americans and distributes its limited resources unequally across many programs. Most Americans are eligible for employment assistance through one of two laws: the Wagner-Peyser Act of 1933 or the Workforce Investment Act (WIA) of 1998. The programs enacted under these laws lack sufficient funding to provide every worker with individual assistance or training, however. Another program, Trade Adjustment Assistance (TAA), which provides employment

Unequal Opportunity

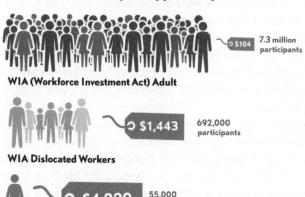

$104 — 7.3 million participants

WIA (Workforce Investment Act) Adult

$1,443 — 692,000 participants

WIA Dislocated Workers

$4,229 — 55,000 participants

Trade Adjustment Assistance

Per-capita funding for worker-assistance programs, FY2015

The most generous program helps workers who lose their jobs to trade competition. But they are a small portion of the unemployed.

Percentage of program participants receiving training, FY2015

And workers who lose their jobs to trade competition have greater access to training.

services and retraining for workers who lose their jobs to international competition, has generous benefits for those who qualify. At the same time, it has narrow eligibility requirements and a difficult application process. More than forty smaller programs provide employment services to specific groups that face significant economic disadvantages.

The Wagner-Peyser Act and the Workforce Investment Act form the backbone of the federal worker-assistance system. The Wagner-Peyser Act was a Great Depression–era law that matched individuals seeking work with New Deal public-works programs through a nationwide network of public employment offices known as the Employment Service. Today, the original Wagner-Peyser Employment Service still exists and provides job-search assistance and counseling for any worker seeking new employment.

Throughout the twentieth century, U.S. employment services became more complex as new programs were created to assist specific groups. Congress overhauled the existing system when it passed the WIA in 1998. The law introduced a system of One-Stop Career Centers designed to coordinate the various services offered across different programs. The WIA also established three large employment and training programs: WIA Adult, which provides employment services to any adult; WIA Displaced Workers, which provides services to workers who have lost their jobs through no fault of their own; and WIA Youth, which offers services to workers younger than twenty-one. The WIA Adult and WIA Displaced Workers programs provide similar services, and decisions about whether a worker should participate in the Adult or Displaced Worker program are generally made by local One-Stop Career Center staff. Both programs provide three levels of service: core, intensive, and training. Core services include job-search assistance, skill assessments, and labor-market information, and can be combined with or delegated to the Employment Service. Intensive services include individual employment-plan development, counseling, and case management. Users need to exhaust both core and intensive services without finding employment to be eligible for training. As a result, only 1 to 5 percent of WIA Adult and Displaced Worker participants receive training. Those who do get access to training can take subsidized courses offered by a local college (often community or technical colleges) or an industry-sponsored training center. States and municipalities often limit what occupations are eligible for subsidized training. When participants complete training, they generally receive industry-recognized certification.

When the bill passed in 1998, the economy was growing strongly and unemployment was low, around 4 percent and dropping. There were many job openings and relatively few job seekers, so the primary focus of the One-Stop Centers was matching unemployed workers with available jobs rather than providing training or other skill development. Congress reauthorized WIA in 2003, but did not make any substantive updates until the new Workforce Investment and Opportunity Act became law in July 2014. But the U.S. labor market changed substantially during that time, particularly with rising long-term unemployment.

The Employment Service and WIA programs account for about 80 percent of worker-assistance participants. The remaining workers receive assistance through one of nearly four dozen narrowly tailored programs; TAA, for example, provides enhanced unemployment benefits, job-search assistance, and retraining services for workers who lose their jobs to foreign competition. In addition to standard unemployment benefits, TAA-qualified workers are eligible to receive a federally funded credit to take part in up to two years of job training, an additional seventy-eight weeks of income support once unemployment benefits expire, a job-search allowance, and a relocation allowance. TAA-qualified workers who take a pay cut to return to the labor force quickly may also choose to forgo their benefits for wage insurance. If a worker's new salary is less than fifty thousand dollars, wage insurance provides half of the difference between a worker's previous salary and new salary for two years, up to a cap of ten thousand dollars.

Other smaller programs provide specific services tailored to needy populations. For example, in its 2011 report, the GAO highlighted two distinct youth training programs: Job Corps, which provides job training to at-risk youth on federally funded campuses, and YouthBuild, which provides skill development and service opportunities to at-risk youth in their own communities.[19] Although these programs offer similar services to overlapping populations, the different styles of service delivery may provide advantages for different individuals. For example, Job Corps provides services such as on-campus health care and child care for participants who otherwise would not be able to afford them. YouthBuild gives participants the opportunity to take part in housing construction for low-income families, as well as other service activities, to build stronger ties with their local community.[20]

Several major problems exist with the current U.S. active labor-market system, including uneven benefits among programs, inconsistent funding streams for different programs, and a scarcity of performance measurement.

Trade Adjustment Assistance offers more generous benefits than other programs, such as guaranteeing workers retraining if needed and providing financial support while workers undergo retraining. But workers can become permanently displaced by technological changes as well as global competition. Treating workers who lose their jobs to foreign competition better than those who lose their jobs to other factors does not make sense from an economic standpoint. And not every worker who loses a job to international competition can demonstrate eligibility for TAA. As a result, only about fifty-five thousand workers of more than 7.9 million unemployed participated in TAA in 2015. TAA is generally used as a political tool to garner support for trade agreements rather than as part of the wider worker-assistance system. As a result, TAA does not have permanent funding and must be regularly reauthorized by Congress.

The different programs have different funding sources. This creates inconsistency and prevents the worker-assistance system from working as effectively as possible during downturns. For example, the Employment Service has a dedicated funding mechanism through the federal unemployment tax (which also funds unemployment benefits), whereas the WIA programs are funded through annual appropriations, which can be held up by political battles in Congress.

Performance measurement is scarce among all programs. Most programs track outcome measures such as the number of participants who found jobs, retained employment, or saw a wage gain. However, only five of the forty-seven programs between 2004 and 2011 had undergone a comprehensive impact study to determine whether workers' employment and wage outcomes could actually be attributed to the program, according to the GAO. Furthermore, the GAO reported that half of the programs had not received a performance review in the previous seven years.[21] The absence of effective program measurement limits the ability of policymakers to compare programs and determine which ones are worthwhile investments.

DENMARK AND GERMANY: MODELS FOR REFORM

The United States handles worker assistance differently than many other industrialized countries. In the United States, worker training is fragmented into numerous programs of varying sizes. Additionally, training and employment services are rarely linked with income support or other passive unemployment measures. Two countries provide models for potential U.S. reforms: Demark maintains a flexible labor market by ensuring near-universal access to worker training and tying income support to employment services; and Germany has kept unemployment low and labor-market participation high by promoting innovative work sharing and apprenticeships for young workers.

Danish flexicurity: flexible labor market and a strong safety net. The Danish system of worker assistance is known as *flexicurity* and consists of three core pillars: labor-market flexibility, income security, and active labor-market policies. Labor-market flexibility refers to a company's ability to easily hire and fire workers. The Danish labor market has characteristics of both liberal market economies like the United States and continental economies such as France. Denmark's level of employee protection falls between those two extremes. Income security means that although companies are able to easily fire employees, substantial financial support is immediately available for displaced workers. Unemployment benefits cover approximately 60 percent of the average income in the country and can last up to two years. Denmark's active labor-market policies center on individualized job training. Job centers work closely with companies to tailor programs toward skills in demand in the local labor market.

Both the Danish and American economies are highly flexible, but Denmark offers significantly wider access to training and employment services, and provides more generous unemployment benefits. Unemployed workers begin meeting with a personal counselor at a local job center immediately after losing their jobs, and must continue to meet with the counselor every three months until employed. It is the counselor's job to ensure that the worker is actively seeking work and to connect the worker with additional retraining programs as necessary. These labor-market services are combined with generous unemployment benefits for the duration of a worker's unemployment or retraining, to ensure income stability while workers learn new skills. Access to these services is nearly universal, and they are funded by a dedicated payroll tax, which ensures consistent funding.[22] As a result, the system works as an automatic stabilizer that has little need for discretionary action during a downturn.[23] This helps buffer Danish labor-market policy from political interference.

Few Resources, Unknown Effectiveness

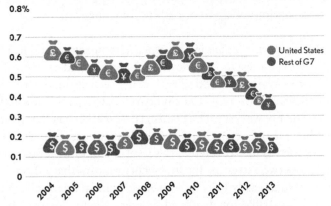

Public expenditure on active labor-market policies as a percentage of GDP

Compared with other rich countries, the United States devotes far
fewer resources to help the unemployed find jobs.

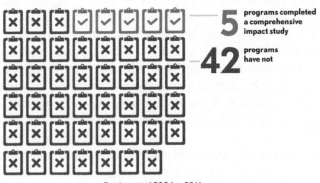

For the period 2004 to 2011

The effectiveness of many U.S.
worker-assistance programs remains unknown.

Denmark's model fosters a high level of employment security—the ability to find a new job after displacement without a significant drop in salary. This is an important distinction between Denmark and several other major continental European economies. France, for example, emphasizes job security, which makes it extremely difficult to fire a worker. Employment security acknowledges that labor-market turnover is essential and instead focuses on ensuring that displaced workers are rehired without a substantial decrease in income.

Flexicurity faced its greatest test during the late-2000s downturn and has shown mixed results in response. Unemployment increased quickly throughout 2008 and 2009, although given the country's low pre-crisis unemployment and relatively flexible labor market, this did not come as a surprise. Unemployment continued to increase at a slower rate for several years, before ultimately peaking at 7.9 percent in May 2012, below both the EU average and U.S. peak unemployment. Over the past three years, it has gradually fallen.[24] Overall, Danish labor-market participation has dropped very little since the onset of the downturn. Additionally, although the proportion of unemployed workers who have been out of work for more than six months has grown, the rate is still among the lowest in Europe.[25]

However, the country's generous benefits strained Danish finances during the downturn. In June 2010, the government halved the duration of its unemployment benefits, cutting eligibility from four years to two. Studies showed that unemployed workers tended to find new jobs much more frequently just after losing a job or just before benefits expired, which indicated that workers were not conducting the most thorough job searches possible.[26]

Germany: low unemployment through work sharing and apprenticeships. Germany withstood the downturn without a major increase in unemployment. Since 2009, Germany's unemployment rate has actually decreased substantially, and it is now one of the lowest among major economies.[27] Germany has also maintained a relatively low unemployment rate among young workers.[28] Its use of work sharing, facilitated by wage subsidies and flexible worker schedules, has helped prevent widespread worker displacement. Additionally, the country's apprenticeship system allows young workers to acquire credentials other than a college degree, facilitating their access to high-paying jobs in manufacturing and other skilled trades.

Extensive use of wage subsidies and payment flexibility also helped German companies retain employees during the worst periods of the downturn. If a company chooses to drop employees from full time to part time rather than to lay them off, the German government will provide the worker with 60 percent of the difference between the two wages (67 percent for workers with children).[29] This policy, known as short-time work, helped employers keep workers on the payroll even as company bottom lines deteriorated from the recession. Firms can thus preserve an experienced work force and minimize recruitment and training costs once recovery begins. For workers, a wage subsidy is usually preferable to collecting unemployment benefits or entering retraining because it minimizes income loss and preserves their longer-term career prospects.

In addition to short-time work, German firms use a flexible work schedule known as work-time accounts to minimize layoffs. Work-time accounts are not a government benefit, but rather an agreement between employers and employees that rewards companies that offer part-time employment rather than laying off workers. During boom times, employees work extra hours but forgo overtime pay. In exchange, the extra hours are tracked in a work-time account. During economic downturns, a company can reduce an employee's hours, but cannot reduce his pay or lay him off until the work-time account is depleted.[30] This gives the employer an incentive to keep the worker employed, or else face a large payout. A 2007 Federal Labor Court ruling said that firms could not lay off a worker if another employee doing equivalent work had a work-time account surplus. This decision strengthened the incentive for employers to shift workers to part time rather than lay them off.[31]

At the height of the crisis in 2009, more than 1.5 million workers held short-time positions. One assessment projected that without short-time work, German unemployment would have risen by twice as much as it did in 2009.[32] Another study estimated that short-time work saved roughly 400,000 jobs and work-time accounts saved an additional 320,000.[33]

In addition to maintaining a relatively stable labor market at the height of the recession, Germany has not experienced a youth unemployment crisis like many other developed economies. This is largely credited to the German dual system apprenticeship model, which combines traditional education with vocational training for young adults. About 60 percent of German sixteen- to nineteen-year-olds participate in apprenticeships, which combine classroom training in a public vocational school with on-the-job training in a specific industry.[34] After students complete their mandatory years of education, they are eligible to apply to a private company for a two- or three-year training contract. Those who are accepted receive on-the-job training provided by the company, and subsidized classroom training through publicly funded vocational schools.[35] Graduates receive an industry-recognized certificate that is widely accepted within the chosen field. They gain technical skills for a specific job, as well as broad knowledge of an industry as a whole. Some 330 different professions sponsor apprenticeships.[36]

Because training and vocational education are only available to individuals who receive an apprenticeship offer from a firm, the system ensures that every enrollee will have a job during the program and good career prospects on graduation. Six in ten apprentices stay with the company where they trained, and those who do not bring an industry-accepted credential to any similar job.[37]

Limitations of these models. Several features of the German and Danish economies may limit their relevance to the United States. The German economy is highly export oriented, whereas the United States still relies on domestic production and consumption for most of its economic growth. Because many manufacturing jobs are export oriented, the demand for industrial-sector workers may be greater in Germany than in the United States.[38] But the United States has millions of job vacancies requiring workers with specialized skills. A German-style apprenticeship program could help companies, in coordination with federal, state, and municipal governments, to fill those openings.

Additionally, both Germany and Denmark have stronger labor representation than the United States. In 2010, union membership stood at 68 percent in Denmark, compared with 11 percent in the United States.[39] In 2010, slightly fewer than 19 percent of German workers were members of trade unions, but collective bargaining agreements cover some 60 percent of the workforce.[40] The relationship between employee representatives, employers, and the government is essential to regulate Danish and German worker assistance. The combination of easy hiring and firing policies with generous unemployment insurance is a long-standing compromise between employers' associations and trade unions in Denmark. The schedule flexibility provided by short-time jobs and work-time accounts in Germany is a similar compromise.

Relatively weak collective bargaining policies in the United States may limit the prospects for establishing Danish- or German-style reforms.

Finally, both Germany and Denmark spend far more on active labor-market policies than the United States. Denmark and Germany allocated 2.3 percent and 0.8 percent of GDP, respectively, to active labor-market policies. The United States, by contrast, spent only 0.1 percent of its GDP on active labor-market policies.[41] Without an increase in spending on the federal, state, or municipal level, it would be difficult to replicate these programs.

WHAT HAS BEEN DONE

OBAMA AND CONGRESS:
COMPROMISE, NO MAJOR REFORMS

Both the president and congressional Republicans have proposed comprehensive worker-assistance reform plans, but the only bill that has managed to gain bipartisan support makes marginal changes to the existing system. In July 2014, Congress passed the Workforce Innovation and Opportunity Act. The WIOA eliminates fifteen small programs, but preserves the existing adult, displaced worker, and youth program models, as well as the Employment Service. It also eliminates the core and intensive service sequence, which it combines into a single career services category, and allows workers to bypass these services and enroll directly in training. Additionally, WIOA puts an increased emphasis on partnerships with business and on-the-job training, reimbursing eligible employers for up to 75 percent of the costs to train workers. The act also strengthens evaluation and data reporting requirements by standardizing them across programs. WIOA received overwhelming bipartisan support, passing 95 to 3 in the Senate and 415 to 6 in the House.

The compromise bill was a positive development, but it largely leaves the existing system intact. During debate on the bill, lawmakers cited their desire to "not let the perfect be the enemy of the good."[42] But WIOA did not address several major issues with the U.S. worker-assistance system, such as eliminating the inequities between TAA and other programs, providing enough funding to guarantee adequate assistance for every worker, or insulating financing from the politics of the congressional appropriations process.

Both the Obama administration and congressional Republicans have proposed more substantial reforms to worker assistance. In his 2012 State of the Union address, the president highlighted "the maze of confusing training programs" that American workers face when they lose their jobs.[43] In response, the Obama administration proposed eliminating Trade Adjustment Assistance and the WIA Dislocated Worker program to establish a new Universal Displaced Worker program that would provide employment services and retraining to all workers who lose their jobs by no fault of their own. A Department of Labor explanation of the proposal noted that there "is simply no economic rationale for treating . . . groups of workers differently based on how they were displaced."[44] Republicans in the House of Representatives originally favored a bill that would have eliminated two dozen existing programs and transformed federal employment services into a block grant system to be administered primarily on the state level.

A Universal Displaced Worker program would combine several elements of the two existing programs. Similar to WIA/WIOA, the program would offer basic and intensive level services to workers, as well as subsidized training in "high-growth, high-demand" occupations for workers who qualify. Like TAA, the program would also provide up to eighteen months of income support for workers in retraining, regardless of whether the worker qualified for unemployment insurance. Workers could also be eligible for job-search allowances and relocation allowances to find a job outside of their home community. Under President Obama's proposal, displaced workers who quickly find a lower-paying job could receive a wage subsidy to cover the difference between their old and new salaries.

Congressional Republicans agree with the president that existing worker-assistance programs should be consolidated. Rather than create a new federally administered program to help displaced workers, however, they support giving greater control over training to state and local workforce organizations. Many Republicans argue that state and municipal officials are more in touch with the needs of the local economy and therefore better positioned to design effective worker-assistance policies.[45] In 2013, the House of Representatives passed a bill to repeal twenty-four federal worker-assistance programs, including the Workforce Investment Act programs and the Employment Service. Instead, the federal government would provide a single block grant to states, giving governors wide discretion on how to use the funding. The act also eliminated core and intensive services,

No Helping Hand
Federal Worker-Retraining Policy

Businesses and Government Are Not Stepping Up to the Plate

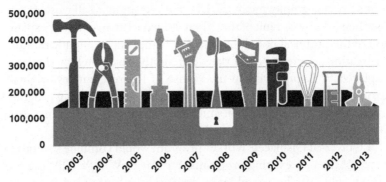

Number of registered apprenticeships

Apprenticeships have declined 40 percent in the last decade.

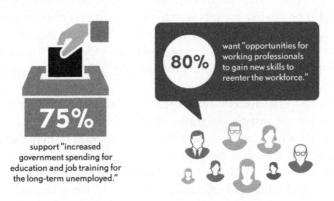

75% support "increased government spending for education and job training for the long-term unemployed."

80% want "opportunities for working professionals to gain new skills to reenter the workforce."

Voters want to see an increased effort by both the government and colleges to help workers gain new skills.

combining them into a single category of work-ready services, and removed the need for a worker to complete these services to be eligible for training. This bill was eventually combined with Senate amendments to become WIOA.

POSITIVE TRENDS ARE EMERGING ELSEWHERE

Outside Washington, state and municipal initiatives show promise for helping workers of all ages and skill levels. South Carolina, for example, has created an apprenticeship reform model that could serve as a template for many other states. And sectoral training programs, which focus on training workers for jobs in high-growth fields, are increasingly popular.

South Carolina has implemented a scalable model to rapidly expand the number of apprenticeships in the state since 2007. Apprenticeship Carolina was created as a partnership among the South Carolina state government, the South Carolina Chamber of Commerce, and the South Carolina Technical College System. The program provides a one thousand dollar annual tax credit to businesses for every apprentice the company takes on, for up to four years per apprentice. In addition, the state provides companies with free services to facilitate hiring apprentices, including marketing apprenticeships, assisting with federal registration paperwork, and identifying core job competencies. The Technical College System works with companies to design a relevant academic and training curriculum, and apprentices take classes while working for the company.[46] Some companies cover tuition for apprentices, whereas other apprentices receive tuition assistance through grants provided by the Technical College System. When Apprenticeship Carolina began, the state had 777 registered apprentices. Since then, more than nine thousand new apprentices have participated in the program, a rapid increase in a time when apprenticeships nationally are growing rarer.[47] Additionally, the number of companies hiring apprentices has risen from ninety in 2007 to more than six hundred today.[48]

The biggest challenge facing Apprenticeship Carolina is its low completion rate. In recent years, the percentage of apprentices completing the program has ranged from the low twenties to the high thirties.[49] In Germany, the completion rate is closer to 80 percent.[50] However, the program is an important first step toward building a wider apprenticeship presence in the United States, and its relatively straightforward model makes use of the existing state Technical College System, which is transferrable to many other states.

The Obama administration has expressed support for expanding regional apprenticeship models like Apprenticeship Carolina. In 2014, President Obama hosted the first White House Summit on American Apprenticeship and called on Congress to fund more apprenticeships.[51] In his 2015 State of the Union address, Obama pledged to expand apprenticeships. His administration has created an American Apprenticeship Grant program that allocates $175 million to create thirty-four thousand new apprenticeships.

In addition to apprenticeships, some states are expanding sectoral training. This model trains participants in a specific industry and gives them a portable skill set that could be applicable to multiple firms in the given industry. Many sectoral training programs focus on high-growth sectors, such as health care or information technology. Training is generally led by vocational schools or community colleges in coordination with local governments or nonprofit organizations, rather than by specific employers. On completion, participants generally receive certification relevant to their industry.

A good example of sectoral training is the Per Scholas program in New York City. Per Scholas provides low-income city residents with computer-technician training. The fifteen-week, five-hundred-hour course offers participants the opportunity to participate in industry-related internships, and participants earn an industry-recognized technician certification.[52] Per Scholas expanded to Columbus and Cincinnati in 2012 and to Washington, DC, and Dallas in 2014.[53] A 2010 study assessing the effectiveness of Per Scholas and several similar programs found that workers in sectoral training programs received 18 percent higher wages and more consistent employment when compared to a control group.[54]

FUTURE PROSPECTS

The Great Recession made Americans more aware of the need for a better-functioning worker-assistance system. A February 2012 Gallup poll found that 75 percent of American workers supported increased government spending for education and job training for the long-term unemployed.[55] And a survey by Northeastern University found that 80 percent of respondents thought it was important for U.S. colleges and universities to focus on "providing opportunities for working professionals to gain new skills to reenter the workforce."[56]

But doing more will cost more. Danish- or German-style reforms cannot be implemented without a big increase in spending on active labor-market policies. The compromise bill that Congress passed does not significantly increase funding for active labor-market programs, and even the president's more ambitious proposal would keep spending below 0.2 percent of GDP, still among the lowest in the OECD. Yet innovative models are being implemented on the state and municipal level, many of which are based on partnerships with the private or nonprofit sectors. Until Congress is willing to invest more in active labor-market policies, these programs could be adopted by other states, or on the federal level, to help fill the gap.

Quality Control: Federal Regulation Policy

INTRODUCTION

The number of federal regulations and hours required to complete federal paperwork have been rising steadily for decades. Under President Obama, the impact of regulations has been increasing, too. New laws enacted by Congress have dramatically changed regulation of the financial and health-care industries, and Obama has continued the long-standing regulatory push to protect the environment and conserve energy. Although a certain level of regulation is needed to keep the environment clean, the public healthy and safe, and markets well-oiled and stable, many policymakers worry that too much regulation can stifle economic growth.

The American public is deeply divided over whether businesses face too many regulations, and Republicans and small-business leaders have grown more concerned over the course of the Obama presidency. Yet when asked about specific regulations, such as standards on air quality, fuel efficiency, or workplace safety, most Americans favor the status quo.

Although regulations may be increasingly costly for U.S. businesses, and for small businesses especially, they do not appear to pose a competitive disadvantage for U.S. companies relative to those based in other advanced economies. Compared with other G7 countries, the United States has consistently been among the easiest places to do business, offering one of the least regulated economies and the least burdensome regulatory systems.

Research on the economic effects of regulation is underdeveloped, though available evidence suggests most regulations have brought benefits that are worth the economic costs. Some of the most costly regulations, which affect air quality, have also produced the biggest benefits. Nevertheless, the federal government could do more to lower burdens on businesses without compromising the objectives of regulation.

In particular, the U.S. regulatory management system, or the way in which federal regulations are designed, could be improved. The system has changed little since the early 1980s and focuses almost exclusively on cost-benefit analysis before regulations are put into place, rather than in hindsight when it is clearer whether or not a regulation is working. As a result, the stock of older regulations accumulates without an institutionalized process for determining which regulations should be repealed or changed. Even the analysis before regulations are implemented could be better informed through empirical research and more sensible and proportionate examination of all draft regulations: some come with overly detailed analysis that impedes decision-making, whereas others escape oversight altogether.

The United States used to be the trailblazer in regulatory reform. The rest of the rich world has caught up, however. Countries such as Australia, Canada, and the United Kingdom can now lay claim to being at the cutting edge of regulatory management. They have implemented systems that better manage the existing stock, for example, with regulatory budgets and automatic reviews, while improving the filter for new regulations through empirical study.

Efforts to revamp the U.S. federal regulatory system are stalled. Regulatory management under President Obama has been hardly distinguishable from that of every other administration since President Jimmy Carter. Dozens of congressional proposals have been made that would bring the U.S. system more in line with countries at the forefront of regulatory innovation. These proposals fall short on several dimensions, however, focusing on more restrictions like regulatory budgets and automatic reviews without directing more resources toward empirical research and improving retrospective analysis.

HOW THE REGULATION SYSTEM WORKS

Regulation is the third principle instrument (along with taxing and spending) that governments use to achieve policy goals.[1] In the United States, Congress passes statutes outlining the broad contours of regulations. Federal departments and agencies within the executive branch then write and enforce specific rules or regulations.

The federal regulatory reach is huge. It affects everything from the food and medicine we consume to the efficiency of the cars we drive, the

safety of our workplaces, the clarity of the air we breathe, and the way
we save for retirement. A full-time federal workforce of three hundred
thousand keeps the regulatory system running. More than three thousand new regulations are issued every year, most of which are minor or
technical, though roughly forty to fifty are economically significant,
which is defined as those with an annual cost to the economy of at least
$100 million.[2] The rate of new rulemaking has been roughly constant
over time, but the number of new statutes passed by Congress has been
decreasing for decades.[3]

More than taxing and spending, regulations do not easily lend themselves to simple and transparent accounting. Regulations are also often
written by civil servants who are not directly accountable to the public.
To keep the quality of regulations in check, governments create regulatory management systems.

In the U.S. federal government, responsibility for overseeing this
quality-control process falls mostly on the executive branch, specifically the Office of Information and Regulatory Affairs (OIRA). Congress has taken a backseat in regulatory management policy, which is
largely set by executive orders issued by the president.[4] But presidential
directives and OIRA's oversight do not cover regulatory agencies that
are technically independent and beyond the president's control, including the Securities and Exchange Commission (SEC), the Federal Communications Commission (FCC), and the Federal Trade Commission
(FTC).

Since 1980, when Congress created OIRA, each president's management framework has been remarkably bipartisan and consistent
across administrations. The system is institutionally designed to
assess and improve the quality of new regulations before they are
implemented. At the heart of the framework is a cost-benefit analysis,
which is calculated by federal agencies and departments for economically significant regulations.[5] All draft regulations (along with any
required cost-benefit analysis) are sent to OIRA for review and final
approval. OIRA sends a majority of draft rules back to departments
with requested changes, sometimes with suggestions for how to
improve submitted cost-benefit analyses. OIRA staffers spend most
of their time collecting and sharing information about best practices
from across the federal government, listening to input from affected
industries and consumer groups, and ensuring that draft regulations
fit with the administration's policy agenda.[6]

IDEOLOGICAL DIVISIONS: BALANCING SOCIETY-WIDE
BENEFITS VERSUS PRIVATE-SECTOR COSTS

Policymakers from across the political spectrum would agree that a
certain level of regulation is needed to keep the environment clean, the
public healthy and safe, and markets well-oiled and stable.

But even if society as a whole ultimately benefits, economic costs are
associated with any regulation. Those costs usually hit businesses first
but are then passed on to employees through lower wages and job cuts
or to consumers through higher prices.

Democrats and Republicans appear most divided over whether the
benefits justify the costs. Republicans tend to worry about the regulatory
burden leveled on businesses and place a higher priority on minimiz-
ing regulatory costs. For example, Rick Perry, the former Republican
governor of Texas, invoked his state's low-regulation environment to
explain its impressive job-growth record.[7] Democrats tend to be more
willing to place regulatory costs on the private sector to achieve what
they believe are larger net benefits for society.

PUBLIC OPINION: DIVIDED ON REGULATIONS
GENERALLY, IN FAVOR SPECIFICALLY

American public opinion on federal regulation falls along partisan lines.
Republicans are far more likely than Democrats to believe there is too
much regulation of business. Since the Great Recession and during the
Obama presidency, the partisan gap has widened considerably—and
is almost entirely explained by growing concern among Republicans.
Today 79 percent of Republicans believe the government regulates business too much; only 26 percent of Democrats agree, a difference of fifty-
three percentage points.[8] During the George W. Bush presidency, the
gap between the two parties was half as large.

A survey of small-business executives mirrors the Republican poll-
ing trend. The share who indicate that "government regulation and red
tape" are their most important problem has been increasing over the
course of the Obama presidency. For the past three years, it was among
the survey's most commonly cited problems.[9] Public criticism of regulations has picked up as well. Between 2007 and 2011, media mentions
of "job-killing regulations" went from just four appearances per year to
seven hundred.[10]

Quality Control
Federal Regulation Policy

Partisan Divide

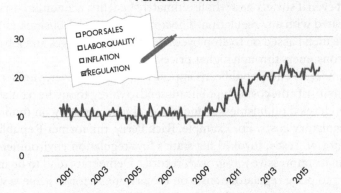

POOR SALES
LABOR QUALITY
INFLATION
REGULATION

Percent of firms selecting regulation as single most important problem

Small businesses have grown more concerned about
regulations under Obama.

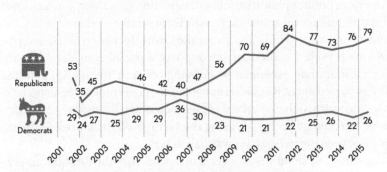

Percent of Americans who say government is overregulated, by party

Over the same period, Republicans increasingly
believed businesses are overregulated.

The public as a whole appears more favorable toward specific regulations, however. In a 2012 Pew survey, the vast majority of Americans (and a clear majority of Republicans) either favored current levels or wanted more regulation for the environment, car safety and efficiency, and workplace safety. Survey results were the same twenty years ago, suggesting public opinion has been remarkably consistent and positive about specific federal regulations.[11]

REGULATION'S AMBIGUOUS EFFECT ON THE ECONOMY

Empirical research remains underdeveloped regarding regulation's effect on the economy. Economists have not settled on a good way to measure overall regulatory burden, often resorting to crude proxies like the number of pages in the list of all federal regulations or the number of restrictive words like *must* or *should* on that list.[12] Because of these data limitations, the best empirical studies take on a specific regulation rather than the full stock of regulations. Largely unknown is how the average business is affected by the cumulative set of regulations, or whether certain regulations harm or help different kinds of business activity, such as innovation or entrepreneurship.

Existing research suggests the political rhetoric blaming economic woes or successes on regulation tends to be overblown. One controversial study, sponsored by the Small Business Administration, found gigantic economic costs, but also failed to measure benefits.[13] No relationship is apparent between the level of regulatory burden among U.S. states and their unemployment rate or their rate of business startups and failures. More prosperous states have more regulation, though this may be because wealthier communities demand it.[14] Studies have not found robust results for the "pollution haven" effect, in which firms are induced to move to regions where environmental regulations are less stringent. This may be in part because the most heavily regulated industries, such as mining, wood products, and energy production, are not very mobile.[15] Michael Porter of Harvard Business School argues that stricter environmental codes can be a competitive advantage because they promote innovation in more efficient production techniques.[16] It makes intuitive sense that regulations are, on average, costlier for smaller businesses because they do not have the advantage of scale.[17] Small business cannot afford to spend the staff time that large businesses can to comply with regulations. But the most costly regulations hit big polluters the most; these polluters tend to be large corporations, not small businesses.[18] Studies that analyze the effect of regulations on job creation have found both positive and negative effects, but they are always small and usually localized.[19] No good research exists on how small-business employment may be affected. At least for larger employers, regulations do not appear to be a significant cause of job loss; employers attribute few mass layoffs of fifty or more employees to government regulation (see table 1).[20]

As for federal regulations, the best evidence suggests nearly all economically significant rules pass the cost-benefit test.[21] Environmental regulations, by far the most costly, carry the greatest benefits by making Americans healthier. The Clean Air Act, enacted in 1970 and tightened with stricter pollution standards ever since, dramatically reduced the fine-particle matter in the air that Americans breathe. As a result, Americans have fewer asthma and heart attacks, miss fewer days of school and work, and live longer. The act also gradually eliminated lead from gasoline, which impairs children's cognitive abilities. Since 1980, the Environmental Protection Agency (EPA) estimates that the lead regulation decreased the level of lead in Americans' bloodstreams by more than 90 percent.[22]

For some regulations that do not pass the monetary cost-benefit test, regulators can decide that human benefits nonetheless justify the high cost. Take a recent regulation that required rear-view cameras in new cars by 2018. Although it will cost an estimated $140 per car to install, even auto manufacturers supported the measure as a way to prevent horrific accidents, such as parents backing over their infant children.[23]

Past government cost-benefit analyses of draft environmental regulations have generally overestimated both costs and benefits, with no

TABLE 1. SURVEY OF REASONS FOR MASS LAYOFF EVENTS

	2012	2011	2010	2009	2008	2007
Number of mass-layoff events	6,500	6,596	7,247	11,824	8,259	5,363
Percentage of mass layoffs attributed to government regulations	0.3	0.2	0.2	0.1	0.3	0.3

Source: Bureau of Labor Statistics (2013).

systemic bias in either direction.[24] The costs are overestimated in large part because government agencies undercount the private sector's ability to adapt and innovate in response to regulation.[25] The Clean Air Act's phaseout of chlorofluorocarbons (CFCs), for example, which harm the ozone layer, ended up being much less costly to manufacturers than had been anticipated because scientists quickly developed new chemical compounds to replace CFCs.

WHERE THE UNITED STATES STANDS

The total number of federal regulations has been increasing at a fairly steady pace since the government started keeping track in the mid-twentieth century.[26] However, compared with the Bill Clinton and George W. Bush administrations, the cost of new regulations is up.[27] An average of fifty-five new economically significant rules have been enacted per year during the Obama administration, versus an average of forty per year under George W. Bush. Although the average significant rule has been more costly under Obama, official government figures suggest benefits have also been higher.[28] According to one analysis, the Obama administration added more new regulatory restrictions (both big and small) than any other president since Carter.[29]

The paperwork collection burden, which includes time spent filling out forms online, has been rising, too.[30] Although information technology should enable streamlined data collection, technology has not yet put a dent in the hours Americans spend doing federal paperwork.

OBAMA-ERA POLICY LEGACY: MORE REGULATION
OF FINANCE, HEALTH CARE, AND THE ENVIRONMENT

The federal government has dramatically extended the federal regulatory reach into finance and health care over the past five years. The 2010 Dodd-Frank bill, for example, was designed to avert future financial crises and prevent banks from being "too big to fail," necessitating government bailouts. The bill covers everything from consumer protection and private hedge funds to how banks trade derivatives, take on systemic risk, and write mortgages. The regulatory burden and paperwork costs have been significant. The bill created three

Quality Control
Federal Regulation Policy

By the Numbers

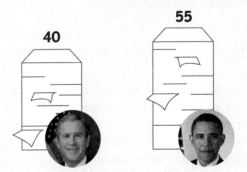

Average annual number of new major regulations

Under Obama, the average annual number of new
major economic regulations is up.

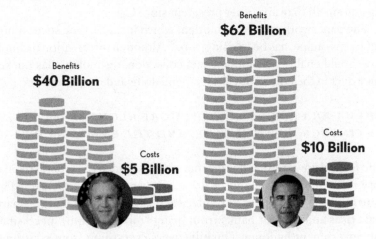

Annual average of new major regulations, 2015 dollars

But the net benefits are also up.

new regulatory offices, including the Consumer Financial Protection Bureau with roughly one thousand employees. The bill itself was 848 pages long and could lead to more than ten thousand pages of new regulations or rules, some 20 percent of which has not yet been finalized.[31] Supporters of Dodd-Frank, however, insist that the burden is justified if it helps to avert financial crises like the most recent one, which lowered net U.S. household wealth by $16 trillion, or 24 percent, between 2007 and 2009.[32]

The 2010 Affordable Care Act (ACA), commonly known as Obamacare, is the biggest change to government health-care policy since the creation of Medicare and Medicaid in 1965. It aims to decrease the share of uninsured Americans while trying to dampen spiraling and unsustainable public and private health-care costs. The health insurance industry, which must now accept more clients regardless of preexisting conditions, is most affected. Critics worry about how the employer mandate will affect medium-sized businesses, given that it will force them to buy health insurance for their full-time employees. Although the rollout of the online application and insurance market exchanges was marred by technical glitches, the system is now up and running. The uninsured rate has declined. But it is too soon to tell whether the ACA will produce a sustained slowdown in health-care costs, which had already begun to slow during the Great Recession.[33]

Although Dodd-Frank and the ACA dominate the headlines, some of the most economically significant regulations during Obama's presidency—and nearly every previous administration for decades—have involved protecting the environment and improving energy efficiency. Obama has continued to strengthen Clean Air Act restrictions on pollutants and was the first to use the Clean Air Act to regulate carbon dioxide (CO_2) emissions that cause climate change. The rule, finalized in 2015, aims to lower CO_2 emissions from existing coal power plants, which are responsible for the largest share of the country's CO_2 output, by 30 percent by 2030.[34] Historically, new standards applied only to new plant construction. Industry groups have promised to fight them hard, claiming it will lead to higher electricity prices for consumers and job losses in coal-producing states like West Virginia. But proponents claim that natural gas or cleaner-energy industries will meet the electricity demand and create new jobs. Obama has also increased energy efficiency standards on cars, motors, and electrical appliances such as microwaves, laundry machines, and light bulbs.

U.S. BUSINESSES FACE LOWER REGULATORY BURDEN
THAN COMPETITORS

Although no data directly compares regulatory and paperwork burdens
across countries, available evidence suggests that U.S. companies are
not more burdened than their competitors abroad. The U.S. economy
has long been among the least regulated in the world. The United States
is currently the top-ranked large rich country in the World Bank's Ease
of Doing Business Index, and has been so for every year but one since
the index was first compiled in 2001.[35] The index is a composite of a
host of objective variables, including how long it takes to start a business, availability of credit, procedures for registering property, and
the enforcement of contracts—which, taken together, are a reasonable starting point for comparing regulatory burden. OECD indicators
broadly corroborate the index; the United States scores better than any
other G7 country by having less complex regulatory procedures, fewer
administrative burdens, and lower entrepreneurship barriers, though
other English-speaking countries are close behind.[36] Unfortunately no
similar indicators compare regulation benefits between countries.

U.S. REGULATORY MANAGEMENT: AN OUTDATED SYSTEM

The United States used to be the trailblazer in regulatory quality management. In 1969, it was the first country to mandate environmental
impact assessments, and the EPA developed some of the original cost-
benefit analytical methods. In 1980, the United States was the first to set
up an oversight body (OIRA), the first to institutionalize cost-benefit
analysis, and the first to make paperwork reduction an explicit goal.
The rest of the world looked to the United States for the gold-standard
model in regulatory management. Since the early 1980s, some marginal improvements have been made to the U.S. system, such as more
transparency and more attention to the effects on small business and
of unfunded federal mandates on state and local budgets. But its fundamental architecture has not changed in more than thirty years, and the
system should be improved.

Most importantly, the U.S. system does not have an institutionalized
process for analyzing and updating the existing stock of regulations.
A cost-benefit analysis is produced before a regulation is enacted and
therefore must rely on uncertain assumptions. Almost no analyses are

Quality Control
Federal Regulation Policy

Burdens

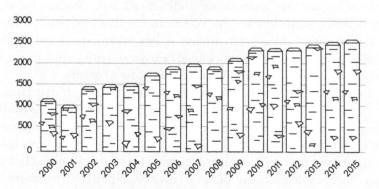

Government-wide paperwork hours (no treasury), billions of hours

The number of hours Americans spend dealing
with federal paperwork has been going up.

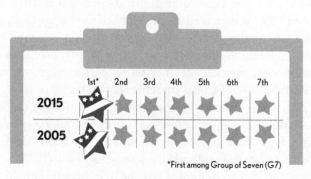

*First among Group of Seven (G7)

Ease of doing business

But when compared internationally, the United States
is consistently among the easiest places to do business.

conducted afterward, however, to determine whether those assumptions
were correct and whether the regulation is having its intended effects.[37]
Nonetheless, federal regulators update many rules at their discretion,
often in response to criticisms from businesses or interest groups.[38]
Every president since Carter has directed the federal bureaucracy to
review old regulations and cut away any excess. But these reviews have
been ad hoc and their methodology rudimentary, in part because the way
the federal government designs regulations does not lend itself to retrospective review.[39] Ideally, provisions for data collection to measure any
impact and a review timeframe should be written into a statute from the
beginning. Such preparation, however, almost never occurs.

Except for those that apply to food and medicine, U.S. regulations
are not empirically tested, although regulations are more empirically
informed than in the past.[40] Behavioral economics research has shown,
for example, that information framing and data presentation can have
a significant effect on consumer behavior. This has been embodied in
fuel-efficiency disclosure displays on new cars at the dealer, which try to
overcome the human tendency to favor short-term over long-term gains.
Five-year fuel-savings estimates need to be presented in a clear and concrete way so that consumers can focus more on long-term savings even
if more fuel-efficient cars have a higher upfront price tag. There is also
a general understanding that market-based approaches (e.g., cap-and-
trade emission programs) or choice-based "nudges" (e.g., default savings
accounts) work better than command-and-control mandates. A small
government office was created in 2014, dubbed the Nudge Unit, to apply
behavioral economics principles to make existing regulations more
effective. According to the unit's first report in 2015, they have already
had some success; for example, they set up personalized text message
reminders to help low-income students stay on track for college.[41] An
even smarter system would test the specific regulations in randomized
controlled trials, teasing out cause and effect and taking out as much
uncertainty as possible in any cost-benefit analysis. This is already standard procedure for the Food and Drug Administration (FDA).

The way the U.S. system uses cost-benefit analysis should also be
more sensible and proportionate. For draft regulations where both
costs and benefits can be quantified and monetized, the U.S. impact
analyses are among the best in the world.[42] Some scholars even argue
there is too much of an emphasis on quantification in the U.S. system;
it does not always lead to more informed policy decisions and can come

at the expense of considering alternative options.[43] It is often impossible to quantify in dollars the effects of a specific regulation. Indeed,
the assessments for most major regulations do not monetize both costs
and benefits, and usually for understandable reasons. In one famous
case, a federal regulation forced prisons to take dramatic steps to reduce
prison rape. Economists were hamstrung trying to quantify the benefits
in dollars, though few doubted the regulation's worth and it was eventually approved. In other situations, economists are only able to construct
such dense calculations that hardly anyone can judge the merits.[44]

Impact analyses can also be gamed or ignored, depending on the
goals of the administration at the time. Regulations that are higher priorities for the current administration tend to elicit less rigorous cost-
benefit analyses.[45] This held true for the George W. Bush administration
regarding homeland security, just as it did for the Obama administration with health care. For these signature policies, the White House
was involved in designing the regulations and the process was rushed—
tight deadlines, no public comment period, and only a few days at OIRA
to check for analytical rigor.[46] A crucial 2015 Supreme Court decision
could set the bar higher for cost-benefit analyses in the future: the ruling
struck down a new EPA regulation on mercury pollutant standards on
the grounds that costs were overlooked.[47]

Although some regulations receive extremely detailed analytical treatment, others receive none. Only economically significant regulations fall
under OIRA oversight and require a cost-benefit analysis. Smaller individual regulations, which encompass 99 percent of all regulatory actions,
rarely receive any impact analysis, even simple back-of-the-envelope calculations.[48] Independent agencies, many of which are responsible for
writing hugely expensive regulations, are beholden to fewer analytical
requirements, ostensibly to preserve their political and institutional independence. The quality of their analysis, when done, is consistently lower
than that of other agencies under OIRA oversight.[49] The independent
SEC, for example, provided impact analysis for Dodd-Frank regulations
that was widely criticized as late, poor, and incomplete.[50]

OBAMA'S MANAGEMENT LEGACY: MORE OF THE SAME, BUT COMMITTED TO IMPROVEMENT

Obama's signature regulatory oversight policy—a retrospective review
that required agencies to sift through old regulations and eliminate

obsolete ones—was not so new.[51] Perhaps the only difference from every other presidential-sponsored review since Carter is that Obama required each department to publish assessment plans twice a year, thus cementing reviews into bureaucratic calendars. But the methods have been no better than those of the past; data and analytical methods are still insufficient.[52] Once again, independent agencies were exempt.

To the disappointment of many Republicans, the review plans contained not just regulatory cuts, but also enhancements to make regulations more effective. After four years of review plans, the White House claims the cumulative cuts totaled $22 billion in compliance cost savings.[53] But when the enhancements are also factored in, there may have been an overall increase in burden. In the most recent set of reviews from July 2015, there is actually a net increase in costs of $14.7 billion, and in paperwork hours of thirteen million, just two agencies planning to reduce overall burdens.[54] The plans contain few new or original look-backs; nearly 90 percent of the rulemakings in the July 2015 report were recycled from previous reports. Although data limitations make comparisons difficult, a tally of net changes in the pages of federal regulations suggests Obama's look-back accomplished less burden reduction than previous efforts (see figure 1).[55] And as in earlier reviews, only a very small percentage of the existing stock was taken off the books (see figure 2).

The Obama administration says it is committed to improving how retrospective reviews are conducted and to empirically testing more draft regulations. The White House has instructed regulators to design new regulations in a way that allows for easier subsequent reviews.[56] But according to an assessment of eighteen proposed rules in 2014, none prepares for retrospective analyses.[57] In their 2011 retrospective review plans, the Departments of Transportation, Labor, and the Interior promised to use more randomized-controlled experiments in their regulation-design process.[58] It remains to be seen, however, whether they follow through on their commitments, especially without dedicated funding for experimental trials.

OTHER COUNTRIES NOW INNOVATING MORE ON REGULATORY MANAGEMENT

The rest of the rich world, and much of the developing world, has caught up with the United States in regulatory management, creating their

FIGURE 1. NUMBER OF PAGES IN THE CODE OF FEDERAL
REGULATIONS (1974–2014)

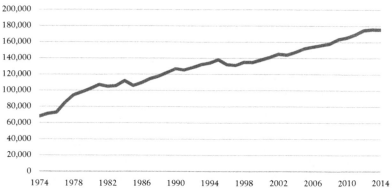

Source: Office of the Federal Register (2015).

FIGURE 2. CHANGE IN THE NUMBER OF PAGES IN THE CODE OF
FEDERAL REGULATIONS (1974–2014)

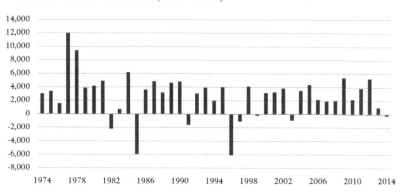

Source: Office of the Federal Register (2015).

own oversight bodies and standardizing impact analysis.[59] Many countries are better than the United States at reviewing the accumulation of
outdated regulations.

In 2009, the United Kingdom dramatically overhauled its system
when the Cameron government came to power. It created the Behavioral Insights Team—the original Nudge Unit—to carry out empirical
research on regulatory best practices. The UK became the first country

to put in place a regulatory budget, originally called one-in, one-out, which later became one-in, two-out, every new regulatory burden now requiring twice the amount of regulatory reduction. Australia, Canada, France, and several smaller European countries now follow regulatory budgeting principles. Although regulatory budgets may unfairly tie future regulations to past regulations, they do force bureaucracies to more carefully weigh regulatory decisions and systematically analyze the existing regulatory stock.

The Netherlands has led the way in reducing administrative burdens. In the mid-2000s, it developed a simple metric for red-tape costs, instructed all agencies to cut those costs by 25 percent within four years, and installed an independent commission to keep tabs on progress. At least officially, the red-tape reduction effort was a success, and several countries are modeling their own cost-cutting efforts after the Dutch.

Australia and Canada have claimed the mantle of regulatory leadership from the United States by implementing a wide range of cutting-edge policies. For example, both countries require across-the-board expiration, known as sunsetting, of all new major regulations within a defined timeframe, usually five to seven years, in the absence of a thorough retrospective review. Australia uses a smart approach to evaluating and managing the stock of old regulations. Instead of siloing retrospective reviews within single government agencies, the regulatory body periodically does "stockade" reviews of the cumulative set of regulations that affect a given industry, which is how businesses actually experience the regulatory system.

The European Union's approach, though not as advanced in managing its stock of regulations as some other governments are, does differ from the U.S. approach in several ways. In the United States, impact-scoring of draft regulations is done by federal departments only after Congress votes on laws. The EU, by contrast, scores the regulatory impact of every piece of legislation before any parliamentary debate or vote. It also scores all draft regulations, big and small, scaling up the analytical detail in proportion to the rule's economic significance.

Many of these policy ideas were originally developed in the United States. Going back to the 1970s, U.S. states have enacted sunsetting provisions. President Carter wanted to require built-in retrospective evaluation plans for all new regulations, and the first head of OIRA in 1980 floated the possibility of establishing a regulatory budget.

Quality Control
Federal Regulation Policy

Pace of Reform

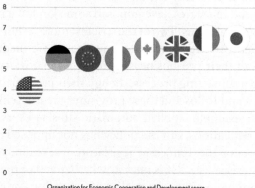

Organization for Economic Cooperation and Development score,
out of eight, for updating regulations

Many other developed countries, however, are doing a
better job at following OECD best practices in
regulatory quality management.

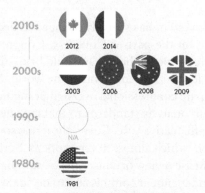

Dates of major regulatory overhauls

And other developed countries have been overhauling and
modernizing their regulatory management systems, while the
U.S. system has changed little in more than thirty years.

U.S. STATES: UNCLEAR WHETHER REFORM
INITIATIVES ARE WORKING

Many U.S. states have their own regulatory management systems that include assessment standards and an oversight body. Many of these states have taken steps in recent years to lower regulatory burdens; since the Great Recession, twenty-five states have established new reviews of existing laws, and ten states have imposed some kind of a moratorium on issuing new regulations. Two of the strictest moratoriums are in Arizona and Indiana, where Republican governors have made the policy a cornerstone of their pro-business agendas. As of 2011, twenty-three states still had a sunsetting process, though their popularity has ebbed since the 1970s and 1980s and these provisions are unevenly enforced. Tennessee, for example, applied automatic sunsets every year to all existing state regulations. But the policy has not imposed rigor on the regulatory process; the Tennessee legislature just extends the full list of regulations every year.[60] It is unclear whether any of these state initiatives are improving either the quality of regulations or the business climate. One study found that states' reform initiatives have generally failed at lowering regulatory burden.[61]

CONGRESSIONAL PROPOSALS: BIG ON RESTRICTIONS,
SHORT ON IMPROVEMENTS

Although the U.S. system has scarcely changed in decades, this is not for want of trying on the part of Congress. Congressional Republicans have regularly proposed bills that would bring the United States more in line with leading systems around the world. Most of the proposals would ramp up congressional oversight, ranging from imposing stricter cost-benefit-analysis standards to making any new major rule contingent on an affirmative vote. Currently, a rule stands unless Congress votes it down, which almost never happens. Some proposals call for either an automatic review or sunsetting of new major rules. Others would install an independent commission to decide which regulations should be repealed, because federal regulators may have a conflict of interest when grading and rolling back their own regulations. The most far-reaching bill, sponsored by Senator Marco Rubio (R-FL), would impose a budget on all federal regulation costs and paperwork, among many other changes.

The bill that has had the most success in the Republican-controlled House of Representatives—the Regulatory Accountability Act (passed in 2011, 2013, and 2015)—would place more layers of requirements on cost-benefit analysis and extend them to independent agencies such as the SEC, as well as mandate ten-year reviews for new major regulations. Similar provisions have not passed in the Senate.

Democrats tend to be against more restrictive measures, particularly blanket caps on the level of regulation. They are keen on keeping the analysis and review decisions with the regulators, who often know the subject matter best, rather than creating a separate commission. Democrats also worry more about bureaucratic ossification—that more layers of requirements would simply slow down the governance process—though research has not found any evidence of ossification yet.[62]

A prominent Democratic proposal for regulatory reform, sponsored by Senator Amy Klobuchar (D-MN), would create an OIRA counterpart within the legislative branch to analyze major draft regulations and then review those regulations five years later. The office would not perform regulatory impact estimates on possible legislation, like the Congressional Budget Office does with budget scoring. But it would add a dose of bureaucratic competition similar to that of the CBO, which many believe benefited the quality of fiscal accounting coming from the Office of Management and Budget after the CBO's formation in 1975.

FUTURE PROSPECTS

These proposals fail to address three fundamental challenges facing the U.S. regulatory system: retrospective reviews that are not informed by relevant data collection and planning, a lack of empirical testing of regulations, and inconsistent requirements for cost-benefit analysis. Most proposals would make cost-benefit analyses more detailed, quantified, and monetized. But complexity can be the enemy of good decision-making. And the benefits of cost-benefit analysis beforehand, no matter how detailed, will never have the certainty of empirical testing or retrospective analysis. Many prominent congressional proposals mandate retrospective analysis, but none would improve how such analysis is conducted. Reformers are correct to widen the scope of these analyses to include independent regulatory agencies, but legislators should also consider increased EU-style proportionate analysis of smaller regulations along with an increase in initial analysis. An overall cap on the regulatory burden may be hard to justify, especially if most new regulations are easily passing a cost-benefit test. A paperwork budget would make more sense for good governance, however, and it is an idea that could garner support from both Democrats and Republicans.[63]

What is certain is that a serious overhaul of the regulatory management system will require more resources. Performing empirical trials will cost money. Doing careful and thorough retrospective reviews of all major regulations will cost *a lot* of money, which is perhaps one reason why reviews to date have been so poorly executed. No one in Congress has called for a funding boost for regulatory management, even though it would likely pay for itself by improving the cost effectiveness of regulations. In 2000, Congress approved an office in the legislative branch (along the lines of Senator Klobuchar's bill) to undertake impact analyses, but the whole plan fell through when Congress failed to authorize funding in the order of several million dollars.[64] Unless Congress is willing to put some cash toward new initiatives, progress on regulatory reform may have to wait.

Balance Owed:
Federal Debt and Deficits

INTRODUCTION

The U.S. government faces an unsustainable long-term debt trajectory. Following the Great Recession of 2008–2009, the federal government accumulated significant new debt, with the ratio of debt to gross domestic product reaching levels not experienced since the 1950s. This debt growth was sharper in the United States than in most other large rich countries. In 2000, the United States had a lower debt burden than most other G7 members, but by 2015 it had nearly caught up to the G7 average. The good news is that U.S. annual budget deficits have fallen from highs of over $1 trillion annually from 2009 to 2012, or nearly 10 percent of GDP, to $435 billion in 2015, about 3 percent of GDP. But while the U.S. debt-to-GDP ratio is projected to be relatively flat in the near term, it will grow rapidly again in about a decade as entitlement spending rises with the aging population. By 2040, the ratio is projected to reach unprecedented peacetime levels. Among the G7 countries, only Japan is projected to have a higher debt-to-GDP ratio than the United States.

The danger posed by U.S. debt is not an outright default, which is highly unlikely, but rather a gradual slowing of the economy. Public debt consumes capital that may be more productively invested elsewhere. And if investors perceive that investing in U.S. debt is becoming riskier, they could charge higher interest rates. This would make it more expensive for the U.S. government to borrow. It would also raise market interest rates, making borrowing more expensive for home buyers, businesses, and consumers. For now, investors remain bullish on U.S. debt. But the consensus is strong among economists and policymakers that the long-term trend of debt growing at a faster rate than the economy is not sustainable.

Although Congress and the Obama administration have made progress in reducing annual budget deficits, they have not taken steps to bend the long-term debt curve, which would require significant reforms to cut spending or increase taxes. Spending on entitlement programs such as Medicare and Social Security, which are becoming increasingly costly, has been left mostly untouched while discretionary spending, which was set to decline anyway, has been slashed. Although these discretionary cuts did lower the current deficit, they did little to alter the long-term debt trend.

Entitlement reform is politically difficult because the programs are broadly popular. But other large rich countries are making dramatic reductions in their entitlement programs, even though they do not share the United States' advantages of a younger population, wealthier elderly who depend less on government support, and more room to raise taxes. Although both Democrats and Republicans agree that the U.S. government's current debt situation is untenable, the country is still far from agreeing on the best path to a sustainable fiscal policy.

PROS AND CONS OF GOVERNMENT DEBT

Government debt is not necessarily a problem. It provides the private market with liquid, risk-free investments and, at least in the case of U.S. debt, acts as a marker to gauge the riskiness of other investments. As with any kind of debt—public, personal, or business—whether it is prudent depends in large part on how the borrowed money is spent. Debt gives governments some spending cushion in unexpectedly difficult times, such as during an armed conflict or a recession when tax revenues fall and unemployment insurance claims rise. Government borrowing and spending can help maintain economic growth at times when private-sector investment or consumer spending is weak. Although it is true that future taxpayers will foot the bill for current debt obligations, governments can borrow to invest in ways that promote future economic growth. If debt is owned by domestic savers instead of foreigners, the direct net effect on a nation's wealth is not as significant because the debt is a future transfer from domestic taxpayers to domestic bondholders. Interest payments leave the country only if debt is foreign owned. And if the economy experiences strong growth, a debt burden can actually grow more manageable because more resources are available to draw on to pay it off.

But there is also a downside to taking on too much debt or allow-ing debt to grow too fast. Investors charge a higher interest rate if they believe buying government debt is increasingly risky—if, for instance, inflation is expected to rise or they question a government's ability to pay back the loan. Higher interest rates from investors make borrowing money more expensive for governments, worsening the debt situation. As a result, interest rates across the country rise, increasing the costs of mortgages, corporate loans, and credit card debt, all of which slow the economy. According to standard macroeconomic theory, government debt "crowds out" private investment; in other words, the debt absorbs private investment that would be more productively spent elsewhere. Studies suggest that higher debt levels correlate strongly with slower economic growth.[1] However, one influential study found that the debt trajectory is what matters, with debt having no effect on economic growth if the debt-to-GDP ratio is declining.[2]

The most sustainable debt situation therefore is one in which the overall debt level is low or, if it is high, it at least represents a steady or declining share of the economy. Debt reduction can also have a down-side, however: spending cuts or tax increases can slow an economy, reversing any macroeconomic advantage from debt reduction. A slower economy can place greater demands on public services and reduce tax revenues, worsening the debt situation. Debt obligations placed on future taxpayers should be weighed against service or entitlement obli-gations to current and future citizens. But debt that grows faster than an economy's ability to pay it off cannot continue to accrue forever. At some point, a policy change is needed to place public debt on a more manageable trajectory.

WHERE THE UNITED STATES STANDS

For most national governments in modern history, including the United States, the norm has been to run annual budget deficits. The U.S. fed-eral government has posted a deficit nearly every year since 1940, except for a few pockets in the late 1940s and late 1990s. Thanks to strong eco-nomic growth and small budget deficits, the huge public debt accumu-lated during World War II gradually fell as a share of GDP through the 1970s. Deficits spiked in the 1980s following the Reagan tax cuts and

Balance Owed
Federal Debt and Deficits

Recent Debt Growth

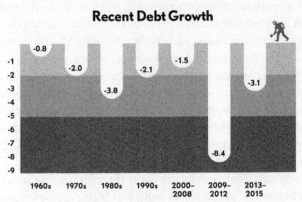

Average annual deficits as a percentage of GDP

Following the Great Recession of 2008–2009, the federal
government ran historically large annual deficits.

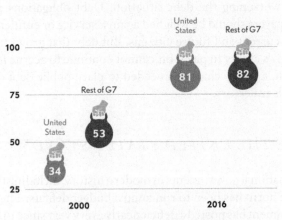

Net public debt as a percentage of GDP

The United States was in a relatively better debt
position compared with other big wealthy
countries in 2000, but this is no longer the case.

spending increases, but then declined in the 1990s, the result of a combination of spending cuts, tax hikes, and a booming economy.

RECENT PAST (2009–2013): BIG DEBT GROWTH AFTER THE GREAT RECESSION

It was not until the Great Recession that budget deficits again became a serious concern, driven mostly by the weak economy.[3] From 2009 to 2012, the average annual deficit level was 8.4 percent of GDP, far exceeding average deficits of previous decades.[4] In 2000, U.S. public debt was 34 percent of GDP. As recently as 2007, it was still about 35 percent. By 2016, it had more than doubled to 81 percent, higher than any period since the early 1950s.[5]

The U.S. debt-to-GDP ratio has increased more than in most other large rich countries. The United States began the 2000s with a lower debt-to-GDP ratio than the average for other G7 countries.[6] Since then, U.S. levels have increased by more than twice the average rate of the rest of the G7 countries. The United States is now in a similar debt position to European countries like France that have long had higher public debt.

PRESENT AND NEAR FUTURE (2014–2025): HIGH BUT RELATIVELY STEADY DEBT

Despite the huge deficits caused by the recession, the federal government is set to have reasonably healthy finances over the next decade. By 2014, the deficit had fallen to 3 percent of GDP, which is close to the forty-year historical average.[7] A recovering economy has certainly helped boost federal finances. But so too have legislative changes since 2011, particularly cuts to discretionary spending and some small tax increases. Relative debt levels, however, are projected to increase a few percentage points by 2025. Relative debt levels will thus remain extremely high compared with the U.S. historical norm.

LONG-TERM FUTURE (BEYOND 2025): UNSUSTAINABLE DEBT GROWTH

The danger zone for U.S. debt is in the long term. By 2040, if current laws remain unchanged, public debt is projected to reach nearly 110 percent, equal to the highest levels reached during World War II.[8] Under more realistic policy and economic assumptions, it could reach 175 percent or higher.[9]

Driving these trends will be growth in entitlement spending programs such as Medicare, Medicaid, and Social Security, without a commensurate increase in tax revenues to pay for them. Entitlement spending has been increasing for decades, but it will grow even more rapidly as baby boomers draw from their old-age entitlements with fewer workers to pay for them. Medicare's cost growth will be greatest of all, not only because the elderly will be more numerous, but also because individuals are consuming more health-care services and health-care prices are rising, even if not as fast as in previous projections because health-care cost growth has recently slowed. Interest payments, too, will require a larger share of the budget to pay for past debt obligations, though the growth here will be more gradual. Revenues are projected to rise, mostly because of bracket creep, where inflation should move more incomes into higher tax brackets, but these higher revenues will not be enough to cover the spending increase.

Before the recession, the United States had one of the lightest debt burdens in the G7; by 2040, it is projected to have one of the heaviest. Beyond 2025, if current trends continue, U.S. debt-to-GDP levels are set to rise above nearly every other large rich country, with the sole exception of Japan.[10] The United States will not fare much better compared with all thirty-four members of the OECD; it is on pace to have the second-highest relative debt, again behind Japan.[11]

MORE FOREIGN-OWNED U.S. DEBT
AND CHINA'S GROWING ROLE

Foreigners have a significant stake in U.S. debt that is much larger than it was in the past. Although growth in the share of foreign-owned U.S. debt has flattened during the 2010s, it is still higher than it was in 2000. Roughly half of U.S. debt available for purchase is currently owned by foreigners.[12] China and Japan are the largest owners by far; China in particular has been buying U.S. debt with zeal. The Chinese share of foreign-owned U.S. debt in 2015 was 21 percent—nearly four times what it was in 2000.[13] China has replaced Japan as the single largest investor in U.S. debt.

The geopolitical implications of foreign-owned U.S. debt are unclear. The United States may be more vulnerable if U.S. and Chinese

Balance Owed
Federal Debt and Deficits

Long-Term Debt Problem

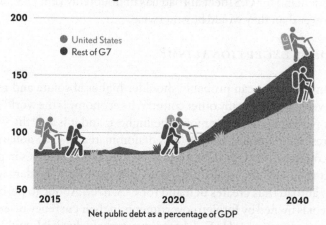

- United States
- Rest of G7

Net public debt as a percentage of GDP

Although U.S. debt as a share of GDP will be steady
in the near term, it will skyrocket in the long term to
levels higher than average for peer countries.

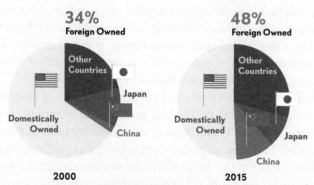

34%
Foreign Owned

Other Countries

Japan

Domestically Owned

China

2000

48%
Foreign Owned

Other Countries

Japan

Domestically Owned

China

2015

Share of U.S. public debt that is foreign owned

An increasing share of U.S. debt is being owned by
foreigners, with uncertain geopolitical consequences.

ambitions clash in the future. But because other countries own U.S. debt, they are also vulnerable to U.S. government policy. With so much Chinese money placed in U.S. debt, for example, China is eager to see the U.S. dollar remain stable and U.S. debt as a reliable investment. There are also mutual benefits—Chinese purchases of U.S. dollars have helped keep its currency weaker, promoting its exports, while the strong demand for U.S. debt abroad has undoubtedly kept U.S. interest rates lower than they would be otherwise.

U.S. DEBT EXCEPTIONALISM?

The United States can probably shoulder higher absolute and relative debt levels better than any other country. Its economy is the world's largest, its per-capita GDP is among the highest, and it issues the world's main reserve currency. U.S. debt is denominated in U.S. dollars, and other countries buy U.S. debt to stock up their dollar reserves in part to protect their currencies against speculative outflows. The demand for dollars abroad thus creates demand for U.S. debt. About 30 percent of U.S. debt is owned by foreign governments in their currency reserves.[14] The other advantages of U.S. debt for investors are that it is liquid, meaning that it can be sold quickly, and it is deep, meaning that because so much U.S. debt is in circulation investors can buy and sell large amounts without affecting the price. The strong demand for dollars abroad also means that the U.S. government is in an enviable and unique position among indebted countries: it can print more dollars without worrying as much about inflation. Indeed, the Federal Reserve Bank's recent monetary policy, called quantitative easing, pumped massive amounts of new dollars into the economy with no appreciable effect on inflation. If anything, economists warn inflation may be too low.

Although investors know the U.S. debt trajectory is unsustainable, they are clearly banking on the U.S. government eventually getting its fiscal house in order. Governments are not losing faith in the stability of the dollar. The share of global reserves in dollars is down some from its peak in 2000, but the dollar is still the preferred reserve currency by a hefty margin (see figure 1).[15] The interest rate investors are receiving is still at historic lows, though this could be because of economic uncertainty elsewhere rather than improvements in the U.S. situation (see figure 2).[16] Whatever the reason, investors continue to consider U.S. debt to be among the world's safest bets, and it has never been cheaper

FIGURE 1. PERCENTAGE OF WORLD'S ALLOCATED
FOREIGN EXCHANGE RESERVES, BY CURRENCY

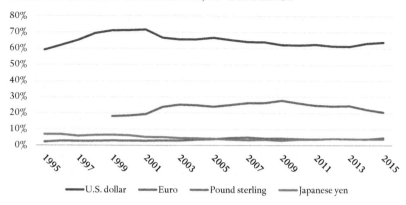

Source: IMF.

FIGURE 2. INTEREST RATE FOR U.S. TEN-YEAR TREASURY BONDS

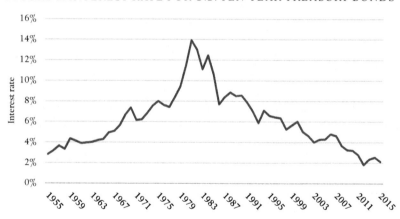

Source: U.S. Federal Reserve.

for the U.S. government to borrow money. Given that net interest payments as a share of GDP are back at the levels of the 1970s, roughly 1.5 percent, taking on more debt would appear to be affordable for the United States.[17]

But the U.S. government should not assume this solid investor confidence will last forever; most economists expect interest rates to rise. According to CBO estimates, under the current debt trajectory, the U.S.

GDP would be 2 percent smaller in 2040 because of debt's crowding-out effect on investment.[18] Former White House Chief of Staff Erskine Bowles, who chaired a government panel on federal debt, put it perfectly: "We face the most predictable economic crisis in history."[19] But lowering debt will be harder than in the past. Debt will be as high as during the era just after World War II, but the United States cannot count on the same conditions that helped draw down that era's debt. Economic growth in coming decades is not expected to be anywhere near as strong as the period from 1950 to 1980. The country's population is much older, making entitlement spending both more socially necessary and politically harder to cut.

That most other OECD countries are in a similarly high-debt position is no consolation if everyone will experience slower economic growth. The effects will spread across the global economy as rich-world investors and consumers spend less money than they otherwise would.

WHAT HAS BEEN DONE SO FAR

Following the gaping deficits caused by the Great Recession and growing public concern over the debt burden, it seemed possible that leaders of both parties would come together on the tough decisions needed to fix future government finances. Yet for all the rhetoric over the past several years, the U.S. government has failed to solve the long-term debt problem.

CRISES: FISCAL UNCERTAINTY
AND DEBT-CEILING SHOWDOWNS

Since 1917, Congress has set the absolute level, or dollar amount, of debt the federal government can take on. If the U.S. government reaches the debt limit and Congress fails to raise it, the U.S. Treasury would no longer be able to pay the bills, including on interest payments, causing a debt default.[20] Debt-ceiling adjustments are so normal that it is estimated that the ceiling has been raised nearly eighty times since 1960 and spread evenly among presidencies.[21]

Although no other country has chosen to adopt such a system, a debt ceiling arguably has an upside. It could in theory impose some form of fiscal accountability, requiring the government to take action visible to public scrutiny before it borrows more. Deficit-reduction negotiations may be more likely because of the debt ceiling; confrontations over raising the debt ceiling in 1997 and 2011 did lead to austerity measures. It may also make changes to entitlement programs easier to enact because entitlement (or mandatory) spending falls outside the annual appropriations process but is subject to the debt limit.

However, the period from August 2011 to February 2014 was an era of fiscal uncertainty unmatched in modern times. During that two-and-a-half year stretch, four debt-ceiling standoffs brought the country within days of default when the Republican-led House refused to raise the debt limit without concessions from the president. At the end of 2012, the country nearly plunged off a fiscal cliff that would have triggered tax hikes and spending cuts, although last-minute bills tempered the tax increase and delayed the cuts for three months. Then, a government shutdown ensued in the fall of 2013 because Congress could not agree on a budget in time. According to one analysis, the fiscal uncertainty level since 2011 is 50 percent higher than the 1986–2010 period.[22] This affects business and consumer behavior; companies and households are less likely to take risks and more likely to sit on their cash. The fiscal uncertainty since 2010 may have shaved off a cumulative 1 percent of real U.S. GDP, or about $150 billion every year.[23]

To be sure, U.S. creditworthiness weathered the fiscal storm relatively unscathed. There was no big sell-off of U.S. debt when, during the initial debt-ceiling crisis in August 2011, one of the three major credit rating agencies downgraded U.S. debt for the first time. Nevertheless, fiscal uncertainty and debt-ceiling crises can only harm the attractiveness of U.S. debt and the dollar as the reserve currency.

MAKING THE WRONG CUTS: SLASHING DISCRETIONARY SPENDING

In an effort to end the debt ceiling crisis, a supercommittee, split evenly between both parties, was formed in 2011 to craft a carefully calibrated austerity package that would have cut $1.5 trillion from projected debt levels over ten years. Built into the deal were stiff consequences called sequestration if the supercommittee could not agree to a package. Sequestration required across-the-board cuts totaling $1.2 trillion over eight years, almost entirely to discretionary spending. The consequences were designed to be so unpalatable to both parties that

Balance Owed
Federal Debt and Deficits

Entitlements vs. Investments

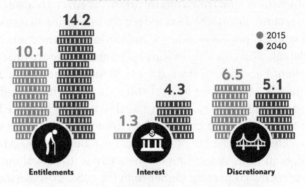

Federal spending categories as a percentage of GDP

Entitlement programs and interest payments on public
debt are driving increases in federal spending.

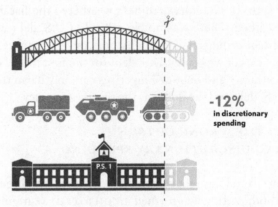

For the period 2011–2024

But recent debt-reduction measures have primarily
affected discretionary spending, most of which goes
toward investments that promote economic growth.

members of the supercommittee would have no alternative except to act as responsible stewards. But in the end, the supercommittee accomplished nothing, and spending cuts that few policymakers wanted or thought wise as actual policy came into effect in 2013. Budget deals in 2014 and 2015 have moderated the cuts in the short-term, but left the original sequestration cuts largely in place after 2016.

The target of the sequestration, discretionary spending, is not the current or future cost problem in the federal budget. Discretionary spending—which, in contrast to mandatory spending like entitlements, is the part of the federal budget appropriated every year by Congress— is just one-third of all federal outlays. It is this portion of the budget that goes toward infrastructure, education, research and development, and other government spending that promotes future economic growth.

The other two options for decreasing deficits—cutting entitlements or increasing tax revenues—were largely left off the table. For the 2011– 2025 period, recent deficit-reduction legislation will have the cumulative effect of reducing entitlements by less than 1 percent, increasing tax revenue by nearly 2 percent, and decreasing discretionary spending by 12 percent.[24]

Yet entitlements will account (along with interest payments) for nearly all new federal spending in the future. Medicare has been cut somewhat, but nothing close to the amount that was sheared from education or defense. Entitlement funds disproportionately go to older Americans and this applies to projected federal health-care spending even after the Affordable Care Act fully kicks in.[25] Whereas in 2010 spending on entitlements and discretionary programs was roughly equal, by 2040 nearly three-times more will be spent on entitlements than on discretionary programs.[26]

Getting U.S. public debt on a sustainable path will require more sacrifice from the American public. Just to slow debt growth to the rate of GDP growth (or a steady debt-to-GDP ratio) from today through 2040, changes to current policy would have to be dramatic: cut entitlements by 10 percent or cut discretionary spending by 24 percent or increase tax revenue by 6 percent, or some combination of the three.[27] Adjustments to actually lower the debt-to-GDP ratio would be even more painful.

Ideally, the debt-reduction burden would be shared by all Americans. But one thing is certain—less generous entitlement programs and tax increases will need to be part of any balanced solution.

PUBLIC OPINION: FOR A BALANCED BUDGET,
BUT AGAINST SACRIFICES TO BALANCE THE BUDGET

Changes in entitlement programs and tax increases, however, collide with an American public that largely wants neither. Almost as a rule, Americans support a balanced federal budget. But public opinion moves decisively in the other direction when Americans are asked about the specific actions necessary to balance the budget.[28]

Entitlement programs are broadly popular. Although most Americans understand that entitlements have a financing problem, they oppose making them less generous. When given the choice between preserving entitlements and reducing the deficit, Americans prefer the status quo. A solid majority, or 69 percent, would rather keep entitlements as they are and incur the debt consequences, whereas only 23 percent say the country should take steps to reduce the budget deficit that would include entitlement cuts.[29] It is understandable that older Americans are more inclined than their younger counterparts to want to preserve entitlements. But even so, most Americans age eighteen to twenty-nine, who will foot the future debt interest bill, still favor entitlement preservation over debt reduction. Perspectives differ depending on party affiliation: Republicans are more likely than Democrats to favor making deficit reduction a priority.

There may be a "tax more" option. Americans do appear to favor increasing taxes on the rich, though Democrats more so than Republicans.[30] It is unclear, however, whether Americans would favor raising their own taxes to cover their entitlement expenses. This suggests a fundamental disconnect between the services Americans want and what they are willing to pay in taxes to fund them.

A SMARTER PATH: GRADUAL CHANGES
THAT AFFECT LONG-TERM COSTS

Some liberal economists believe debt reduction should not be an urgent policy priority.[31] The debt crisis, they argue, is not immediate. With a still-weak economy, the government should continue to spend more than it receives in tax revenues to spur consumer spending. Short-term austerity can be counterproductive if it harms economic growth. Sequestration, they argue, was a foolish form of austerity because it cooled an already weak economy in the short term, disinvested in

Balance Owed
Federal Debt and Deficits

Painful Choices

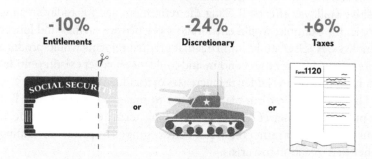

-10%	**-24%**	**+6%**
Entitlements	Discretionary	Taxes

or   or

For the period 2011–2025

To keep the current level of debt steady as a share of GDP through 2024, policy changes today would have to be dramatic.

23% Taking steps to reduce budget deficit.

69% Keeping entitlements as they are.

But such policy changes will be difficult, since Americans prefer keeping the status quo.

long-term economic growth, and failed to make a serious dent in the long-term debt situation.

But there are ways to sensibly reduce debt. The longer the country waits to make adjustments, the more dramatic any reform will have to be. Act now and reform can be more gradual, spreading the burdens of service cuts and tax hikes more equally across generations. It would give the public and the economy more time to adapt to the change, with potentially positive spillover effects. Raising the retirement age for today's young people, for example, would encourage more private savings and longer work lives. A CBO study confirms that gradual reforms would produce more net benefits for the economy and could better cover existing entitlement promises than sudden tax increases or a sudden cut in benefits.[32]

The politics of reform may be easier to manage if a crisis hits. But the public will be better off if the tough, long-term debt-reduction decisions come sooner rather than later and are guided by prudent planning rather than reaction to a crisis.

PEER COUNTRIES: DOING MORE
TO TACKLE ENTITLEMENT-COST GROWTH

Over the last decade, other G7 countries have made more dramatic changes to their pension programs than the United States has to Social Security.[33] Germany and Japan have put automatic stabilizers into their public pension systems so that the pension benefits rise or fall automatically with the country's ability to afford them. Italy linked pension age eligibility to life expectancy, while France indexed part of its public pension system to price inflation. These changes amount to huge spending cuts by 2040 compared with previous law—roughly 30 percent in France, 40 percent in Germany and Japan, and nearly 50 percent in Italy.[34] Some of the reforms were delayed because of the recession. Nonetheless, the public broadly understands that future benefits should be cut, and the push for reform has come equally from the Left and the Right. The United States, meanwhile, has not managed to pass a major Social Security reform in thirty years.

Other G7 countries have also done a better job of keeping health-care costs under control (see figure 3). Germany, Italy, and Japan, whose populations are among the oldest in the world, are projected to have almost no growth in public health-care costs, apart from costs related to unavoidable population aging.[35] The United States has long had the

FIGURE 3. PROJECTED INCREASE IN PUBLIC-HEALTH SPENDING, 2013–2030

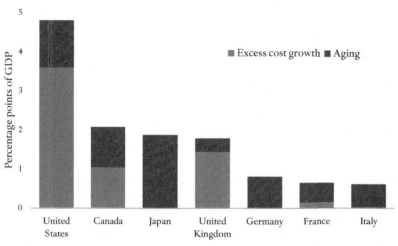

Source: IMF (2013).

fastest-growing health-care costs (private and public) in the rich world. Though cost growth has slowed in recent years, this is mostly because of the recession rather than a structural change in the health-care cost curve. At least for public health-care costs, the high cost-growth trend is expected to return in coming decades—and a disproportionate share of that growth will come from preventable excess costs.

Yet the United States enjoys certain advantages compared with other G7 countries that should make changing entitlement programs easier (see table 1).[36] First, its population is younger, which means more working-age people will continue paying into Social Security. And though the poverty rate among the elderly is higher in the United States than other G7 countries, the average older American is wealthier than his or her counterparts in other countries. The elderly tend to have longer work lives and depend less on public pensions. The United States has a mature private pension system, and the share of elderly income coming from private pensions is higher than in any other OECD country. The United States also has more room to raise taxes. If the country decided to tax itself enough to pay for all projected federal outlays in 2040, even without making any cuts to entitlement benefits, the tax burden in comparison with the size of the economy would still be below the current

TABLE 1. UNITED STATES COMPARED WITH THE REST OF THE G7
IN 2040: YOUNGER POPULATION, WEALTHIER ELDERLY, MORE
TAX ROOM

	2040 United States	Rest of G7
Elderly share of the total population	26%	35%
Elderly to non-elderly total income ratio	1.4:1	1:1
Tax revenues (as percentage of GDP) needed to cover the total increase in elderly benefits	41%	48%

Source: Center for Strategic and International Studies (2012).

level of most European countries. And economists expect economic growth to be stronger in the United States than in nearly every other G7 country.

Other G7 countries may have been forced to act sooner than the United States on entitlement reform. They have much more expensive old-age entitlement systems, and they have been dealing with older populations and higher public debt for longer. But most have placed smart cost controls on their systems, while also managing to pay for a larger share of the expense. The United States spends less on old-age benefits, but the projected growth in those benefits is much steeper, and no real plan is in place to pay for it all. Barring significant policy changes, the United States will end up in a worse debt situation in 2040 than the European welfare states that offer more generous old-age benefits.

FUTURE PROSPECTS

Recent bipartisan deals have offered at a least a pause in the political conflicts over fiscal policy, though there are no prospects for any larger deal. After four years of continuing resolutions and no annual budgets, Congress agreed to two-year budget deals in early 2014, and then again in late 2015 that loosened sequestration caps, but otherwise kept taxation and expenditures at roughly existing levels. In 2014, the Republican-led House voted to raise the debt limit without any conditions, the first so-called clean increase since 2009. They did so again in 2015.

The Obama administration and congressional Republicans have submitted long-term budget proposals that would moderate the debt trajectory, albeit to different degrees. Obama's plan would slow debt growth in the long term; the Republican plan would set debt on a downward long-term trajectory, eventually leading to a zero-debt balance.[37]

Both parties agree that Medicare costs should be controlled. The main cost savings in Obama's plan target Medicare. The Republican plan would squeeze even more cost savings out of health-care entitlements in the long term, mostly from means-testing Medicare and raising its eligibility age, along with cutting spending for Medicaid.

But plenty of disagreement between the two parties remains. The Obama and Republican plans differ on taxes and discretionary spending. Obama's plan relies mostly on higher revenues from tax hikes on the wealthy to lower the debt-to-GDP ratio. It would also considerably boost discretionary spending, busting the sequestration caps. The Republican plan relies only on spending cuts—and the cuts to discretionary programs would be deep, amounting to four times what the original sequestration bill was going to slash.[38] Social Security, meanwhile, takes no budget hit in either plan. Obama has even backtracked on Social Security reform since his previous budget, choosing in his recent budget plans not to propose a less-generous measure of inflation to calculate benefits.

Although both parties agree that the current debt situation is unsustainable, they are still far from agreeing on how to resolve it. Even if they can reach agreement on a reform plan, the biggest challenge may be to persuade the American public of its merits.

Keeping the Edge:
U.S. Innovation

INTRODUCTION

The United States outperforms its peers in technological innovation, which drives rising living standards in rich countries that are already at the cutting edge in inventing and adopting technology. Although China and some other developing countries are ramping up research and development, and are graduating many more scientists and engineers than a decade ago, they remain far behind the United States in combining innovation quality and quantity. But the challenges are growing, particularly when it comes to scientific research whose full benefits are not usually felt until decades later. Such research is essential for keeping the United States at the technological frontier, and it is also where the government has the most critical role. Addressing gaps in U.S. innovation policy could help ensure that the United States remains the leading innovation center for decades to come.

A successful innovation system is a complex web that requires substantial investment and brings together business, universities, and human capital. Few countries are seriously challenging the United States in any of those areas in quality or scale. U.S. government policy, though not without flaws, deserves credit for creating a nurturing innovation environment and for directly promoting innovation where the private market cannot. The U.S. government is relatively generous in supporting research funding for business and, unlike European governments, relies more on direct subsidies instead of tax incentives, which helps the smaller start-ups that disproportionately drive innovation. Big defense R&D budgets and government procurement also spur innovation in ways that no other country has matched. Recently, President Obama has focused new efforts on bolstering advanced manufacturing and clean energy, two areas where the United States could be performing better.

The United States also has an entrepreneurial culture, a limited regulatory regime, a developed venture capital industry, and a continent-wide

single market, all of which gives U.S. businesses an edge at commercializing innovations. U.S. companies are especially successful in the global
information technology (IT) market, and technology-intensive industries form a larger share of the economy of the United States than the
economies of its peers. It has top-notch universities that produce more
of the highest-quality scientific research than any other country, and a
science and technology workforce that recruits the best foreign talent.

Yet a number of weaknesses should concern U.S. policymakers. Current trends point to a future of fewer scientific breakthroughs and less
transformative innovation. Over time, U.S. businesses have been investing less in basic scientific research with distant market relevance, academics have been doing more "sure thing" research instead of high-risk but
potentially high-return studies, and the public universities where most
scientific discoveries take place are under historic financial pressure.

Federal policies could be improved in the following areas:

- The federal government should be increasing basic research funding
  at least in equal proportion to the amount the private sector has been
  cutting basic research funding. The federal government had increased
  funding for many years, but funding has remained flat for a decade.

- R&D incentives should be better targeted away from older established firms and toward young firms.

- Research expenditures should be rebalanced among the sciences.
  The life sciences currently receive twice as much federal funding
  support as all the other sciences, including engineering, physics, and
  computer science.

- Patent property lines for IT should be made clearer and so-called
  patent trolls reined in.

- The immigration visa system should do more to help employers
  attract the top scientific talent from around the world.

INNOVATION AND THE ECONOMY

In advanced economies, innovation is an important driver of economic
growth and rising living standards. Growth comes either from adding
labor and capital inputs—such as workers, the number of hours worked,
worker education levels, and buildings and infrastructure—or by
making these inputs more efficient or productive through innovation,

which can be defined as new ideas, technology, or business methods. Rising living standards in developing countries such as India and China are driven less by innovation; these countries are still catching up to the developed world, increasing labor or capital inputs and adopting technologies designed elsewhere. But for rich economies already at the leading edge of technological progress, with slow-growing, well-educated workforces and modern infrastructure and buildings, innovation is more important for raising living standards further. It is at the heart of competitive advantage among rich countries.

Of course, Americans do benefit from innovations that occur elsewhere. The benefits of medical research, for example, transcend borders. So do breakthroughs in clean energy technology that may mitigate climate change. The United States has borrowed, improved, and commercialized plenty of technologies that were invented elsewhere; British inventors such as Alan Turing laid the foundation for modern computers, but it was Americans who fashioned computers into a profitable product. Similarly, Asian countries are adopting, manufacturing, and profiting from technologies first invented in the United States, such as semiconductors. A smart innovation strategy should include adopting and improving on innovations that occur elsewhere, as well as being the first to invent. Those who invent first get the first crack at making money from their inventions with the resulting business profits and well-paying jobs.

Some innovations are novel products that push the technological frontier forward, such as personal computers and cellular phones. Some are incremental improvements on existing products, where computer chips become faster or cellular phones become "smart" with Internet access and a touchscreen. Innovations can also be new processes, such as Dell's global supply-chain model where each computer is made to order for each customer rather than manufactured in bulk and held in stock for an order, which dramatically lowered expensive inventory holdover times. These innovations all enhance productivity.

Invention is only the first step in the process. Transforming an idea into a practical application for consumers is where innovation adds the most value to the economy. In other words, scientists and researchers are at the beginning of the innovation pipeline; businesspeople and entrepreneurs then figure out the best way to turn inventions into profit. This pipeline can take decades from beginning to end, and the end point is often initially unclear. For example, the computer was invented in the

1950s, yet it was not until the 1980s and 1990s that the digital economy began to take shape.

Young firms or start-ups are usually better at breakthrough innovations, especially in immature industries, which offer more room to grow.[1] Examples include Uber for ride-sharing or Amazon in the early days of online retail. Unlike larger firms, entrepreneurs are not bound by more rigid corporate institutions or an existing customer base. Large firms have always spent the majority of the country's business R&D funding, but these established firms tend to excel at incremental innovation.

WHERE THE UNITED STATES STANDS

The United States stands out as a leader in technological innovation, but the landscape is becoming more crowded. Although no rule of thumb is in place for how much governments should be spending on R&D, major Asian economies, including Korea, Taiwan, and Japan, devote a significantly larger portion of their gross domestic product to it than the United States does. Sometime around 2020, China will likely surpass the United States as the world's biggest R&D spender.[2] Although their academic standards may not be as high, China and India are churning out science and engineering graduates at a pace that the United States could not hope to match, given a population one-quarter their size. China is also positioning itself to become a leader in some emerging areas of scientific discovery like the human genome. Yet these challengers still remain far behind the United States in combining innovation quantity with quality.

R&D FUNDING OVERALL:
THE UNITED STATES IS NEAR THE TOP

The United States, as a whole, spends the most on R&D in absolute terms and also more than most wealthy countries on R&D relative to GDP. At 2.8 percent of GDP, U.S. national R&D expenditures are currently higher than at any time since their peak in the early 1960s, when the costly U.S. space program took off. China has made rapid gains, albeit from a much lower spending base. Among G7 countries and as a percentage of GDP, only Japan has consistently outspent the United States on R&D (see figure 1). Scale and absolute spending

FIGURE 1. NATIONAL R&D EXPENDITURES
AS A PERCENTAGE OF GDP (2000–2013)

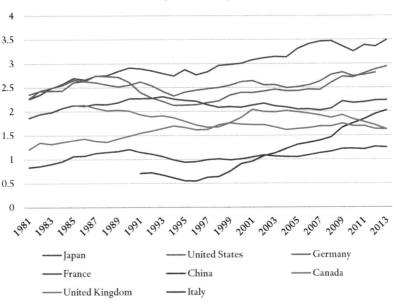

Source: OECD Main Science and Technology Indicators (2015).

levels matter, too, and here U.S. spending dwarfs every other country. The United States still spends twice as much in absolute terms as the second-highest spender, China.

The makeup of U.S. R&D spending has shifted over time. In the 1960s, the government was responsible for two-thirds of national R&D, and businesses most of the rest. Now the shares have flipped: businesses make up two-thirds of R&D spending decisions. Across the wealthy world, businesses now outspend governments on R&D.

Businesses are closer to the market and therefore usually better positioned to decide the most efficient ways to allocate R&D dollars for the economy. But businesses tend to invest in ways that help their bottom line instead of what might be most beneficial to society. The bulk of business R&D is geared toward applied, or practical, research and especially development, which readies a product for the market.

Government funds are critical for basic research, which tackles fundamental scientific questions in fields such as particle physics or astronomy. This research often has long-term value for society but may not have much immediate market value. About one-sixth of all U.S. R&D goes toward basic research, a share that has held steady for three decades. Although data is poor, the United States appears to be devoting a higher share of its R&D resources to basic research than most G7 countries.[3]

U.S. CORPORATE LEADERSHIP
IN ADVANCED INDUSTRIES

U.S. corporations have been highly successful in the global marketplace in those industries most associated with innovation, such as IT. Private-sector performance is one good way to assess a country's innovative prowess, because the market should reward new technologies that consumers want and business methods that are most effective.

U.S. businesses are strongest in industries where innovation plays a large role—in IT (e.g., Apple, Google, Microsoft), pharmaceuticals (Pfizer, Merck), financial services (JPMorgan Chase & Co., Wells Fargo), and industrials (General Electric, Boeing).[4] A greater share of the U.S. economy is knowledge-based (meaning industries linked to science and technology) than any other economy, and the share is growing faster than that of its peer competitors.[5]

In business management, which is important for incremental innovation, the United States outperforms as well.[6] U.S. firms invest more in IT management strategies and are more effective at extracting productivity gains from IT than non-U.S. firms.

Among the world's publicly traded firms, U.S. businesses are gaining ground. With U.S. businesses taking the lead in high-growth and innovative sectors, U.S. companies are taking over more of the top spots in the global marketplace even as the U.S. share of the global economy has declined over time (see table 1).[7] California-based Apple is the world's most valuable publicly traded company, having quadrupled its market capitalization since 2009. In market capitalization rankings, U.S. companies have become more dominant. Of the top one hundred publicly traded companies in 2014, forty-seven were U.S.-based, up from forty-two in 2009. Overall, European business rankings have been flat while Japanese and Chinese businesses have fallen.

U.S. business R&D also continues to expand. Of the top two thousand corporations that spend the most on R&D, the U.S. share has risen slightly while European and Japanese shares have been decreasing (figure 2). According to a recent business survey, the average U.S.

*TABLE 1. MARKET VALUE OF TOP ONE HUNDRED GLOBAL FIRMS,
BY COUNTRY OF ORIGIN*

	2009	2014
United States	45%	54%
Europe	27%	27%
Japan	4%	2%
China	15%	8%
Other	8%	9%

Source: PwC, Top Global 100 Companies (2014).

corporation planned to boost research spending in 2015 by nearly twice
the rate of its international competitors.[8]

Better entrepreneurial climate. Although many top U.S. companies are
global in terms of operations and revenue, they all benefited from a
start-up launching pad in the United States that is among the best in
the world. It is easier to take business risks and try something new in
the United States because bankruptcy laws are more forgiving to business failure, it is easier to hire and fire workers, and capital markets are
deep and broad. The United States consistently ranks among the easiest
places in the world to do business, and its regulatory barriers to start-
ups are among the lowest.[9] All these factors are strongly correlated with
more knowledge-intensive and innovative economies.[10] This regulatory
environment may be a big reason why U.S. firms grow and contract
more quickly than European firms, a process that enhances efficiency
and productivity.[11] The U.S. economy is also better at allocative efficiency—channeling the best workers and resources toward the most
innovative and productive firms.[12]

U.S. start-ups benefit from highly developed venture capital and
angel investing industries. They give seed money to start-ups, most of it
in information and biotechnology industries, and investors offer their
business acumen to steer start-ups toward success. The U.S. venture
capital industry has grown from $1 billion in 1980 to more than $100
billion today. Except for Israel, venture capital industries in other countries are tiny and mostly rely on public funding because private sources
have been less willing to participate.[13]

FIGURE 2. GLOBAL R&D SHARES OF TOP 2,000 R&D-INVESTING
FIRMS, BY COUNTRY OF ORIGIN (2004–2013)

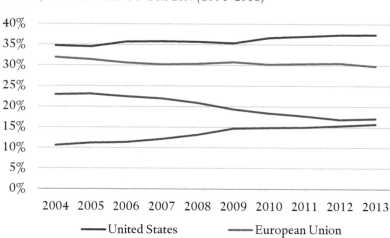

Source: EU Industrial R&D Investment Scoreboards (2005–2014).

Americans appear more culturally inclined than their peers to take business risks, too. Some economists describe Americans as adventurous consumers, giving innovators more room to experiment with new products.[14] Compared to their international peers in surveys, American entrepreneurs display more confidence in their abilities and less fear of failure, signal greater intention to hire new staff, and produce more innovation by offering novel products or services.[15]

Less private-sector basic research. U.S. businesses are devoting less of their R&D budgets to long-term basic research than in the past.[16] This is especially true of corporate technology firms, which in the 1960s and 1970s supported giant in-house research labs, including the legendary AT&T Bell Labs and Xerox PARC. Google and Microsoft still do this kind of research, but it is a smaller slice of their R&D spending compared with the big technology firms of the past. Business R&D has indeed exploded in recent years, but the growth has been almost entirely focused on the development of products for immediate market opportunities rather than the research to invent new products. From a profitability standpoint, this shift makes sense; in the 1980s, corporate returns on basic research began to decline, so corporations allocated their resources elsewhere.[17] The same is happening with venture capital, which is shifting toward less risky (e.g., software instead of capital-intensive hardware) and shorter time-horizons (e.g., later-stage instead of seed-stage) projects.

Shift in research to smaller firms. Although corporations are investing less in their own long-term innovative capacities, they are increasingly willing to buy inventions developed by other, usually smaller, firms with highly specialized scientific research niches.[18] Silicon Valley firms such as Facebook are buying out start-ups like WhatsApp rather than competing by developing in-house products. Although small firms in the U.S. economy are less numerous than in the past, they are bearing more of the R&D burden than ever.[19]

This evolving research hierarchy may make more market sense. Smaller firms have a track record of conducting more cost-effective R&D, claiming more lucrative patents, and taking up much of the slack left by the overall relative decline in corporate research compared to development.[20] But small firms are unlikely to fill the basic research gap. These businesses have more immediate profit concerns and can make more money by pursuing patentable applied research.

More business R&D going abroad. U.S. corporations are also shifting more of their research and manufacturing abroad, which could lead to less innovative capacity within the United States. More than 80 percent of U.S. business R&D funding is still spent in the United States, but that share is gradually falling. For decades, U.S. corporations have been increasing R&D investment abroad at twice the rate of investment at home. This could lead to a hollowing out of the innovation infrastructure within the United States, weakening the network of innovative researchers and start-ups.

This location debate is most developed when it comes to trade in consumer electronics. Although the consumer electronics supply chain is now almost entirely based in Asia, most of the value of high-end goods comes from the design process (for example, at Apple headquarters in Cupertino, California) rather than the final assembly (in China). But at a certain point, the production—with all the tinkering and expertise honed on and around the manufacturing floor—could pull innovation activity and capacity away from the design headquarters. In a classic

Keeping the Edge
U.S. Innovation

Research Spending Growing Overseas

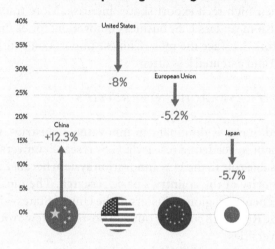

Change in percentage share of global R&D expenditures, 1996–2011

With the rise of China, the U.S. share of global R&D is falling.

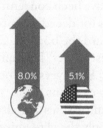

Share of U.S. multinational R&D in the United States   U.S. multinational R&D annual growth rate, by location

Although U.S. multinationals still mostly invest in the
United States, that share is declining, which might mean
more innovation potential is leaving the country.

case, the initial offshoring of consumer electronics production in the 1980s to Japan, South Korea, and Taiwan then turned into dominance decades later in the design and production of lithium-ion batteries and flat-screen panels. And more than most peer countries, the United States has been losing ground on manufactured high-tech exports as a percentage of total U.S. exports.[21] France and Germany, meanwhile, have seen their high-tech export shares increase. More trade competition may also mean less U.S. business innovation; for example, U.S. firms in sectors that face the most Chinese import competition spent less on R&D and patented less often.[22]

TOP-NOTCH RESEARCH UNIVERSITIES

If the United States is dominant in innovative industries, it is even more dominant in academic research. U.S. research universities play an indispensable role in the U.S. innovation system because they conduct the majority of the country's basic research. The most innovative, entrepreneurial regional clusters in the United States—in Silicon Valley and the Route 128 corridor outside Boston—grew around existing elite universities.

The quality of U.S. research is unrivaled. Many other countries are investing heavily in creating academic research systems; the number of academic publications coming from outside the United States, and particularly from China, is growing rapidly. Yet when comparing citations, which can be a good proxy for research quality, U.S. articles have been concentrated in the top percentiles across all scientific fields for decades, European articles in the middle, and Japanese ones toward the bottom. China is making gains in quality, but not at the highest level.[23] The same goes for university rankings by research quality; U.S. universities occupy sixteen of the top twenty spots when ranked by citations.[24]

U.S. universities are also better at monetizing their research. To be sure, only the elite universities—for example, Harvard, Massachusetts Institute of Technology, and Stanford—make big profits. And direct university spinoffs into successful companies have been rare, the major exception being in the emerging biotechnology industry, where hardware-intensive university labs have given spinoffs a leg up on the competition. But no other country has universities that exploit their research for profit as effectively as those in the United States do.[25] Many

European countries are adopting U.S.-style regulations in the hopes that their universities can make U.S.-level profits.[26]

The U.S. university system is organized—with decentralized and autonomous administration, diversity, and competition-based funding—to promote research productivity and innovation.[27] University resources are more diversified in the United States, the money coming from institutional endowments, public coffers, and private donors. In many other countries, university systems are centrally administered by the government and funding is apportioned based on formula rather than merit. European countries have tended to rely more on bureaucratic national research institutes instead of universities to carry out basic research. Europe has been trying to move closer to the U.S. model, downsizing national research institutes and decentralizing university systems. One natural endowment also gives the United States an edge—a single-language academic market for U.S. researchers and publications. Only China can claim the same scale for its academic community.

Growing risk aversion in academic basic research. Yet such intense competition, coupled with more demands from funders for results, could be making U.S. academic research more risk averse.[28] The federal government has become more vigilant about funding accountability, attaching shorter review cycles and more deliverable requirements to research grants. Because success rates for winning federal grants have been on the decline for decades, researchers are more likely to propose research ideas that are less risky and more likely to succeed. Private and philanthropic funders, who have become larger factors in academic research, are also more exacting about results. This could make transformative innovation less likely. According to one analysis, funding schemes that reward early failure and long-term over short-term results produce more outside-the-box and high-impact research.[29] And, perhaps, as a result of choosing more research with guaranteed results, federal grants are increasingly being rewarded to older, established researchers. These scientists tend to produce less transformative scientific discoveries, whereas young researchers have more difficulty getting a start.[30]

Currently well funded, but a financial squeeze is coming. The United States spends generously on its universities and, until recently, university R&D funding had been increasing steadily for decades. On a

Keeping the Edge
U.S. Innovation

Dominant in Quality

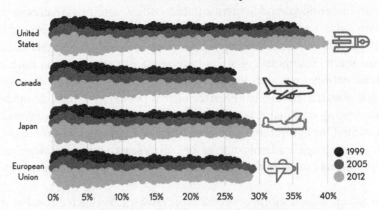

Share of GDP devoted to knowledge-intensive services or high-technology manufacturing

The U.S. economy is more knowledge-intensive than its competitors and no one is catching up.

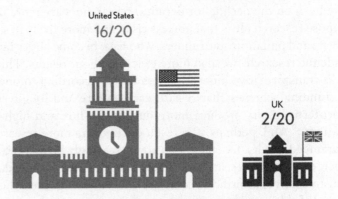

Top twenty universities by research impact, 2015

The United States has the most high-quality research universities.

per-student basis, only Canada devotes more resources to its higher education system.[31] Going back to the early 1990s, the university R&D expenditure growth rate has outpaced that of business R&D.[32] Between 2000 and 2010, universities increased their R&D expenditure budgets by one-third, with federal funding boosts accounting for most of that increase.

But university research funding has been under pressure. Many state governments have been cutting back on their general support, although some universities rely much more on public funding than others. Elite private universities with deep-pocketed endowments will be fine. But for public universities doing first-rate research—such as the University of California, University of North Carolina, Ohio State University, University of Texas, Texas A&M, University of Washington, and University of Wisconsin—any institutional funding squeeze would affect research programs. Public universities like these conduct most of the country's academic basic research and graduate the majority of students with advanced degrees who go on to do further innovative research. However, reductions in federal spending required under sequestration and discretionary spending caps could precipitate further budget cuts for university research.

HIGH-QUALITY HUMAN CAPITAL

Human capital has historically been the most critical component driving economic growth, and here again the United States comes out on top.[33] Compared with other countries, a larger percentage of U.S. workers are researchers.[34] Although U.S. K–12 students do not perform especially well on international math, science, and technology tests, the U.S. adult workforce produces a disproportionate share of scientific breakthroughs, and these researchers are paid handsomely compared with their peers. Across the public, private, and nonprofit sectors, American scientists earn about one-third more than European scientists—more than in any other rich country when adjusted for cost of living.[35] The impact, measured by number of citations, of U.S. scientific authors is higher than anywhere else in the world.[36] The United States is also home to 60 percent of Nobel laureates, and the share continues to rise.

STEM professionals and technology entrepreneurs are disproportionately foreign born. Much of American innovation talent is foreign born. If it were not for foreigners, the U.S. Nobel Prize rankings would look markedly different: roughly 30 percent of U.S. prizes go to foreign-born researchers. These researchers are especially concentrated among science, technology, engineering, and mathematics (STEM) fields. Foreign-born residents are one-eighth of the U.S. population but roughly one-half of STEM PhD students, most of whom end up staying in the United States.[37] They also tend to make more exceptional research contributions than U.S.-born researchers, perhaps because American universities attract the most elite talent from abroad.[38]

According to one measure, the U.S. innovation system seems to benefit the most from the international migration of scientists, compared to other countries in the OECD. Of the world's immigrant scientists, those who reside in the United States write the most widely cited scientific articles.[39] And U.S. scientists who study abroad and then return are much more likely to write influential articles than returnees elsewhere. Those U.S. scientists who do leave permanently are no more influential than the ones who stay, unlike in most other countries (figure 3). Another study that compared the United States and the United Kingdom, which is another top destination for immigrant scientists, found that the U.S. system pushed foreigners to reach their full potential more than the UK system.[40]

FIGURE 3. IMPACT OF SCIENTIFIC AUTHORS,
BY CATEGORY OF MOBILITY (1996–2011)

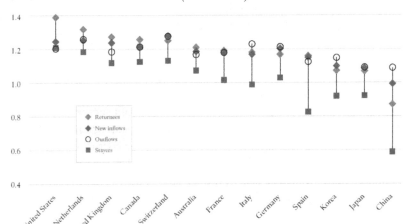

Source: OECD (2013).

The United States is holding up well in the global competition for talent. There is some evidence that Chinese academics are heading back to China in greater numbers than they once did after a stint in the United States.[41] And stay rates for Chinese students, who are the largest group of foreign students in the United States, have declined some in the last decade. Still their rates are higher than for any other nationality—85 percent of Chinese students remain in the United States five years after completing their studies. Many other countries, including Canada, Australia, and the United Kingdom, are aggressively catering to the international student and skilled immigrant markets, making the United States slightly less competitive than it used to be for the average mobile student or professional.[42] Nevertheless, the United States is still the number one destination for nearly every country's emigrant scientists and STEM students, especially for those coming from emerging science powers India and China. The tide of foreign students and skilled workers is not ebbing even as countries like India and China grow more prosperous.[43]

The foreign born are also overrepresented in business clusters. Residents of the counties that make up Silicon Valley are 36 percent foreign born, which is among the highest in the country. Anecdotally, U.S. corporations are much more likely than European or Japanese firms to hire nonnative chief executive officers.[44]

FEDERAL INNOVATION POLICY

The success of the United States as an innovation leader suggests that the U.S. government is getting its innovation policy mostly right. Obama has focused new policy efforts in targeted ways to boost emerging advanced manufacturing practices (e.g., nano-engineering and 3-D manufacturing) and renewable energy research, both sectors with the potential for broad societal gains. Except for R&D tax policy, most rich countries are adopting U.S.-style policies. They are lowering regulatory barriers, making it easier to hire and fire people and to start businesses, and promoting regional technology hubs in hopes of developing their own Silicon Valleys.

But unlike the United States, these countries are also crafting formal national innovation strategies and tasking government innovation agencies to carry them out. In addition, they are generally more comfortable picking winners by using public funds to promote specific industries or applied technologies. This may reflect weakness on their part, but it also means other countries are ramping up their innovation strategies in an effort to erode the U.S. lead.

HOW INNOVATION POLICY WORKS

Innovation policy can be categorized along two dimensions. First, governments set the stage for innovation to develop organically. This would include, for example, the regulatory environment (e.g., patent law and standards for industry research and product testing) and developing human capital (e.g., immigration and education policy). Second, governments can play a more direct role by funding research through grants or tax breaks.

The challenge is to position policy so that business investments in innovation are enhanced rather than impeded or replaced. If government subsidizes a business to carry out research it would do anyway, the subsidy is a waste of public resources. If the government tries to pick winners by investing in applied research or product development that is too narrowly focused and misaligned with market signals so that no business could eventually earn a profit on its own, the investment can be a waste, too.

Government policy should find the sweet spot by funding research and innovation that is valuable to society but that the private sector would not undertake on its own. Private R&D has spillover benefits for the public that are not calculated into private-sector decisions. As a result, businesses do not invest in R&D at a level that would maximize social benefits.[45] A well-designed tax credit can promote private R&D broadly, without picking winners. Governments lead in funding basic scientific research because it generally cannot be protected by patents and the research's market value is too uncertain and distant for most firms to bear the risk. However, basic research also leads to advancements in general-purpose technologies like computers, biotechnology, or synthetic materials that have broader societal benefits.

FEDERAL R&D SPENDING LEVELS: GENEROUS, BUT UNDER HISTORIC PRESSURE

Compared with its peers, the U.S. federal government invests a lot of public dollars in R&D as a percentage of GDP (see figure 4).[46] The

FIGURE 4. PUBLIC R&D EXPENDITURES AS
A PERCENTAGE OF GDP (2000–2012)

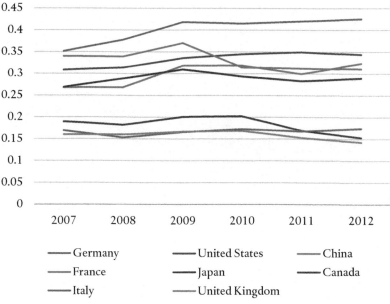

Source: OECD (2014).

same is the case for government R&D support for business, where only France spends more, as well as for basic research.[47] And whereas most other rich countries—including Canada, France, and the UK—slashed R&D spending during the difficult economic period between 2007 and 2012, the U.S. government increased it.

Until the mid-2000s, federal support for basic research—or more academic scientific research—enjoyed steady growth. Today, half of all federal R&D goes elsewhere, to more practical development (mostly for weapons systems). But government development budgets have been cut, especially since the end of the Cold War. Over time, federal R&D dollars increasingly targeted basic scientific research instead of defense-related development. Basic research was less than one-tenth of the federal R&D budget in 1950 (see figure 5). Now it is one-quarter.

The trends, however, began to reverse in the mid-2000s, with development spending boosts along with flat basic research funding. Yet R&D generally has remained a relatively resilient public budget

FIGURE 5. U.S.GOVERNMENT R&D FUNDING SHARE,
BY CHARACTER (1955–2012)

Source: National Science Foundation (2015).

priority compared with other discretionary priorities, such as education or defense.[48]

It is hard to determine the optimal amount of government R&D spending, although government investments have clearly spurred innovation.[49] In a conservative estimate, 88 percent of the top inventions between 1977 and 2006 depended on publicly funded research.[50] Obama (along with most world leaders) uses a benchmark goal that national R&D should be 3 percent of GDP.

Spending still focused on defense. The U.S. government's R&D budget is still heavily oriented toward defense. Roughly half of U.S. government R&D spending goes through the Department of Defense. The UK allocates the next-highest proportion among OECD countries, with about one-third of its research budget spent on defense.

Defense R&D and procurement produce tremendous advantages for the U.S. innovation system even though the commercialization of defense research was never a deliberate policy goal. Many of the technologies that have made U.S. companies global powerhouses—the Internet, global positioning system, touchscreen displays, and voice-recognition software—were initially developed for military purposes. The beginning of the semiconductor industry, which gave Silicon

Valley its name and first technology boom in the 1950s, was almost entirely directed and financed by the Department of Defense. However, defense R&D may be producing fewer spillovers; innovations such as stealth technology grow increasingly specialized and have little consumer value. Nevertheless, defense procurement pumps a huge amount of money into technology research.

FEDERAL BUSINESS R&D SUPPORT FAVORS
DIRECT SUBSIDIES OVER TAX INCENTIVES

The U.S. government uses direct subsidies more than tax breaks to promote business R&D. This is largely a sensible approach. But existing tax breaks favor older, established firms and could be better targeted at young and small firms that need financial help and are disproportionately innovative.

In the United States, tax credits amount to 22 percent of all federal business R&D support, compared with 50 percent in the UK, 70 percent in France and Japan, and 85 percent in Canada. In 1981, the United States was the first country to offer an R&D tax credit. Now, however, the U.S. credit is lower than most other countries except for Germany, which has no R&D credit at all. Additionally, most countries have been sweetening their tax credits over time; the United States has expanded its direct subsidy programs, instead.

Tax incentives versus direct subsidies. Tax breaks are not the most efficient way to promote business R&D, especially for start-ups. Tax breaks have certain advantages: they objectively apply to all qualifying R&D, they are easier to administer than grants, and they let the market decide where and how to allocate R&D, though these preferences are not always the most socially valuable. Empirical studies find that tax breaks may lead to some more business R&D spending, but not beyond what is lost in tax revenue, which is how economists typically compare credits and grants.[51] The United States uses an incremental tax credit, which applies to increases in R&D spending, and this form of tax break delivers slightly more business R&D than the volume-based tax credits favored by most European countries. Still, the U.S. credit does not deliver much more in extra R&D spending than in revenue losses.[52] Tax credits are also easily exploited by clever firms that find ways to bend legal language to qualify. Several countries known for their innovativeness, including Switzerland, Sweden, and Germany, do not even have an R&D tax credit.

The United States could do more to target tax credits toward smaller firms. It is one of only a few rich countries that applies the same R&D credit regardless of firm age or size. Other countries, including France, Canada, and the Netherlands, recently introduced R&D credits specifically for young firms. Small firms, which usually have slimmer profit margins, are more sensitive than large firms to any financial incentive.[53] The U.S. government could start by making the credit refundable. This allows companies with more precarious profit situations, which often include start-ups, to claim the tax credit even when they owe no taxes.

Fortunately, Congress made the tax credit permanent in December 2015. The U.S. R&D credit had previously relied on congressional extensions every few years. Worse, Congress usually missed the expiration deadline and had to retroactively allow companies to claim the credit. Although nearly all politicians supported a permanent credit in theory, budgetary gimmicks had stood in the way.

Direct grants are generally a better approach, even if most of these government programs are focused on fulfilling each agency's specific missions—that is, defending the country (Department of Defense) or educating students (Department of Education)—rather than the general goal of promoting innovation. Direct subsidies are more effective at stimulating business R&D, especially when there is a matching component that requires firms to invest their own money as well.[54] Grants also give governments the ability to direct resources to projects that are more socially valuable.[55] Although there may be a greater administrative burden and some danger of political manipulation, the application process is at least transparent and competitive.

Compared with tax breaks, direct grants are also more helpful for start-ups and small businesses with immediate cash-flow needs.[56] Money up front gets new businesses on their feet or aids them through a tough stretch. Businesses have to wait to collect tax breaks after R&D money has already been spent. Empirical studies confirm that direct subsidies tend to incentivize R&D, whereas tax breaks often work better for companies already carrying out R&D. Studies also suggest tax breaks favor established firms over new entrants, and countries that rely more on such breaks tend to have a less dynamic firm environment (i.e., fewer firm births and deaths, and lower growth) in

R&D-intensive industries.[57] Direct grants appear to be more neutral, favoring young and established firms equally.[58] Winning a government grant can even help young firms attract private investors as a sign of quality.[59]

BUSINESS R&D COMMERCIALIZATION PROGRAMS: MOSTLY EFFECTIVE AND STEADILY EXPANDED

Beginning in the early 1980s, the U.S. government created several programs to help small businesses, universities, and federal labs move their research into commercially viable products. The biggest (by funding allocation) is the Small Business Innovation Research (SBIR) program, which gives early-stage research awards to small businesses.[60] The aim is to help businesses bridge the "valley of death" between good research ideas and commercialization. The government acts as an initial investor in projects that are far from the market and therefore too risky for venture capital or other private investors. Federal agencies with substantial R&D budgets have to allocate 2.8 percent of R&D to the SBIR program, equaling about $2.5 billion per year in awards given out in three phases to roughly 6,500 small businesses.

SBIR is a significant force in the technology start-up scene. According to one estimate, the SBIR program supplies up to one-quarter of all early-stage technology funding.[61] Although venture capitalists and angel investors allocate more seed and early-stage funds in total volume, SBIR spreads its funds to more firms with smaller awards.[62] Many of the best-known technology companies, including Apple, Compaq, and Intel, received SBIR awards in the 1980s.

SBIR has been effective. SBIR firms are better at getting subsequent private investors, are more likely to patent, and outperform non-SBIR firms in the market.[63] The effect is strongest for the earliest phase of funding and for younger firms.[64] Only 3 percent of surveyed SBIR firms indicated they would have undertaken their projects without SBIR funding.[65] The program is politically popular and has been reauthorized relatively easily, most recently through 2017. Over time, the amount of R&D financed through SBIR and the average award size have increased. SBIR-type programs are spreading across the world, from China to Germany, the UK, and Israel.

In the wake of SBIR's success, the federal government has created many other commercialization programs for specific technologies and industries.[66] Many of the programs involving energy and manufacturing, however, take the government further down the research pipeline, away from basic and early-stage and toward applied research and development, where the government has not been as effective.[67] It is too soon to tell whether these programs are working well.

MORE INNOVATION CHALLENGES AND PRIZES

The federal government increasingly uses cash prizes to promote innovation; these have been a great deal for taxpayers because the social benefits vastly exceed government funding costs.[68] The prizes are at most only a few million dollars, and the competition energizes nongovernmental researchers and entrepreneurs to tackle socially significant problems. The Defense Advanced Research Project Agency (DARPA) launched its first "Grand Challenge" in 2004; whoever could design a driverless car that completed a desert course fastest would win one million dollars. No car managed to cross the finish line that day, and no one took home the prize money. The challenge, though, focused brilliant minds on driverless technology. A decade later, Google is close to mastering the technology and most major automakers are working on their own prototypes. Since then, DARPA-sponsored competitions involving humanoid robots and radio communications, among other fields, have multiplied.

Innovation prizes have taken off across the federal government. Legislation in 2009 made it easier for federal agencies to launch their own competitions, specific to their needs and missions, with awards ranging from a few thousand to several million dollars.[69] Since 2010, more than four hundred competitions have been launched with more than one hundred thousand participants.

OBAMA'S MARK: ADVANCED MANUFACTURING AND RENEWABLE ENERGY

Obama has shifted federal resources toward two areas where the United States has historically lagged behind peer competitors: advanced manufacturing and renewable energy.

Manufacturing applied research institutes. Germany is the world's envy in advanced and high-wage manufacturing. The German government

Keeping the Edge
U.S. Innovation

Changing Domestic Priorities

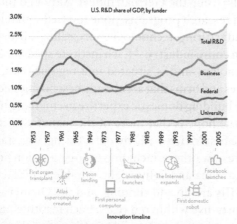

While government R&D as a percentage of GDP has
declined over time, business R&D has risen.

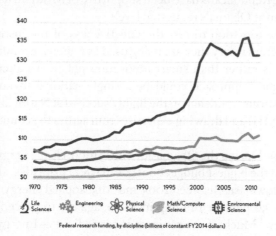

Federal research-funding priorities have become unbalanced, skewing
toward the life sciences and away from the physical sciences.

invests heavily in a network of applied research institutes to support manufacturers. Germany spends 12.7 percent of its national R&D on industrial production and technology research; the United States spends less than 1 percent.[70]

As part of Obama's Advanced Manufacturing Initiative, the federal government is trying to build a network of Manufacturing Innovation Institutes (MIIs) using the German model. Although there were many federal applied research programs, none focused squarely on commercializing manufacturing technologies or scaling up new technology products for an entire industry.[71] Each institute specializes on a specific emerging technology and is situated in a regional hub, collaborating with universities and firms that are already best positioned to exploit the technology. By building domestic expertise in emerging manufacturing technologies, the hope is that more of the manufacturing will stay at home, too. The first MII, for 3-D manufacturing, was started in 2012 in Ohio. There are now others, including next-generation power electronics in North Carolina and lightweight, durable materials in Michigan. So far, eight MIIs are up and running, and the Obama administration is aiming for forty-five within ten years. Each institute must match federal funds from private partners. The institute in Ohio now has twice the private-sector contributions needed to match the federal amount, which suggests that participating firms believe the institutes are a good investment. Republicans have been supportive of MIIs and have agreed to fund them at Obama's requested levels.

It may be too soon to test the effectiveness of the institutes, but some detractors worry they are being used as regional economic development tools rather than smart innovation policy. An alternative or complementary approach could be a single national manufacturing research institute, modeled on the highly successful National Institutes of Health (NIH) and drawing expertise from across the country.

Clean energy. During the Obama administration, clean energy research has received the biggest budget boost of all R&D priorities, albeit from a relatively low base. Between 2005 and 2015, applied energy programs have seen a 50 percent funding increase, against 19 percent for general science.[72] Much of the research is carried out at Energy Frontier Research Centers—the energy version of the Manufacturing Innovation Institutes—which are also based on public-private partnerships and matching private financing. There is now also an energy version of

DARPA, the Advanced Research Projects Agency–Energy (ARPA–E), doing more ambitious energy research at the technological frontier.

New programs within the Department of Energy are working with the private sector to build solar panel production facilities, develop next-generation batteries for electric cars, and conduct biofuel demonstration projects, among other initiatives. Not all have proved profitable, and, arguably, too much public money has gone toward scaling up mature technologies (e.g., solar thermal power plants) rather than emerging technologies that may be more competitive with fossil fuels (e.g., next-generation solar photovoltaic technologies).[73] But Obama's clean energy push is the most serious federal effort to support clean energy innovation since the early 1980s.

The United States has long led the world in clean energy technology innovation—at least when measured by patents—but other countries, such as China, are leading the way in clean energy production and investment.[74] In the 1990s, for example, the United States used to be the top solar panel producer, with 45 percent of the global market share.[75] Today the U.S. share is less than 5 percent and China has a near monopoly. And whereas the United States had the highest annual investment in clean energy as recently as 2008, now China occupies the top spot, investing almost twice as much as the United States.[76] China added more renewable power capacity in 2014 than any other country.[77] China's massive spending spree in clean energy technology could cause the locus of clean energy innovation to shift away from the United States as well.

The benefits of clean energy technology are not just environmental. Business opportunities are huge in exporting clean technologies to giant markets like China and India, which only recently embraced clean energy. The technologies are also becoming more competitive with fossil fuels. For example, the cost of solar panels has dropped more than tenfold since 2000 and the rate of solar deployment has increased by the same factor in just seven years.

But the commercialization of innovation and deployment has not kept pace. New solar technology breakthroughs in U.S. universities and federal laboratories could enable cheap and lightweight solar coatings for diverse new applications, but to date most innovative U.S. start-up companies have failed to achieve scale. Absent success in commercialization of new technologies, the United States will lose out on fast-growing markets in clean energy.

Obama's clean-energy initiative faces considerable obstacles. Republicans are far less keen on supporting renewable energy research than on promoting U.S. manufacturing. And, unlike other emerging technologies in immature industries, the energy sector has stiff competition from extremely successful, established oil and gas companies.

RESEARCH FUNDING ALLOCATION:
TOO SKEWED TO THE LIFE SCIENCES

The federal government allocates three times more money to the life sciences than to any other field of science. It has not always been this way. In 1990, federal allocations were roughly equal across the major science disciplines—life sciences, engineering, physical science, math, computer science, and environmental science. Beginning in the late 1990s, however, NIH funding for life sciences shot up and support for other sciences remained flat.

In principle, most presidents and both political parties have supported putting more public dollars into basic science research. President Ronald Reagan in the early 1980s was the first to pledge a doubling of science funding, a spirit that continued through to the late 1990s, when this was delivered to the NIH in a quick—perhaps too quick—jolt.[78] The 2007 America Competes Act authorized doubling funding over seven years, but only a fraction of the increase was eventually appropriated.[79] Obama entered office with the same doubling pledge, but has since backtracked under the strain of tight budgets. And in the era of sequestration, the non-life sciences are unlikely to see double funding any time soon.

The unbalanced science-funding priorities are difficult to justify.[80] The United States spends more on medical research than any other country by a large margin. As a percentage of GDP, the U.S. government spends much more on medical research than the average for the rest of the OECD.[81] All this money could solidify the U.S. position as the leading medical research nation, and indeed many global pharmaceutical companies are moving their research labs to the United States. But there is no reason to believe the medical sector is uniquely positioned to drive innovation in the future. Additionally, medical research has become less productive over time, every dollar of R&D on average producing fewer medical breakthroughs.[82]

Keeping the Edge
U.S. Innovation

Policy Challenges

36% | 138%
Increase in patents granted | Increase in patent-related lawsuits

2007–2011

Patent litigation is way up, suggesting the U.S. patent system could be functioning more efficiently.

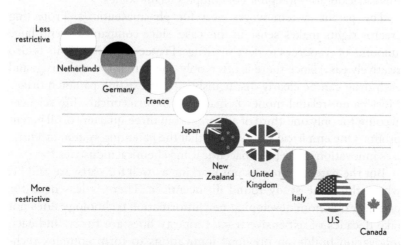

Less restrictive

Netherlands

Germany

France

Japan

New Zealand

United Kingdom

Italy

U.S

Canada

More restrictive

Relative restrictiveness toward high-skilled immigrants, by country, 2012

The United States has a more restrictive immigration system for skilled workers than most other developed countries.

THE PATENT SYSTEM: OUTDATED AND PROBLEMATIC
FOR INFORMATION TECHNOLOGY

The one-size-fits-all patent system is problematic for the IT sector in both hardware and software, where establishing inventor property rights is more difficult. This has led to a litigation morass and impedes IT innovation, with small firms and start-ups getting hit hardest.

Patenting incentives work for pharmaceuticals, not information technology. In theory, protecting creators' rights should encourage innovation. The creator incurs costs in time and money to come up with an invention. If someone else claims credit for those inventions in the marketplace, the value to the original inventor declines and there will be less invention. Empirical evidence suggests that, all else equal and in general, countries with stronger tangible property rights (e.g., land, objects) have experienced more economic growth.[83] The empirical evidence, however, for intangible rights like patents is not as clear.[84] The number of patents being filed and granted has risen sharply in the last thirty years, with no appreciable relationship to productivity growth. Property systems work better when the property and its owner can be clearly defined, and this is trickier for intangibles or complex technologies.

The patent system works best for pharmaceuticals. Protecting creator rights makes sense in this case, since companies spend huge amounts of resources to develop drugs. Protecting those rights is also relatively easy, since there is often only one patent for each drug, and each drug can be clearly distinguished from existing patented drugs. Most patent-related money is made in pharmaceuticals; life sciences account for only one-third of all patents but three-quarters of all patent profits. One empirical study found that the patenting system incentivizes innovation in the pharmaceutical and chemical industries.[85]

But the patent system is not working as well for software and IT, where the same study found disincentives. There is less need for patent protection; developing new information technology does not take decades of expensive tests. Property lines are fuzzy, and each innovation builds on previous innovations to form complex technological systems. Companies must navigate a "patent thicket" to get their products to market. The Apple iPhone, for example, uses 250,000 patents. Copyright faces similar problems—how to manage overlapping software codes, for example. Computer programmers have developed work-arounds through open-source code that is freely available online. Many in the software industry want to do away with intellectual property protections altogether. Yet the general trend over time has been to strengthen the status quo patent regime and inventor rights.

Rising patent litigation costs. Given so many IT patents where property lines are fuzzy, patent litigation costs have exploded. Some of the most high-profile patent litigation cases have involved Apple and Samsung, where each tries to claim broad swathes of technology such as smartphone physical design or automatic search functions. Between 2007 and 2011, the number of defendants tied up in patent lawsuits increased four times faster than the rate of patenting, and the vast majority of that growth involved software-related patents.[86] The average cost of each lawsuit is up, too, and increasing faster than business R&D spending. The defendants tend to be more innovative (measured by number of patents owned and R&D spending) than the plaintiffs doing the suing.[87] Studies have found that patent litigation is especially harmful to start-ups and small firms, whose litigation costs eat into R&D spending more than for larger firms.[88]

Too many patent lawsuits are frivolous and driven by firms that produce no products but do own and enforce patent rights. Nonpracticing entities accounted for half of all patent suits in 2013, up from 5 percent in 2001.[89] They are a problem mostly within the software industry, where they target smaller firms that cannot put up a fight.[90] Of all cases that have gone to court, only 2 percent of defendants have been found guilty. There may be a case for an intermediary patent market that allows inventors to sell and monetize their patents. But it is difficult to argue these nonpatenting entities are adding more to the innovation system than they are extracting in costs, especially given that they hurt small technology firms the most. According to one estimate, litigation costs may total as much as 20 percent of U.S. business R&D spending.[91] No other country has such costly patent litigation.

Some progress on patent trolls, less on fuzzy patents. Momentum is building in Congress to take on these so-called patent trolls. Obama and both parties have publicly expressed a willingness to make frivolous patent lawsuits harder. Legislation in 2011 took some initial steps, forcing patent-infringement suits to be launched against firms individually rather than collectively. The main patent reform bill currently before the House of Representatives proposes shifting the burden of litigation fees from defendants and forcing litigants to disclose more information early on in any legal action.[92] Additionally, some patent system tweaks could help start-ups by fast-tracking some patent applications. But Congress has made much less progress on fuzzy patents, which drive litigation costs and encourage patent lawsuits.

IMMIGRATION SYSTEM: NOT DESIGNED TO SELECT BY SKILL

The United States is fortunate to receive much of the world's top talent despite an immigration system that does not prioritize talent. Under the 1965 Immigration Act that remains in force today, roughly two-thirds of permanent immigration visas are allocated to family members. Only 15 percent are awarded specifically for employment reasons. Exceptionally talented immigrants, such as elite scientists or athletes, have their own visa category, but only a small number qualify.

Highly skilled immigrants without such exceptional résumés face a more difficult problem. Their best bet is to enter the country as students and then marry Americans, which gives them permanent residency.[93] Foreigners who received their college degrees in the United States have a year (two for STEM graduates) to secure employment. Their stay in the United States is not guaranteed, however; their employer must file their application for a temporary work visa, typically the H-1B. The H-1B is capped at eighty-five thousand visas annually and does not adjust with employer demand.[94] In 2014, the limit was reached within a few days, triggering a lottery based on luck rather than qualifications. Employers must take on the several-thousand-dollar cost of applying, incurring the risk that even the most-qualified candidates might lose the lottery. The entire process can take over a year from initial filing before the employee can go on the payroll. Start-ups are at a disadvantage; they do not have the patience or resources to sponsor H-1B applicants, as Google and Microsoft do. The H-1B lasts six years, but the visa holder is usually tied to the same employer for that period. Adjusting from a temporary work visa to a green card normally takes several more years with the same employer. The waits are longest for Indian and Chinese citizens. They hold the majority of H-1B visas, but no one nationality can receive more than 7 percent of green cards each year, resulting in backlogs that can stretch a decade or more. This immigration system has barely changed in twenty-five years.

Other developed countries, meanwhile, have been changing their immigration systems to prioritize worker skills. No other country allocates such a high percentage of permanent visas for family reunification. Most allocate far more based on employment qualifications and have less restrictive skilled-worker immigration systems (figure 6).[95] Many countries, following the lead set by Australia and Canada, now use some combination of employer demand and points-based selection, where immigrants are ranked based on a number of factors—including job offers and skill levels—so that the most qualified are most likely to obtain visas. These countries can adjust the points system year-to-year depending on the needs of their economies rather than setting an absolute and inflexible cap. Moving from a temporary to a permanent work visa is also usually faster in other countries. In part because of their skills-focused immigration systems, the foreign-born in other English-speaking countries tend to be better educated than in the United States (see figure 6).

Congress has failed to make any significant changes to the immigration system even though there is bipartisan support for prioritizing high-skilled immigrants. Several bills have been introduced in recent years that would increase the H-1B cap or increase the number of permanent visas for skilled migrants. The effort, though, has so far languished because Congress has been unable to agree on comprehensive legislation that would address other immigration-related issues, such as border security, low-skilled immigration, and the legal status of unauthorized migrants.

FIGURE 6. SHARE OF PERMANENT VISAS FOR WORK
AND FOREIGN BORN WITH A TERTIARY EDUCATION

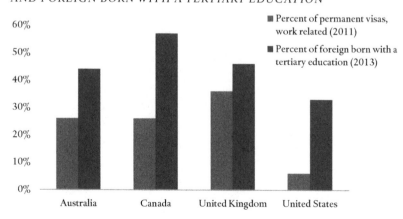

Source: OECD (2014).

FUTURE PROSPECTS

There is a healthy bipartisan consensus on the importance of innovation and much agreement among Washington policymakers about where the problems exist. U.S. scientists and businesses are leading in innovation today and probably will be for the next decade. The challenge is preserving that lead. Where the United States is weakest today—businesses and scientists stepping back from risky but essential scientific research—is also where the government can play the biggest role in ensuring the United States remains dominant for decades to come.

Endnotes

REMEDIAL EDUCATION

1. "Financing Education—Investments and Returns: Analysis of the World Education Indicators," UNESCO Institute for Statistics and the Organization for Economic Cooperation and Development (OECD), 2002, http://www.oecd.org/education/highereducationandadultlearning/2494749.pdf.
2. Doug Lederman, "College for All," *Inside Higher Ed*, February 25, 2009, http://www.insidehighered.com/news/2009/02/25/obama.
3. OECD, "Education at a Glance 2014," tables A1.2a and A1.3a, Education at a Glance 2014," tables A1.2a and A1.3a, http://www.oecd.org/edu/Education-at-a-Glance-2014.pdf.
4. There has been a reported recent uptick in the U.S. high school graduation rate, but there is some disagreement over whether this is driven by improvements in the education system, because of changing employment conditions for teenagers, or because of a change in how graduation numbers are being calculated. See Anya Kamenetz, "High School Graduation Rates: The Good, the Bad, and the Ambiguous," *NPR*, June 9, 2015, http://www.npr.org/sections/ed/2015/06/09/412939852/high-school-graduation-rates-the-good-the-bad-and-the-ambiguous; and Michael Muskal, "U.S. high school graduation rate hits highest level in decades," *Los Angeles Times*, January 23, 2013, http://www.latimes.com/news/nation/nationnow/la-na-nn-high-school-graduation-rate-increasing-20130122,0,3444079.story.
5. James J. Heckman and Paul A. LaFontaine, "The Declining American High School Graduation Rate: Evidence, Sources, and Consequences," *NBER Reporter: Research Summary* no. 1, 2008, http://www.nber.org/reporter/2008number1/heckman.html. In figure 1, the high school equivalency shares are calculated based on National Center for Education Statistics (NCES) data and applied to OECD high school graduation rates. High school equivalency shares calculated by dividing the graduation rate of seventeen-year-olds by the status completion rate. For graduation rates of seventeen-year-olds, see NCES, "Digest of Education Statistics 2013," table 103, http://nces.ed.gov/pubs2015/2015011.pdf. For status completion rates, see NCES, "Trends in High School Dropout and Completion Rates in the United States: 1972–2012," June 2015, table 10, p. 46, http://nces.ed.gov/pubs2015/2015015.pdf.
6. OECD, "Education at a Glance 2014," table C2.1.
7. NCES, "Digest of Education Statistics 2014," table 302.20, https://nces.ed.gov/programs/digest/d14/tables/dt14_302.20.asp.
8. For historical data on on-time graduation rates, see John Bound et al., "Why Have College Completion Rates Declined? An Analysis of Changing Student Preparation and Collegiate Resources," *American Economic Journal of Applied Economics* 2, no. 3, July 2010, http://www.ncbi.nlm.nih.gov/pmc/articles/PMC3140225/; also see Anthony

Carnevale and Jeff Strohl, "How Increasing College Access Is Increasing Inequality, and What to Do About It," in *Rewarding Strivers*, ed. Richard D. Kahlenberg (New York: The Century Foundation, 2010), p. 74, http://www.tcf.org/assets/downloads/tcf-CarnevaleStrivers.pdf.

9. For enrollment rates, see OECD, "Education at a Glance 2014," table C3.1a; for college dropout rates, see OECD, "Education at a Glance 2013," table A4.1.

10. Valerie Strauss, "What the national drop in 2015 NAEP test scores really means," *Washington Post*, October 28, 2015, https://www.washingtonpost.com/news/answer-sheet/wp/2015/10/28/what-the-national-drop-in-2015-naep-test-scores-really-means.

11. OECD, "Education at a Glance 2014," chart B1.4.

12. NCES, "Digest of Education Statistics, 2013," table 236.55, https://nces.ed.gov/programs/digest/d13/tables/dt13_236.55.asp.

13. College Board, "Trends in College Pricing 2014," figure 16b, http://trends.collegeboard.org.

14. OECD, "Education at a Glance 2014," table B5.1.

15. College Board, "College Pricing 2014," table 2.

16. For math scores, see Ina V.S. Mullis et al., "TIMSS 2007 International Math Report," TIMSS and PIRLS International Center at Boston College, p. 34, http://timss.bc.edu/TIMSS2007/PDF/TIMSS2007_InternationalMathematicsReport.pdf. For science scores, see Michael O. Martin et al., "TIMSS 2007 International Science Report," TIMSS and PIRLS International Study Center at Boston College, p. 34, http://timss.bc.edu/TIMSS2007/PDF/TIMSS2007_InternationalScienceReport.pdf.

17. As measured by the proportion who are high-achieving. See Michael J. Petrilli and Janie Scull, "American Achievement in International Perspective," Thomas B. Fordham Institute, March 2011, p. 4, http://www.edexcellencemedia.net/publications/2011/20110315_EdShorts_PISA/PISA_final.pdf.

18. NCES, "Digest of Education Statistics, 2013," table 225.40, https://nces.ed.gov/programs/digest/d13/tables/dt13_225.40.asp?current=yes.

19. *U.S. News & World Report*, "Best Global Universities Rankings," 2015, http://www.usnews.com/education/best-global-universities/rankings?int=a27a09.

20. Michael E. Porter and Jan W. Rivkin, "An Economy Doing Half Its Job: Findings of Harvard Business School's 2013–14 Survey on U.S. Competitiveness," September 2014, http://www.hbs.edu/competitiveness/Documents/an-economy-doing-half-its-job.pdf.

21. For historical National Assessment of Education Progress (NAEP) scores, see http://nces.ed.gov/nationsreportcard.

22. Sean Reardon, "The Widening Academic Achievement Gap Between the Rich and the Poor: New Evidence and Possible Explanations," in *Whither Opportunity? Rising Inequality, Schools, and Children's Life Chances*, ed. Greg J. Duncan and Richard J. Murnane (New York: Russell Sage Foundation, 2011), p. 92.

23. Bailey and Dynarski, *Whither Opportunity?* p. 117. But some new evidence indicates that the income gap may be narrowing slightly for school readiness among kindergarteners after having widened for decades; see Sean F. Reardon and Ximena A. Portilla, "Recent Trends in Socioeconomic and Racial School Readiness Gaps at Kindergarten Entry," CEPA Working Paper no. 15-02, September 2015, http://cepa.stanford.edu/content/recent-trends-socioeconomic-and-racial-school-readiness-gaps-kindergarten-entry.

24. OECD, "Economic Policy Reforms 2010: Going for Growth." See figure 5.3 for the influence of parental socioeconomic background on student secondary achievement.

25. Reardon et al., "Race, income, and enrollment in highly selective colleges, 1982–2004," Center for Education Policy Analysis working paper, August 3, 2012, http://cepa.

stanford.edu/sites/default/files/race%20income%20%26%20selective%20college%20
enrollment%20august%203%202012.pdf.

26. The Pell Institute, "Indicators of Higher Education Equity in the United States: 45
Year Trend Report," 2015, indicator 5a, http://www.pellinstitute.org/downloads/
publications-indicators_of_Higher_Education_Equity_in_the_US_45_Year_Trend_
Report.pdf.

27. Julie Renee Posselt et al., "Access Without Equity: Longitudinal Analyses of Institutional
Stratification by Race and Ethnicity, 1972–2004," *American Education Research Journal*
49, no. 6, December 2012.

28. Reardon et al., "Race, Income, and Enrollment in Highly Selective Colleges."

29. OECD, "Viewing Education in the United States Through the Prism of PISA," figure
2.3, http://www.oecd.org/unitedstates/46579895.pdf.

30. Caroline M. Hoxby, "The Changing Selectivity of American Colleges," *Journal of
Economic Perspectives* 23, no. 4, Fall 2009, http://www.nber.org/papers/w15446.

31. Anthony Carnevale and Jeff Strohl, "How Increasing College Access Is Increasing
Inequality, and What to Do About It," in Richard D. Kahlenberg, eds., *Rewarding
Strivers* (Century Foundation: New York, 2010), pp. 92, 150, http://www.tcf.org/assets/
downloads/tcf-CarnevaleStrivers.pdf.

32. Bound et al., "Why Have College Completion Rates Declined?"

33. Anthony Carnevale et al., "Career and Technical Education: Five Ways That Pay Along
the Way to a B.A.," Georgetown University Center on Education and the Workforce,
September 2012, figures 7 and 8, http://www.insidehighered.com/sites/default/
server_files/files/CTE_FiveWays_FullReport_Embargoed.pdf.

34. See, for example, Harry J. Holzer and Robert I. Lerman, "The Future of Middle-Skill
Jobs," Brookings' Center on Children and Families Brief no. 41, p. 4, http://www.
brookings.edu/~/media/research/files/papers/2009/2/middle%20skill%20jobs%20
holzer/02_middle_skill_jobs_holzer.

35. NCES, "Institutional Retention and Graduation Rates for Undergraduate Students,"
May 2015, http://nces.ed.gov/programs/coe/indicator_cva.asp. *Sub-bachelor's* refers
here to two-year institutions. Four-year degree cohort is for the 2007 incoming class
and the two-year degree cohort is for the 2010 income class.

36. Sandy Baum et al., "Trends in Public Higher Education: Enrollment, Prices, Student
Aid, Revenues, and Expenditures," Trends in Higher Education Series, College Board,
May 2012, table 3, http://trends.collegeboard.org/sites/default/files/trends-2012-
public-higher-education-expenditures-brief.pdf. *Low-income student* is defined here
as a student whose family income is less than $60,000.

37. John Immerwahr and Jean Johnson, "Squeeze Play 2010: Continued Public Anxiety on
Cost, Harsher Judgments on How Colleges Are Run," A Joint Project of the National
Center for Public Policy and Higher Education and Public Agenda, February 2010,
http://www.highereducation.org/reports/squeeze_play_10/squeeze_play_10.pdf.

38. Brandon Busteed and Stephanie Kafka, "Most Americans Say Higher Education Not
Affordable," *Gallup*, April 16, 2015, http://www.gallup.com/poll/182441/americans-
say-higher-education-not-affordable.aspx.

39. W. Steven Barnett et al., "The State of Preschool 2014," National Institute for Early
Education Research, 2015, p. 8, http://nieer.org/sites/nieer/files/Yearbook2014_
full2_0.pdf.

40. W. Steven Barnett et al., "The State of Preschool 2011," National Institute for Early
Education Research, 2012, p. 6, http://nieer.org/sites/nieer/files/Yearbook2014_
full2_0.pdf; http://nieer.org/sites/nieer/files/2011yearbook.pdf.

41. W. Steven Barnett, "Preschool Education and Its Lasting Effects: Research and Policy
Implications," National Institute for Early Education Research, Rutgers University,
September 2008, http://nieer.org/resources/research/PreschoolLastingEffects.pdf.

42. See, for example, Lawrence J. Schweinhart et al., "Lifetime Effects: The High/ Scope Perry Preschool Study Through Age 40," High/Scope Education Research Foundation, 2005, http://www.highscope.org/content.asp?contentid=219.

43. This three-to-one benefit-cost ratio is the estimate from the Abcedarian Project. It is the lowest of the three model programs with long-term studies. The others are the Chicago Child-Parent Centers ($7.14) and the High Scope/Perry Preschool project ($5.15 to $17.1). All figures obtained from Julia Isaacs, "Research Brief #4: Model Early Childhood Programs," Impacts of Early Childhood Programs, Brookings Institution, September 2008, http://www.brookings.edu/~/media/Research/Files/ Papers/2008/9/early%20programs%20isaacs/09_early_programs_brief4.PDF.

44. Michael Puma et al., "Head Start Impact Study Final Report," U.S. Department of Health and Human Services, January 2010, http://www.acf.hhs.gov/sites/default/files/ opre/executive_summary_final.pdf; and for results that showed no impact in third grade, see Michael Puma et al., "Third Grade Follow-up to the Head Start Impact Study," U.S. Department of Health and Human Services, October 2012, http://www. acf.hhs.gov/sites/default/files/opre/head_start_report.pdf.

45. See David Deming, "Early Childhood Intervention and Life-Cycle Skill Development: Evidence from Head Start," *American Economic Journal: Applied Economics*, vol. 1, no. 3, July 2009, http://people.fas.harvard.edu/~deming/papers/Deming_HeadStart.pdf.

46. William T. Gormley Jr. et al., "Head Start's Comparative Advantage: Myth or Reality?" *Policy Studies Journal* 38, no. 3, August 2010.

47. Haskins and Barnett, "Introduction: New Directions for America's Early Childhood Policies," pp. 4–5.

48. Anna D. Johnson et al., "Child-Care Subsidies: Do They Impact the Quality of Care Children Experience?" *Child Development* 83, no. 4, July/August 2012.

49. Elaine Maag, "Taxation and the Family: How Does the Tax System Subsidize Child Care Expenses?" *The Tax Policy Briefing Book*, Urban-Brookings Tax Policy Center, 2010, http://www.taxpolicycenter.org/briefing-book/key-elements/family/child-care-subsidies.cfm.

50. In 2014, Congress chose not to reauthorize Race to the Top Early Learning Challenge. In its place now exists a very similar program called Preschool Development Grants, funded at about half the level as Race to the Top Early Learning Challenge.

51. Barnett, "The State of Preschool 2014," p. 6.

52. NCES, "Digest of Education Statistics," table 3, http://nces.ed.gov/programs/digest/ d07/tables/dt07_003.asp. Most states have mandatory attendance laws up until age fifteen or sixteen. Enrollment is not 100 percent universal for K–12 because some students drop out or are homeschooled.

53. For a good overview of how U.S. education funding works, see "PreK-12 Financing Overview," New America Foundation, June 29, 2015, http://atlas.newamerica.org/ school-finance.

54. Michael Hout and Stuart W. Elliott, eds., "Incentives and Test-Based Accountability in Education," National Academy of Sciences and National Research Council, 2011, http://www.nap.edu/catalog.php?record_id=12521.

55. Also, one Bush-era competitive grant program, School Improvement Grants (SIG), for the lowest-performing schools, was rejuvenated with stimulus funds and later appropriations to the tune of $4.6 billion. Applicants must pick from four school reorganization models in which to invest their grant money, ranging from relatively mild ("turnaround," with a new principal and staff changes) to dramatic ("restart" as a charter or "closure," with enrollment of students elsewhere).

56. Daniel Weisberg et al., "The Widget Effect: Our National Failure to Acknowledge and Act on Differences in Teacher Effectiveness," the New Teacher Project, 2009, p. 4, http://widgeteffect.org/downloads/TheWidgetEffect_execsummary.pdf.

57. Raj Chetty et al., "The Long-Term Impacts of Teachers: Teacher Value-Added and Student Outcomes in Adulthood," NBER Working Paper no. 17699, December 2011, http://www.nber.org/papers/w17699.

58. Broadly, and especially at the elementary-school level, teacher academic credentials and cognitive ability have had no effect on student achievement. But at the secondary-school level, in higher-level math and science courses, teachers' substantive expertise and cognitive ability are more significant factors. For a review of research on what makes a good teacher, see Dan Goldhaber, "The Mystery of Good Teaching," *Education Next* 2, no. 1, Spring 2002, http://educationnext.org/the-mystery-of-good-teaching.

59. C. Kirabo Jackson, "Teacher Quality at the High-School Level: The Importance of Accounting for Tracks," *Journal of Labor Economics* 32, no. 4, October 2014, http://www.nber.org/papers/w17722.

60. See, for example, Sarena Goodman and Lesley Turner, "Teacher Incentive Pay and Educational Outcomes: Evidence from the NYC Bonus Program," Program on Education Policy and Governance Working Papers Series, PEPG 10–7, May 2010, http://www.hks.harvard.edu/pepg/MeritPayPapers/goodman_turner_10-07.pdf; and Matthew G. Springer et al., "Teacher Pay for Performance: Experimental Evidence from the Project on Incentives in Teaching," National Center on Performance Incentives, September 21, 2010, http://www.hechingerreport.org/static/pointstudy. pdf. But there is one recent evaluation of the Washington, DC, pay-for-performance scheme that found especially generous rewards did have an impact on performance, even if the high level of pay may not be fiscally sustainable across the country: James Wyckoff and Thomas Dee, "Incentives, Selection, and Teacher Performance: Evidence from IMPACT," NBER Working Paper no. 19529, October 2013, http://www.nber.org/ papers/w19529.

61. OECD, "Strong Performers and Successful Reformers in Education: Lessons from PISA for the United States," 2011, http://www.oecd.org/pisa/46623978.pdf.

62. Motoko Rich, "Enrollment in Charter Schools Is Increasing," *New York Times*, November 14, 2012, http://www.nytimes.com/2012/11/14/us/charter-schools-growing-fast-new-report-finds.html.

63. Melissa A. Clark et al., "Do Charter Schools Improve Student Achievement? Evidence from a National Randomized Study," Mathematica Policy Research Working Paper, December 2011, http://www.mathematica-mpr.com/publications/PDFs/education/ charterschools_WP.pdf.

64. Joshua D. Angrist et al., "Explaining Charter School Effectiveness," NBER Working Paper no. 17332, August 2011, http://www.nber.org/papers/w17332.pdf; Christina Clark Tuttle et al., "Student Characteristics and Achievement in 22 KIPP Middle Schools," Mathematica Policy Research, June 2010, http://www.mathematica-mpr. com/publications/PDFs/education/KIPP_fnlrpt.pdf; and "Urban Charter School Study Report on 41 Regions," Center for Research on Education Outcomes, 2015, http://urbancharters.stanford.edu/download/Urban%20Charter%20School%20 Study%20Report%20on%2041%20Regions.pdf.

65. "Chartering a Better Course," *Economist*, July 7, 2012, http://www.economist.com/ node/21558265.

66. John F. Witte et al., "MPCP Longitudinal Educational Growth Study: Fifth Year Report," School Choice Demonstration Project, February 2012, http://www.uark. edu/ua/der/SCDP/Milwaukee_Eval/Report_29.pdf; Patrick Wolf et al., "Evaluation of the D.C. Opportunity Scholarship Program: Final Report," U.S. Department of Education, National Center for Education Evaluation and Regional Assistance, June 2010, http://ies.ed.gov/ncee/pubs/20104018/pdf/20104018.pdf; and Matthew M. Chingos and Paul E. Peterson, "Experimentally estimated impacts of school vouchers

on college enrollment and degree attainment," *Journal of Public Economics* 122, February 2015, http://www.sciencedirect.com/science/article/pii/S0047272714002461.

67. Tom Loveless, "The 2012 Brown Center Report on American Education: How Well Are American Students Learning?" Brookings Institution, February 2012, http://www.brookings.edu/~/media/newsletters/0216_brown_education_loveless.pdf.

68. "Children's Budget 2015," First Focus, 2015, http://firstfocus.org/resources/report/childrens-budget-2015.

69. Title I was always meant to be supplementary to local funding; districts had to fund wealthier and poorer schools equally, and then federal Title I funds could be used on top of the equal funding. But because of loopholes, which, for example, allow districts to exclude teacher salaries from funding figures, funding at the school level is in practice seldom equal. See, for example, Jennifer S. Cohen and Raegen T. Miller, "Evidence of the Effects of the Title I Comparability Loophole: Shining a Light on Fiscal Inequity Within Florida's Public School Districts," Center for American Progress and American Enterprise Institute, March 2012, http://blogs.edweek.org/edweek/teacherbeat/florida_paper.pdf.

70. Baum et al., "Trends in Public Higher Education," p. 2. Also see "Digest of Education Statistics 2014," National Center for Education Statistics, table 303.70, http://nces.ed.gov/programs/digest/d14/tables/dt14_303.70.asp.

71. For percentage of undergraduates receiving federal student aid, see "Digest of Education Statistics 2014," National Center for Education Statistics, table 331.20, http://nces.ed.gov/programs/digest/d14/tables/dt14_331.20.asp.

72. K–12 federal spending was $41.8 billion in 2014; see Julia Isaacs et al., "Kid's Share 2015: Report on Federal Expenditures on Children in 2014 and Future Projections," Urban Institute, September 2015, http://firstfocus.org/resources/report/kids-share-2015. For postsecondary federal spending, the rough breakdown in 2015 was $31 billion for Pell Grants, $11 billion for IRB debt repayment, $32 billion for tax breaks, and $2 billion for community colleges. The real postsecondary federal spending amount would be higher if accounting for veterans' education grants.

73. "Federal Pell Grant Program," New America Foundation, Federal Education Budget Project, May 2015, http://febp.newamerica.net/background-analysis/federal-pell-grant-program.

74. A comparable personal, unsecured loan, which also requires no collateral, would charge between 10 and 13 percent in interest.

75. NCES, "2012–13 National Postsecondary Student Aid Study," August 2013, table 3, http://nces.ed.gov/pubs2013/2013165.pdf.

76. Figures compiled by Mark Kantrowitz at http://www.finaid.org/loans.

77. Jason Delisle, "The Graduate Student Debt Review: The State of Graduate Student Borrowing," New America Education Policy Program Policy Brief, March 2014, https://www.newamerica.org/education-policy/the-graduate-student-debt-review.

78. "Estimates of Total Income Tax Expenditures for Fiscal Years 2014–2024," U.S. Department of Treasury, https://www.whitehouse.gov/sites/default/files/omb/budget/fy2016/assets/ap_14_expenditures.pdf.

79. "Total Student Aid and Nonfederal Loans in 2014 Dollars over Time," Trends in Student Aid 2015, College Board, http://trends.collegeboard.org/student-aid.

80. Jason Delisle and Alex Holt, "Safety Net or Windfall? Examining Changes to Income-Based Repayment for Federal Student Loans," New America Foundation, Federal Education Budget Project, October 2012, http://static.newamerica.org/attachments/2332-safety-net-or-windfall/NAF_Income_Based_Repayment.18c8a688f03c4c628b6063755ff5dbaa.pdf.

81. Jason Delisle, "What Does Incomes-Based Repayment for Student Loans Cost?" New America Foundation, May 21, 2015, http://www.edcentral.org/income-based-repayment-cost.

82. According to Jason Delisle of the New America Foundation, the only tax benefits for most of the 1990s were the scholarship income and personal parental exemptions, which totaled about $2.5 billion, adjusted for inflation.

83. Susan Dynarski, testimony before the U.S. Senate Committee on Finance, July 25, 2012, p. 2, http://www.finance.senate.gov/imo/media/doc/Dynarski%20Testimony.pdf.

84. Jason Delisle and Kim Dancy, "A New Look at Tuition Tax Breaks," New America Foundation, November 2015, http://www.luminafoundation.org/files/resources/a-new-look-at-tuition-tax-benefits.pdf.

85. In 1992–93, 19.7 percent of students took out loans, and in 2007–2008, 34.7 percent of students did. Assuming the historical rate of increase continues through 2012–2013, roughly 40 percent of students have taken out loans this year. Figures used in calculation provided by Mark Kantrowitz of Finaid.org.

86. In 2001–2002, state student grants and tax benefits constituted 26.7 percent of total government student grants and tax benefits. In 2011–2012, the state share decreased to 16.1 percent. Figures provided by Mark Kantrowitz of Finaid.org.

87. See "42nd Annual Survey Report on State-Sponsored Student Financial Aid: 2010–2011 Academic Year," National Association of State Student Grant and Aid Programs, 2012, http://www.nassgap.org/viewrepository.aspx?categoryID=3.

88. Pell Grants covered 77 percent of the cost of a public four-year college in 1979, but 30 percent today.

89. Tamar Lewin, "Senate Committee Report on For-Profit Colleges Condemns Costs and Practices," New York Times, July 29, 2012, http://www.nytimes.com/2012/07/30/education/harkin-report-condemns-for-profit-colleges.html.

90. There was also a proposed "First in the World" competitive-grant program funded at $55 million to promote innovation specifically to boost college completion rates among minorities and low-income students.

91. Scott Jaschick, "Online Penalty," Inside Higher Ed, April 20, 2015, https://www.insidehighered.com/news/2015/04/20/study-finds-student-success-lags-online-california-community-college-students; and Ry Rivard, "Udacity Project on 'Pause,'" Inside Higher Ed, July 18, 2013, https://www.insidehighered.com/news/2013/07/18/citing-disappointing-student-outcomes-san-jose-state-pauses-work-udacity.

92. Ryan Brown, "Community College Students Perform Worse Online Than Face to Face," Chronicle of Higher Education, July 18, 2011, http://chronicle.com/article/Community-College-Students/128281.

93. Jon Marcus, "Poll: Americans give high marks to community colleges for quality, value," The Hechinger Report, October 26, 2015, http://hechingerreport.org/poll-americans-give-high-marks-to-community-colleges-for-quality-value.

94. The Trade Adjustment Assistance Community College and Career Training grant program (TAACCT), http://www.doleta.gov/taaccct.

95. Catherine Rampell, "As Millions Seek Work, an Overhaul in Retraining," New York Times, November 10, 2010, http://www.nytimes.com/2010/11/11/giving/11TRAIN.html.

96. David Deming and Susan Dynarski, "Into College, Out of Poverty? Policies to Increase the Postsecondary Attainment of the Poor," NBER Working Paper no. 15387, September 2010, http://www.nber.org/papers/w15387.pdf; and Eric Bettinger, "How Financial Aid Affects Persistence," NBER Working Paper no. 10242, January 2004, http://www.nber.org/papers/w10242.pdf.

97. See Bridget Terry Long, "The Impact of Federal Tax Credits for Higher Education Expenses," NBER Working Paper no. 9553, March 2003, http://www.nber.org/

papers/w9553.pdf; and Nicholas Turner, "The Effect of Tax-Based Federal Student Aid on College Enrollment," *National Tax Journal* 64, no. 3, September 2011, http://www.ntanet.org/NTJ/64/3/ntj-v64n03p839-61-effect-tax-based-federal.pdf.

98.   The Pell Grant program could be made more cost-effective as well. The complexity and paperwork that comes with a well-targeted, means-tested program lowers benefit take-up rates. A simplified process for applying for aid had the same impact on college enrollment as several thousand dollars in aid. See Eric Bettinger et al., "The Role of Simplification and Information in College Decisions: Results from the H&R Block FAFSA Experiment," NBER Working Paper no.15361, September 2009, http://www.nber.org/papers/w15361.pdf.

ROAD TO NOWHERE

1.   Sylvain Leduc and Daniel Wilson, "Roads to Prosperity or Bridges to Nowhere? Theory and Evidence on the Impact of Public Infrastructure Investment," NBER Working Paper no. 18042, May 2012, http://www.nber.org/papers/w18042.

2.   "Estimated Impact of the American Recovery and Reinvestment Act on Employment and Economic Output from October 2011 Through December 2011," Congressional Budget Office (CBO), February 2012, http://www.cbo.gov/sites/default/files/cbofiles/attachments/02-22-ARRA.pdf.

3.   "The Global Competitiveness Report: 2014–2015," World Economic Forum, 2014, http://www3.weforum.org/docs/WEF_GlobalCompetitivenessReport_2014-15.pdf.

4.   See "United States" profile for Transportation, *The World Factbook*, Central Intelligence Agency, https://www.cia.gov/library/publications/resources/the-world-factbook/geos/us.html.

5.   For improving conditions, see "2013 Status of the Nation's Highways, Bridges, and Transit: Conditions & Performance Report," U.S. Department of Transportation's Federal Highway Administration, 2013, https://www.fhwa.dot.gov/policy/2013cpr/pdfs/cp2013.pdf; for travel mode breakdown, see "Passenger Travel Facts and Figures 2015," U.S. Department of Transportation, 2015, http://www.rita.dot.gov/bts/sites/rita.dot.gov.bts/files/PTFF%20August_2015.pdf; for share of federal transportation spending for highways and transit, see "Public Spending on Transportation and Water Infrastructure, 1956 to 2014," CBO, March 2015, https://www.cbo.gov/sites/default/files/114th-congress-2015-2016/reports/49910-Infrastructure.pdf.

6.   For population growth, see "Population Estimates," U.S. Census Bureau, https://www.census.gov/popest/data/historical; for road lane construction, see "Public Road Mileage, Lane-Miles, and VMT," Office of Highway Policy Information, 2013, http://www.fhwa.dot.gov/policyinformation/statistics/2013/vmt422c.cfm.

7.   "U.S. Driving Hits Historic High in Year's First Half," U.S. Department of Transportation, August 20, 2015, https://www.fhwa.dot.gov/pressroom/fhwa1557.cfm.

8.   David Schrank et al., "2015 Urban Mobility Scorecard," Texas A&M Transportation Institute and INRIX, August 2015, http://d2dtl5nnlpfror.cloudfront.net/tti.tamu.edu/documents/mobility-scorecard-2015.pdf.

9.   "FHWA Forecasts of Vehicle Miles Traveled (VMT): May 2015," Federal Highway Administration's Office of Highway Policy Information, June 5, 2015, https://www.fhwa.dot.gov/policyinformation/tables/vmt/vmt_forecast_sum.pdf.

10. "Total inland transport infrastructure investment (1995–2013)," OECD International Transport Forum, https://stats.oecd.org/Index.aspx?DataSetCode=ITF_INV-MTN_DATA.

11. "2013 Status of the Nation's Highways, Bridges and Transit," Federal Highway Administration, 2013.

12. "Funding Challenges in Highway and Transit: A federal-state-local analysis," Pew Charitable Trusts, February 24, 2015, http://www.pewtrusts.org/en/research-and-analysis/analysis/2015/02/24/funding-challenges-in-highway-and-transit-a-federal-state-local-analysis. The federal data does not includes stimulus spending.

13. For data showing capital investments in highways has fallen off more than other types of infrastructure investment, see "Public Spending on Transportation and Water Infrastructure, 1956 to 2014," CBO, 2015, p. 27.

14. Joseph Kile, "Testimony: The Status of the Highway Trust Fund and Options for Paying for Highway Spending," CBO, June 18, 2015, https://www.cbo.gov/sites/default/files/114th-congress-2015-2016/reports/50297-TransportationTestimony-Senate_1.pdf, pp 9.

15. "Projections of Highway Trust Fund Accounts Under CBO's January 2015 Baseline," CBO, https://www.cbo.gov/sites/default/files/cbofiles/attachments/43884-2015-01-HighwayTrustFund.pdf.

16. "States Delay Many More Projects Amid Highway Trust Fund Uncertainty," American Association of State Highway and Transportation Officials (AASHTO) Journal, March 20, 2015, http://www.aashtojournal.org/Pages/032015delays.aspx.

17. Kile, "Testimony."

18. "Raise the Gas Tax to Fix America's Roads," New York Times, January 10, 2015, http://www.nytimes.com/2015/01/11/opinion/sunday/raise-the-gas-tax-to-fix-americas-roads.html, and Roger C. Altman et al., "Financing U.S. Transportation Infrastructure in the 21st Century," Brookings Institution, May 7, 2015, http://www.brookings.edu/research/papers/2015/05/07-financing-transportation-infrastructure-altman-krueger-klein.

19. "The Life and Death of the Highway Trust Fund: How We Pay for Transportation," ENO Center for Transportation, December 2014, https://www.enotrans.org/wp-content/uploads/2015/09/Highway-Trust-Fund.pdf.

20. "Funding Challenges in Highway and Transit," The Pew Charitable Trusts, 2015.

21. "Excessive Truck Weight: An Expensive Burden We Can No Longer Support," U.S. Government Accountability Office, July 16, 1979, http://www.gao.gov/products/CED-79-94, pp 23.

22. Joseph Kane et al., "Tolls on the rise as highway funding dries up," Brookings Institute, April 6, 2015, http://www.brookings.edu/blogs/the-avenue/posts/2015/04/06-tolls-highway-funding-kane-sabol-puentes.

23. Robert Poole, "Surface Transportation News #130," Reason Foundation, August 20, 2014, http://reason.org/news/show/surface-transportation-news-130.html#a.

24. Robert Dunphy, "Toll Roads: A Problem or a Solution?" UrbanLand, May 28, 2015, http://urbanland.uli.org/infrastructure-transit/toll-roads-problem-solution.

25. "The Consequences of Reduced Federal Transportation Investment," Eno Center for Transportation and Bipartisan Policy Center, September 2012, http://bipartisanpolicy.org/wp-content/uploads/sites/default/files/BPC-Eno%20Transportation%20Report.pdf, p 16.

26. Kile, "Testimony."

27. Ibid.

28. Robert W. Poole, Jr., "Annual Privatization Report 2015: Transportation Finance," Reason Foundation, May 2015, http://reason.org/files/apr-2015-transportation-finance.pdf.

29. Ibid.

30. Aman Batheja, "A G.O.P. Shift Against Toll Roads in Texas," New York Times, July 3, 2014, http://www.nytimes.com/2014/07/04/us/a-republican-shift-against-toll-roads-in-texas.html?_r=0.

31. Joseph Kile, "Testimony: Public-Private Partnerships for Highway Projects," CBO, March 5, 2014, https://www.cbo.gov/sites/default/files/113th-congress-2013-2014/reports/45157-PublicPrivatePartnerships.pdf.

32. William Reinhardt, "The Role of Private Investment in Meeting U.S. Transportation Infrastructure Needs," American Road & Transportation Builders Association's Transportation Development Foundation, May 2011, http://www.pwfinance.net/document/research_reports/0%20artba.pdf.

33. "Fiscal Year (FY) 2015 Redistribution of Transportation Infrastructure Finance and Innovation Act (TIFIA) Funds and Associated Obligation Limitation," Federal Highway Administration, April 24, 2015, http://www.fhwa.dot.gov/legsregs/directives/notices/n4510783.cfm.

34. "Americans' Views on Spending Versus Federal Budget Plans," Center for Effective Government, April 2, 2013, http://www.foreffectivegov.org/fy14-budget-plans-side-by-side.

35. Jacob Anbinder, "Public Seeks Transparency in Infrastructure Investment," Century Foundation, May 7, 2015, http://www.tcf.org/blog/detail/public-seeks-transparency-in-infrastructure-investment; and Rockefeller Foundation Infrastructure Survey, conducted by Hart Research Associates and Public Opinion Strategies, February 14, 2011, http://www.rockefellerfoundation.org/uploads/files/80e28432-0790-4d42-91ec-afb6d11febee.pdf.

36. Rockefeller Foundation Infrastructure Survey.

37. Asha Weinstein Agrawal and Hilary Nixon, "What Do Americans Think About Federal Tax Options to Support Public Transit, Highways, and Local Streets and Roads? Results from Year Six of a National Survey," Mineta Transportation Institute, June 2015, http://transweb.sjsu.edu/PDFs/research/1428-road-tax-public-opinion-poll-2015.pdf.

38. For transit ballot initiatives, see "Transportation Ballot Measures," Center for Transportation Excellence, http://www.cfte.org/elections; For state transportation ballots, calculations derived from data from the Ballot Measures Database, the National Conference of State Legislatures, http://www.ncsl.org/research/elections-and-campaigns/ballot-measures-database.aspx.

39. Abinder, "Public Seeks Transparency."

40. "Quality, Not Just Quantity, of Infrastructure Needs Attention," Wall Street Journal, Greg Ip, May 20, 2015, http://www.wsj.com/articles/quality-not-just-quantity-of-infrastructure-needs-attention-1432138724.

41. "Surface Transportation: DoT Is Progressing Toward a Performance-Based Approach, but States and Grantees Report Potential Implementation Challenges," U.S. Government Accountability Office, January 2015, http://www.gao.gov/assets/670/667939.pdf.

42. "Issue Brief: Obama FY2016 Budget Proposal: Sustainable Energy, Buildings, Transportation and Climate," Environmental and Energy Study Institute, February 4, 2015, http://www.eesi.org/papers/view/issue-brief-2016-budget.

43. For a good review of high-speed rail issues in the United States, see David Randall Peterman et al., "The Development of High Speed Rail in the United States: Issues and Recent Events," CRS Report no. R4284, December 20, 2013, https://www.fas.org/sgp/crs/misc/R42584.pdf.

TRADING UP

1. For 1960 and 1990 figures, see World Bank Databank, http://databank.worldbank.org/data/home.aspx; for 2012 figures, authors' calculations based on Bureau of Economic Analysis data.

2. World Trade Organization, *World Trade Report 2014*, https://www.wto.org/english/news_e/pres14_e/pr728_e.htm. See also Theo Janse van Rensburg, "Developing country growth – The paradox of decoupling," World Bank's Prospects for Development blog, March 28, 2012, http://blogs.worldbank.org/prospects/developing-country-growth-the-paradox-of-decoupling.

3. Bryan Riley and Terry Miller, "2013 Index of Economic Freedom: No Boost in Trade Freedom," Heritage Foundation, October 25, 2012, http://www.heritage.org/research/reports/2012/10/2013-index-of-economic-freedom-no-boost-in-trade-freedom.

4. Robert C. Johnson and Guillermo Noguera, "Fragmentation and Trade in Value Added over Four Decades," NBER Working Paper no. 18186, 2012, http://www.nber.org/papers/w18186.pdf.

5. Robert C. Feenstra and David E. Weinstein, "Globalization, Markups and the U.S. Price Level," National Bureau of Economic Research, February 2010, p. 3, http://www.econ.ucdavis.edu/faculty/fzfeens/pdf/Feenstra_Weinstein_NBER.pdf.

6. World Bank, "Tariff rate, applied, simple mean, all products," http://data.worldbank.org/indicator/TM.TAX. MRCH.SM.AR.ZS. The simple mean tariff is the unweighted average of effectively applied rates for all products subject to tariffs calculated for all traded goods. The other common measure is a weighted average tariff, which is the average of effectively applied rates weighted by the product import shares corresponding to each partner country. The U.S. weighted average tariff in 2012 was 1.6 percent.

7. The United States and Mexico in late 2014 reached an agreement to restrict Mexican sugar exports to the United States following record-level imports of Mexican sugar. The agreement was reached after the U.S. government imposed anti-dumping and countervailing duties on imports of Mexican sugar following complaints by U.S. sugar producers.

8. "The Economic Effects of Significant U.S. Import Restraints," United States International Trade Commission, December 2013, pp. 2–18, http://www.usitc.gov/publications/332/pub4440.pdf; John C. Beghin and Amani Elobeid, "The Impact of the U.S. Sugar Program Redux," Iowa State University, May 2013, https://www.econ.iastate.edu/sites/default/files/publications/papers/p16172-2013-05-07.pdf

9. Randy Schnepf, "Status of the WTO Brazil-U.S. Cotton Case," Congressional Research Service, October 1, 2014, http://nationalaglawcenter.org/wp-content/uploads/assets/crs/R43336.pdf.

10. Edward Gresser, "The Forgotten Tax: The Unequal Burden of Tariffs," Spotlight on Poverty and Opportunity blog, February 15, 2012, http://www.spotlightonpoverty.org/ExclusiveCommentary.aspx?id=b046004d-8940-4caa-afd6-ad45f78f7138.

11. World Bank Databank.

12. Bureau of Economic Analysis, "Summary Estimates for Multinational Companies: Employment, Sales, and Capital Expenditures for 2011," U.S. Department of Commerce, http://www.bea.gov/newsreleases/international/mnc/mncnewsrelease.htm.

13. World Bank Databank.

14. Barry P. Bosworth and Susan M. Collins, "Determinants of U.S. Exports to China," Brookings Institution, April 4, 2008, p.15, http://www.brookings.edu/research/papers/2008/04/04-exports-bosworth-collins.

15. "Economy & Trade," Office of the United States Trade Representative, http://www. ustr.gov/trade-topics/economy-trade.

16. Office of the U.S. Trade Representative, "2014 Annual Report," Annex I, https://ustr. gov/sites/default/files/files/ reports/2015/Annex%20I.pdf, http://www.whitehouse.gov/ sites/default/files/microsites/2011_erp_full.pdf.

17. "International Economic Accounts," Bureau of Economic Analysis, http://www.bea. gov/international/index.htm #services.

18. J. Bradford Jensen, *Global Trade in Services* (Washington, DC: Peter G. Peterson Institute for International Economics, 2011), p 7.

19. Ibid, 3.

20. Ibid, 4.

21. U.S. Bureau of Economic Analysis. All figures are reported on a historical cost basis.

22. David Payne and Fenwick Yu, "Foreign Direct Investment in the United States; Executive Summary," ESA Issue Brief #02-11, U.S. Department of Commerce, Economics and Statistics Administration, June 2011, p. 4, http://www.esa.doc.gov/ sites/default/files/reports/documents/fdiesaissuebriefno2061411final.pdf.

23. Rhodium Group, "China Investment Monitor," http://rhg.com/interactive/china-investment-monitor. This number is significantly higher than the BEA measurement of official stock of Chinese FDI in the United States. For the most recent numbers at time of publication, see http://www.bea.gov/scb/pdf/2014/09%20 September/0914_inward_direct_investment_tables.pdf (page 12, table 8.3). This discrepancy has several causes. First, BEA counts investments on a balance of payments basis, which means it does not capture investment that goes through Hong Kong or other offshore financial centers. Second, BEA only counts capital originating in mainland China, so it does not count capital from Hong Kong or loaned from U.S. or other international banks. Finally, the balance of payments basis that BEA uses measures net stock, which subtracts reverse flows (such as loans from U.S. subsidiaries back to Chinese parents) and sales of assets. Rhodium Group measures gross expenditures, which helps it avoid these shortcomings. The BEA used to have a dataset based on principles similar to Rhodium Group called "outlays on new U.S. establishments," but it was discontinued in 2008 due to lack of budget. For more information, see http://rhg.com/wp-content/themes/ rhodium/interactive/ china-investment-monitor/ RosenHanemann_AnAmericanOpenDoor_2011.pdf, p. 81.

24. Daniel H. Rosen and Thilo Hanemann, "An American Open Door? Maximizing the Benefits of Chinese Foreign Direct Investment," Asia Society, May 2011, p. 16, http:// www.ogilvypr.com/files/anamericanopendoor_ china_fdi_study.pdf.

25. UNCTADSTAT, United Nations Conference on Trade and Development, http:// unctadstat.unctad.org.

26. Organization for International Investment, "Foreign Direct Investment in the United States: 2014 Report," and Deloitte, "The Geography of Jobs, part 3: Mapping the Effects of International Investment Flows," January 2015.

27. "Inward Foreign Direct Investment (FDI) Performance Index," How Canada Performs, Conference Board of Canada, http://www.conferenceboard.ca/hcp/details/economy/ inward-fdi-performance.aspx.

28. "FDI Regulatory Restrictiveness Index, 2012" Organization for Economic Cooperation and Development, November 2012, http://www.oecd.org/daf/inv/ColumnChart-FDI_RR_Index_2012.pdf.

29. "The 2013 A. T. Kearney Foreign Direct Investment Confidence Index," A.T. Kearney, 2013, p. 16, http://www.atkearney.com/documents/10192/1464437/Back+to+Business+-+Optimism+Amid+Uncertainty+-+FDICI+2013.pdf/96039e18-5d34-49ca-9cec-5c1f27dc099d; "The 2014 A.T. Kearney Foreign Direct Investment Confidence Index,"

A. T. Kearney, 2014, pp. 12–14, http://www.atkearney.com/documents/10192/4572735/ Ready+for+Takeoff+-+FDICI+2014.pdf/e921968a-5bfe-4860-ac51-10ec5c396e95.

30. "Special Report: Outsourcing and Offshoring," *The Economist*, January 19, 2013.

31. Ayse Bertrand and Emilie Kothe, "FDI in Figures," Organization for Economic Cooperation and Development, April 2013, p.1, http://www.oecd.org/daf/inv/FDI%20 in%20figures.pdf.

32. Matthew J. Slaughter, "American Companies and Global Supply Networks; Driving U.S. Economic Growth and Jobs by Connecting with the World," Business Roundtable, the United States Council for International Business and the United States Council Foundation, January 2013, p. 5, http://www.uscib.org/docs/2013_ american_companies_and_global_supply_networks.pdf.

33. World Bank, "Tariff rate, applied, simple mean, all products," http://data.worldbank. org/indicator/ TM.TAX.MRCH.SM.AR.ZS.

34. Ibid.

35. "USCBC 2012 China Business Environment Survey Results: US Companies Report Continued Growth and Profitability; Tempered Optimism Due to Rising Costs, Competition, and Market Barriers," U.S.-China Business Council, October 10, 2012, http://www.uschina.org/advocacy/press/uscbc-2012-china-business-environment-survey-results-us-companies-report-continued.

36. "World Trade Report 2012," World Trade Organization, 2012, p.105, http://www.wto. org/english/res_e/ booksp_e/anrep_e/world_trade_report12_e.pdf.

37. Ibid., pp. 134–59.

38. "Trade as a Driver of Prosperity," Commission staff working document, European Commission, 2010, p. 44, http://trade.ec.europa.eu/doclib/docs/2010/november/ tradoc_146940.pdf.

39. Gary Clyde Hufbauer et al., *Figuring Out the Doha Round* (Washington, DC: Peterson Institute for International Economics, 2010), p 125.

40. Authors' calculations based on data from the International Trade Administration, http://www.trade.gov/mas/ian/build/groups/public/@tg_ian/documents/ webcontent/tg_ian_003368.pdf and http://www.trade.gov/mas/ian/build/groups/ public/@tg_ian/documents/webcontent/tg_ian_003364.pdf.

41. Data from Census Bureau and Department of Commerce.

42. Jeffrey Zients, Investor-State Dispute Settlement (ISDS) Questions and Answers, http://www.whitehouse.gov/ blog/2015/02/26/investor-state-dispute-settlement-isds-questions-and-answers.

43. Jeffrey M. Jones, "Americans Shift to More Positive View of Foreign Trade," Gallup, February 28, 2013, http://www.gallup.com/poll/160748/americans-shift-positive-view-foreign-trade.aspx.

44. Gallup, "International Trade/Global Economy," PollingReport.com, http://www. pollingreport.com/trade.htm.

45. Harris Poll, "Americans See Inequality as a Major Problem," Harris Interactive, April 5, 2012, http://www.harrisinteractive.com/NewsRoom/HarrisPolls/tabid/447/ctl/Read Custom%20Default/mid/1508/ArticleId/1002/Default.aspx.

46. Congressional Research Service, "Export-Import Bank: Frequently Asked Questions, November 26, 2014, http://fas.org/sgp/crs/misc/R43671.pdf

47. Stephen J. Ezell, "Understanding the Importance of Export Credit Financing to U.S. Competitiveness," Information Technology and Industry Foundation, June 2011, http://www.itif.org/files/2011-export-credit-financing.pdf.

48. Drewry, "DREWRY: U.S. Exports Miss Target," Marine Link, http://www. marinelink.com/news/exports-drewry-target356658.aspx.

49. Chris Rasmussen and Martin Johnson, "Jobs Supported by Exports, 2014: An Update," Office of Trade and Economic Analysis, U.S. Department of Commerce, http:// www.trade.gov/mas/ian/build/groups/public/@tg_ian/documents/webcontent/tg_ ian_005406.pdf.

50. Francisco Sánchez, "Foreign Direct Investment and SelectUSA," Testimony before the House Committee on Energy and Commerce, Subcommittee on Commerce, Manufacturing, and Trade, April 18, 2013, http://trade.gov/press/testimony/2013/ sanchez-041813.asp.

51. Joseph Francois et al., "Reducing Transatlantic Barriers to Trade and Investment: An Economic Assessment," Centre for Economic Policy Research, March 2013, p. vii, http://trade.ec.europa.eu/doclib/docs/2013/march/tradoc_150737.pdf.

52. Pater A. Petri et al., "The Trans-Pacific Partnership and Asia-Pacific Integration: A Quantitative Assessment," Peterson Institute for International Economics, November 2012; European Commission, "Transatlantic Trade and Investment Partnership: The Economic Analysis Explained," November 2013.

53. Edward Alden, "Opportunity Knocks for Obama on Trade," *World Politics Review*, January 8, 2013.

STANDARD DEDUCTIONS

1. The U.S. average effective tax rate is roughly on par with the weighted OECD average effective tax rate. See Jane G. Gravelle, "International Corporate Tax Rate Comparisons and Policy Implications," CSR Report no. R41743, December 28, 2012, p. 3, https://www.fas.org/sgp/crs/misc/R41743.pdf. For a corroboration of Gravelle's findings, see Martin A Sullivan, "U.S. Effective Corporate Tax Rate Higher Than Foreign Competitors? Not Really," *Taxanalysts*, March 23, 2015, http://www. taxanalysts.com/taxcom/taxblog.nsf/Permalink/UBEN-9TCN3X?OpenDocument.

2. "Revenue Statistics: Corporate Tax on Profit as a Percentage of GDP," Organization for Economic Cooperation and Development, https://stats.oecd.org/Index. aspx?DataSetCode=REV; Mark P. Keightley and Molly F. Sherlock, "The Corporate Income Tax System: Overview and Options for Reform" Congressional Research Service Report R42726, September 13, 2012, http://www.fas.org/sgp/crs/misc/ R42726.pdf.

3. Office of Management and Budget, Historical Tables, table 2.1, http://www.whitehouse. gov/omb/budget/HISTORICALS.

4. For the $2 trillion figure, see Dena Aubin, "U.S. companies' overseas earnings hit record $1.9 trillion: study," Reuters, May 8, 2013, http://www.reuters.com/article/2013/05/08/ us-usa-taxes-oveseas-idUSBRE9470Z920130508; for foreign effective tax rate, see Melissa Costa and Jennifer Gravelle, "Taxing Multinational Corporations: Average Tax Rates," presented at an American Tax Policy Center conference, October 2011, http://www.americantaxpolicyinstitute.org/s/pdf/Costa-Gravelle%20paper.pdf.

5. Costa and Gravelle, "Taxing Multinational Corporations: Average Tax Rates."

6. For the $2 trillion figure, see Aubin, "U.S. companies' overseas earnings"; for foreign effective tax rate, see Costa and Gravelle, "Taxing Multinational Corporations."

7. Martin A. Sullivan, *Corporate Tax Reform: Taxing Profits in the 21st Century* (New York: Apress, 2011), pp. 22–23.

8. A bonus to the normal depreciation credit was added during the recession in 2008, greatly expanding its generosity. The R&D credit has been gradually expanded since

the 1980s. The domestic production credit, which was introduced in 2004, replaced a much less generous credit called the extraterritorial income regime, or ETI.

9. "Target's Annual Effective Tax Rate," Csimarket.com; and "General Electric Co., effective income tax rate (EITR) reconciliation," https://www.stock-analysis-on.net/NYSE/Company/General-Electric-Co/Analysis/Income-Taxes#EITR. For more background on the disparity in effective corporate tax rates, see the U.S. House of Representatives, Committee on Ways and Means, Testimony of Martin A. Sullivan, January 20, 2011, http://waysandmeans.house.gov/uploadedfiles/sullivan_written_testimony_wm_jan_20.pdf.

10. Martin Sullivan, "The Problem with the Research Tax Credit," *Forbes*, October 30, 2013, http://www.forbes.com/sites/taxanalysts/2013/10/30/the-problem-with-the-research-tax-credit.

11. Sullivan, *Corporate Tax Reform*, p. 19.

12. Ibid, p. 106.

13. Steven Pearlstein, "Marty Sullivan figured out how the world's biggest companies avoided billions in taxes. Here's how he wants to stop them," *Washington Post*, October 26, 2013, http://www.washingtonpost.com/blogs/wonkblog/wp/2013/10/26/marty-sullivan-figured-out-how-the-worlds-biggest-companies-avoided-billions-in-taxes-heres-how-he-wants-to-stop-them.

14. "Taxing Businesses Through the Individual Income Tax," Congressional Budget Office, December 2012, p. 15, http://www.cbo.gov/sites/default/files/cbofiles/attachments/43750-TaxingBusinesses2.pdf.

15. "Treasury Conference on Business Taxation and Global Competitiveness: Background Paper," U.S. Department of the Treasury, July 23, 2007, http://www.treasury.gov/press-center/press-releases/Documents/07230%20r.pdf.

16. Martin A. Sullivan, "JCT Report Provides New Insight on Competitiveness," *Taxanalysts*, February 3, 2015, http://www.taxanalysts.com/taxcom/taxblog.nsf/Permalink/UBEN-9TCN3X?OpenDocument.

17. Martin A. Sullivan, "Foreign Tax Profile of Top 50 U.S. Companies," *Taxanalysts*, July 25, 2011, http://www.taxanalysts.com/www/features.nsf/Articles/022A377AEFD25A52852578D8006F1EAC?OpenDocument.

18. Sullivan, *Corporate Tax Reform*, p. 96.

19. Mark Keightley, "An Analysis of Where American Companies Report Profits: Indications of Profit Shifting," Congressional Research Service Report R42927, January 18, 2013, https://www.fas.org/sgp/crs/misc/R42927.pdf.

20. Jane G. Gravelle, "Tax Havens: International Tax Avoidance and Evasion," CSR Report no. R40623, January 15, 2015, p. 1, https://www.fas.org/sgp/crs/misc/R40623.pdf.

21. Martin Sullivan, telephone interview, September 26, 2013.

22. Alex Heber, "Australia will get a 'Google tax' in the federal budget," *Business Insider Australia*, May 11, 2015, http://www.businessinsider.com.au/australia-will-get-a-google-tax-in-the-federal-budget-2015-5.

23. Stephanie Soong Johnston, "EU to Investigate Apple, Starbucks, and Fiat Tax Rulings," *Taxanalysts*, June 13, 2014, http://www.taxanalysts.com/www/features.nsf/Features/E41550AF2BBC6FD985257CF6005FB324?OpenDocument.

24. President Obama's 2010 Jobs Act did tighten some rules about taxing foreign profits, but it will raise only an extra $1 billion a year for ten years.

25. Terry Macalister, "Starbucks pays corporation tax in UK for first time in five years," *Guardian*, June 23, 2013, http://www.theguardian.com/business/2013/jun/23/starbucks-pays-corporation-tax.

26. Nigel Morris, "I'll make 'damn sure' big companies pay their tax, says David Cameron," *Independent*, January 4, 2013, http://www.independent.co.uk/news/uk/politics/ill-make-damn-sure-big-companies-pay-their-tax-says-david-cameron-8439137.html.

27. "Report to the G20 Leaders: Global Forum Update on Effectiveness and Ongoing Monitoring," Organization for Economic Cooperation and Development, September 2013, http://www.oecd.org/tax/transparency/progress_report__G20.pdf.

28. Tom Bergin and Maya Dyakina, "G20 backs fundamental reform of corporate taxation," *Reuters*, July 19, 2013, http://www.reuters.com/article/2013/07/19/g20-tax-corporate-idUSL6N0FP25A20130719.

29. Paul Hannon and Sam Schechner, "OECD Rewrites Corporate Tax Rule Book," *Wall Street Journal*, October 5, 2015, http://www.wsj.com/articles/oecd-rewrites-corporate-tax-rule-book-1444046845.

30. Klaus Schwab, ed., *The Global Competitiveness Report 2014–2015* (Geneva: World Economic Forum, 2014), p. 378, http://www3.weforum.org/docs/WEF_GlobalCompetitivenessReport_2014-15.pdf.

31. Ibid, p. 379.

32. Jan W. Rivkin et al., "The Challenge of Shared Prosperity: Findings of Harvard Business School's 2015 Survey of U.S. competitiveness," Harvard Business School, September 2015, p. 7, http://www.hbs.edu/competitiveness/Documents/challenge-of-shared-prosperity.pdf.

33. Reuven Avi-Yonah and Yaron Lahav, "The Effective Tax Rate of the Largest US and EU Multinationals," Law & Economics Working Paper no. 41, 2011, http://repository.law.umich.edu/law_econ_current/art41.

34. David Cay Johnston, "U.S. Corporations Are Using Bermuda to Slash Tax Bills," *New York Times*, February 18, 2002, http://www.nytimes.com/2002/02/18/business/us-corporations-are-using-bermuda-to-slash-tax-bills.html?pagewanted=all&src=pm.

35. Eric J. Allen and Susan C. Morse, "Tax Haven Incorporation for U.S. Headquartered Firms: No Exodus Yet," *National Tax Journal* 66, 2013, http://papers.ssrn.com/sol3/papers.cfm?abstract_id=1950760.

36. Patrice Hill, "Whopper of a corporate tax ate fries Burger King and others seeking tax inversions," *Washington Times*, September 4, 2014, http://www.washingtontimes.com/news/2014/sep/4/burger-kings-tax-inversion-deal-just-latest-move-f/?page=all.

37. "Fact Sheet: Treasurey Actions to Rein in Corporate Tax Inversions," U.S. Department of the Treasury, September 22, 2014, http://www.treasury.gov/press-center/press-releases/Pages/jl2645.aspx.

38. Kimberly A. Clausing, "Multinational Firm Tax Avoidance and Tax Policy," *National Tax Journal* 62, no. 4, December 2009, http://www.ntanet.org/NTJ/62/4/ntj-v62n04p703-25-multinational-firm-tax-avoidance.pdf.

39. Nahid Kalbasi Anaraki, "Does Corporate Tax Rate Affect FDI? Case Study of Core European Countries," *Journal of Global Economics* 11, no. 2, 2015, http://www.rcssindia.org/jge/index.php/jge/article/view/394.

40. "Macroeconomic Analysis of Various Proposals to Provide $500 Billion in Tax Relief," Joint Committee on Taxation, March 1, 2005, https://www.jct.gov/publications.html?func=startdown&id=1611; and U.S. Senate Joint Economic Committee, "Lessons From Reagan: How Tax Reform Can Boost Economic Growth," Testimony of Jane Gravelle, July 31, 2013, p. 3, http://www.jec.senate.gov/republicans/public/?a=Files.Serve&File_id=a4971933-7917-4392-bc16-ee1cf2a21112.

41. Åsa Johansson, Christopher Heady, Jens Arnold, Bert Brys, and Laura Vartia, "Tax and Economic Growth," OECD Economics Department Working Paper no. 620, July 11, 2008, http://www.oecd.org/tax/tax-policy/41000592.pdf.

42. Jonathan Weisman, "Plan to Curb U.S. Taxation of Overseas Profit Finds Bipartisan Support," *New York Times*, July 8, 2015, http://www.nytimes.com/2015/07/09/business/end-to-us-taxation-of-overseas-profit-finds-bipartisan-support.html.

43. Jim Puzzanghera, "Bipartisan support grows for corporate tax change tied to Highway Trust Fund," *Los Angeles Times*, July 14, 2015, http://www.latimes.com/business/la-fi-corporate-tax-plan-20150714-story.html.

44. Office of Tax Policy, *Approaches to Improve the Competitiveness of the U.S. Business Tax System for the 21st Century*, U.S. Department of the Treasury, December 2007, http://www.treasury.gov/resource-center/tax-policy/Documents/Approaches-to-Improve-Business-Tax-Competitiveness-12-20-2007.pdf.

45. Luke A. Stewart and Robert D. Atkinson, "Restoring America's Lagging Investment in Capital Goods," Information Technology & Innovation Foundation, October 2012, http://www2.itif.org/2013-restoring-americas-lagging-investment.pdf.

46. Michael Mundaca, "Just the Facts: The Costs of a Repatriation Tax Holiday," U.S. Department of Treasury, http://www.treasury.gov/connect/blog/Pages/Just-the-Facts-The-Costs-of-a-Repatriation-Tax-Holiday.aspx.

47. "Consumption Tax Trends," Organization for Economic Cooperation and Development, table 1.1, http://www.oecd-ilibrary.org/taxation/consumption-tax-trends-2012_ctt-2012-en.

48. John Ydstie, "Apple CEO Faces Senate Panel's Accusations of 'Tax Gimmickry'," NPR, May 21, 2013, http://www.npr.org/2013/05/21/185688463/ceo-cook-to-defend-apple-before-senate-committee-hearing.

49. Carroll Doherty, "Public Wants Reform. But What Kind of Reform?" Pew Research Center, May 22, 2013, http://www.pewresearch.org/fact-tank/2013/05/22/public-wants-tax-reform-but-what-kind-of-reform.

NO HELPING HAND

1. "Multiple Employment and Training Programs: Providing Information on Colocating Services and Consolidating Administrative Structure Could Promote Efficiencies," Government Accountability Office, p. 5, http://www.gao.gov/products/GAO-11-92.

2. Jun Nie and Ethan Struby, "Would Active Labor Market Policies Help Combat High U.S. Unemployment?" Federal Reserve Bank of Kansas City, pp. 43–44, https://www.kansascityfed.org/publicat/econrev/pdf/11q3Nie-Struby.pdf.

3. Carolyn J. Heinrich, "Targeting Workforce Development Programs: Who Should Receive What Services? And How Much?" University of Texas, November 2013, pp. 10–11, http://umdcipe.org/conferences/WorkforceDevelopment/Papers/Workforce%20Development_Heinrich_Targeting%20Workforce%20Development%20Programs.pdf.

4. Ibid., 12.

5. Ibid., 11–12.

6. "Worker Displacement: 2011–2013," Bureau of Labor Statistics, p. 2, http://www.bls.gov/news.release/pdf/disp.pdf.

7. Interview with Christopher King, senior research scientist and director, Ray Marshall Center for the Study of Human Resources, Lyndon B. Johnson School of Public Affairs, University of Texas at Austin, July 2, 2014.

8. "Better Skills Better Jobs Better Lives: A Strategic Approach to Skills Policies," OECD, 2012, p. 36, http://skills.oecd.org/documents/OECDSkillsStrategyFINALENG.pdf; see also "Innovation in Skills Development in SMEs," OECD, p. 3, http://www.oecd.org/cfe/leed/TSME%20Highlights%20FINAL%20formatted.pdf.

9. Gary Burtless, "America: One-Time Home of the 'Employment Miracle,'" Brookings, October 22, 2013, http://www.brookings.edu/research/opinions/2013/10/22/america-

one-time-home-employment-miracle-burtless; see also "LFS by Sex and Age—Indicators,"OECD,http://stats.oecd.org/Index.aspx?DataSetCode=LFS_SEXAGE_I_R#.

10. John Merline, "The Sharp Rise in Disability Claims: Are federal disability benefits becoming a general safety net?" Federal Reserve Bank of Richmond, 2012, http://www.richmondfed.org/publications/research/region_focus/2012/q2-3/pdf/feature3.pdf.

11. OECD, "Public expenditure on active labour market policies, Percent of GDP," http://www.oecd-ilibrary.org/employment/public-expenditure-on-active-labour-market-policies_20752342-table9.

12. Wendy Dunn, "The U.S. Labor Market Recovery Following the Great Recession," OECD, p. 13, http://www.oecd-ilibrary.org/docserver/download/5k4ddxp3xlvf.pdf.

13. Ben Olinsky and Sarah Ayres, "Training for Success: A Policy to Expand Apprenticeships in the United States," Center for American Progress, November 2013, p. 19, http://cdn.americanprogress.org/wp-content/uploads/2013/11/apprenticeship_report.pdf.

14. Ibid.

15. U.S. Department of Labor, "Apprentices," http://www.doleta.gov/oa/apprentices.cfm.

16. However, some U.S. companies do not register their apprenticeship programs, preventing them from being counted. Olinsky and Ayres, "Training for Success," p. 19.

17. Nelson D. Schwarz, "Where Factory Apprenticeship Is Latest Model from Germany," New York Times, November 30, 2013, p. 16, http://www.nytimes.com/2013/12/01/business/where-factory-apprenticeship-is-latest-model-from-germany.html; Olinsky and Ayres; and Nancy Cook, "Should the U.S. Adopt the German Model of Apprenticeships?" National Journal, April 11, 2014, http://www.nationaljournal.com/next-economy/solutions-bank/should-the-u-s-adopt-the-german-model-of-apprenticeships-20140411.

18. Olinsky and Ayres, "Training for Success," p. 33.

19. Government Accountability Office, "Multiple Employment and Training Programs: Providing Information on Colocating Services and Consolidating Administrative Structure Could Promote Efficiencies," GAO-11-92, pp. 16-17, http://www.gao.gov/products/GAO-11-92.

20. Adrienne L. Fernandes-Alcantara, "Vulnerable Youth: Employment and Job Training Programs," CRS Report no. R40929, May 11, 2014, pp. 9, 27, http://fas.org/sgp/crs/misc/R40929.pdf.

21. GAO, "Multiple Employment and Training Programs," p. 11.

22. According to a study from the Economic Council of the Labour Movement, 85 percent of employed workers in Denmark would qualify for unemployment benefits or social security if they became unemployed ; Per Kongshøj Madsen, "'Shelter from the storm?' Danish flexicurity and the crisis," p. 13, http://www.izajoels.com/content/pdf/2193-9012-2-6.pdf.

23. Ibid.

24. Eurostat, "Unemployment rate by sex and age groups—monthly average, percent," http://appsso.eurostat.ec.europa.eu/nui/show.do?dataset=une_rt_m&lang=en.

25. OECD, "Incidence of unemployment by duration," http://stats.oecd.org/Index.aspx?DataSetCode=DUR_I.

26. Liz Alderman, "Why Denmark Is Shrinking Its Social Safety Net," New York Times, August 16, 2010, http://economix.blogs.nytimes.com/2010/08/16/why-denmark-is-shrinking-its-social-safety-net.

27. OECD, "Short-Term Labour Market Statistics: Unemployment Rates by Age and Gender," http://stats.oecd.org/index.aspx?queryid=36499.

28. Selected "Unemployment rate, aged 15–24, all persons" from "Short-Term Labour Market Statistics: Unemployment Rates by Age and Gender."

29. Ulf Rinne and Klaus F. Zimmerman, "Another economic miracle? The German labor market and the Great Recession," p. 19, http://ftp.iza.org/dp6250.pdf.

30. Elisabeth Jacobs, "Growth Through Innovation: Lessons for the United States from the German Labor Market Miracle," Brookings, pp. 6–7, http://www.aimcmp.com/73044_0113_jobs_jacobs.pdf.

31. Ibid., p. 7.

32. Rinne and Zimmerman, "Another economic miracle?" p. 12.

33. Ibid., p. 13.

34. Thomas Deißinger, "Germany: The Culture of a Long-Established Apprentice System," in *The Future of Vocational Education and Training in a Changing World*, ed. Matthias Pilz (Wiesbaden: Springer, 2012), p. 309.

35. Michael Dolgow, "Would German-Style Apprenticeships Work in the U.S.?" *Bloomberg Businessweek*, July 19, 2012, http://www.businessweek.com/articles/2012-07-19/german-vocational-training-model-offers-alternative-path-to-youth.

36. Nelson D. Schwartz, "Where Factory Apprenticeship Is Latest Model From Germany," *New York Times*, November 30, 2013, http://www.nytimes.com/2013/12/01/business/where-factory-apprenticeship-is-latest-model-from-germany.html.

37. Andy Eckardt, "In Euro Zone Crisis, Germany Benefits From Apprentices," CNBC, November 27, 2012, http://www.cnbc.com/id/49976017.

38. Rinne and Zimmerman, "Another economic miracle?" pp. 12–13.

39. OECD, "Trade Union Density," http://stats.oecd.org/Index.aspx?DataSetCode=UN_DEN.

40. "Germany: Key Facts," European Trade Union Institute, http://www.worker-participation.eu/National-Industrial-Relations/Countries/Germany; corroborated by Nicola Düll, "Collective wage agreement and minimum wage in Germany," European Employment Observatory, http://www.eu-employment-observatory.net/resources/reports/1-Germany-NationalAdHocResponseMinimumWage-final.pdf; John Logan, "Union Recognition and Collective Bargaining: How Does the United States Compare With Other Democracies?" UC Berkeley Labor Center, http://laborcenter.berkeley.edu/laborlaw/union_recognition09.pdf.

41. "Public expenditure on active labour market policies, percent of GDP," OECD, http://www.oecd-library.org/employment/public-expenditure-on-active-labour-market-policies_20752342-table9.

42. Maggie Severns, "Workforce bill clears Senate," *Politico*, June 25, 2014, http://www.politico.com/story/2014/06/federal-workforce-programs-jobs-senate-bill-108310.html.

43. The White House, "Remarks by the President in State of the Union Address," http://www.whitehouse.gov/the-press-office/2012/01/24/remarks-president-state-union-address.

44. Seth Harris, "Streamlining Services for Displaced Workers," U.S. Department of Labor, http://social.dol.gov/blog/streamlining-services-for-displaced-workers.

45. "Just the Facts: The SKILLS Act Encourages Local Control, Flexibility," House Education and Workforce Committee, March 6, 2013, http://edworkforce.house.gov/news/documentsingle.aspx?DocumentID=322244.

46. Olinsky and Ayres, "Training for Success," p. 37.

47. Apprenticeship Carolina, "Apprenticeship Carolina," SC Technical College System, http://www.apprenticeshipcarolina.com.

48. Olinsky and Ayres, "Training for Success," p. 37.

49. Ibid.

50. Jim Campbell, Emily Thomson, and Hartwig Pautz, "Apprenticeship Training in England: Closing the Gap?" *Journal of Contemporary European Studies*, p. 36, http://www.academia.edu/1094235/Modern_Apprenticeships_in_the_UK_and_Germany_with_Emily_%20

Thompson_and_Jim_Campbell; Hillary Steedman, "The State of Apprenticeship in 2010," p. 24, http://cep.lse.ac.uk/pubs/download/special/cepsp22.pdf.

51. Tom Perez and Jeff Zients, "The First-Ever White House Summit on American Apprenticeship," The White House, July 14, 2014, https://www.whitehouse.gov/blog/2014/07/14/first-ever-white-house-summit-american-apprenticeship-helping-american-workers-punch.

52. Carol Clymer, Maureen Conway et al., "Tuning In to Local Labor Markets: Findings From the Sectoral Employment Impact Study," Public/Private Ventures, July 1, 2010, p. 3, http://www.issuelab.org/resource/tuning_in_to_local_labor_markets_findings_from_the_sectoral_employment_impact_study.

53. Per Scholas, "Our Communities," http://perscholas.org/our-communities-per-scholas.

54. Carol Clymer, Maureen Conway et al., p. 12. For additional reading on the positive wage effects from a different sectoral training program, see Tara Carter Smith and Christopher T. King, "Exploratory Return-on-Investment Analysis of Local Workforce Investments," Austin: Ray Marshall Center for the Study of Human Resources, Lyndon B. Johnson School of Public Affairs, University of Texas at Austin, June 2011, http://www.utexas.edu/research/cshr/pubs/pdf/Capital_IDEA_ROI_Final_Aug_23_2011.pdf; for a summary and the research brief, see http://www.capitalidea.org/downloads/RayMarshall_Brief_May2011.pdf.

55. Lymari Morales, "Republicans, Democrats Favor Tax Breaks to Win Back U.S. Jobs," Gallup, February 1, 2012, http://www.gallup.com/poll/152396/republicans-democrats-favor-tax-breaks-win-back-jobs.aspx.

56. "Preparing Graduates for Global Success Toplines Report," Northeastern University, August 2013, http://www.northeastern.edu/innovationsurvey/pdfs/toplines_report.pdf.

QUALITY CONTROL

1. Susan E. Dudley and Jerry Brito, *Regulation: A Primer* (Washington, DC: Mercatus Center at George Mason University, 2012).

2. Office of Information and Regulatory Affairs, data pulled from http://www.reginfo.gov/public/. For quick reference, see https://regulatorystudies.columbian.gwu.edu/sites/regulatorystudies.columbian.gwu.edu/files/downloads/2014%20Presidential%20Years_0.PNG.

3. Steve Benen, "Obama Blasts 'Least Productive Congress in Modern History,'" *MaddowBlog*, April 1, 2014, http://www.msnbc.com/rachel-maddow-show/obama-blasts-least-productive-congress.

4. Congress can place requirements on the regulation-design process that applies to all federal departments and agencies, including independent regulatory agencies. But they are largely toothless or unenforced. For example, the Administrative Procedures Act sets a low bar for establishing need and purpose for a draft regulation. The Regulatory Flexibility Act requires a ten-year review for any regulation that has a "big" impact on small business, but then leaves the decision of whether any regulation's impact would qualify to the regulators themselves, and as a result, regulators can easily skirt the requirement. There is no penalty if federal regulators violate the Paperwork Reduction Act. The Congressional Review Act gives Congress the power to block a regulation that OIRA approves with a majority vote, but this has only happened once.

5. "Economically significant" regulations are defined by the federal government as having an impact of at least $100 million annually.

6. For a good summary of how OIRA works, see Cass Sunstein, *Valuing Life: Humanizing the Regulatory State* (Chicago: University of Chicago Press, 2014), pp. 11–46.

7. Alec MacGillis, "Rick Perry's Entry Sets up a Clarifying Contrast," *Washington Post*, August 12, 2011, http://www.washingtonpost.com/politics/rick-perrys-entry-sets-up-a-clarifying-contrast/2011/08/10/gIQAum32AJ_story.html.

8. Andrew Dugan, "In U.S., Half Still Say Gov't Regulates Too Much," Gallup, September 18, 2015, http://www.gallup.com/poll/185609/half-say-gov-regulates-business.aspx.

9. William C. Dunkelberg and Holly Wade, "NFIB Small Business Economic Trends," National Federation of Independent Business Research Foundation, September 2015, http://www.nfib.com/Portals/0/pdf/sbet/sbet201510.pdf.

10. Michael A. Livermore and Jason A. Schwartz, "Analysis to Inform Public Discourse on Jobs and Regulation," in *Does Regulation Kill Jobs?* ed. Cary Coglianese et al. (Philadelphia: University of Pennsylvania Press, 2013), p. 244.

11. "Auto Bailout Now Backed, Stimulus Divisive: Mixed Views of Regulation, Support for Keystone Pipeline," Pew Research Center for the People and the Press, February 23, 2012, p. 15, http://www.people-press.org/files/legacy-pdf/2-23-12%20Regulation%20release.pdf; Stuart Shapiro and Debra Borie-Holtz, *The Politics of Regulatory Reform* (New York: Routledge, 2013), pp. 68–92.

12. See, for example, "RegData," compiled by Patrick McLaughlin and Omar Ahmad Al-Ubaydli, George Mason University Mercatus Center, November 12, 2014, http://mercatus.org/publication/regdata-numerical-database-industry-specific-regulations.

13. Nicole V. Crain and W. Mark Crain, "The Impact of Regulatory Costs on Small Firms," Office of Advocacy, Small Business Administration, September 2010, https://www.sba.gov/sites/default/files/advocacy/The%20Impact%20of%20Regulatory%20Costs%20on%20Small%20Firms%20%28Full%29_0.pdf.

14. Shapiro and Borie-Holtz, *The Politics of Regulatory Reform*, pp. 64–67.

15. Josh Ederington et al., "Footloose and Pollution-Free," *Review of Economics and Statistics* 87, no. 1, 2005, http://www.mitpressjournals.org/doi/abs/10.1162/0034653053327658#.VJMWM14AOQ.

16. Michael Porter, *Competitive Advantage of Nations* (New York: The Free Press, 1990).

17. Crain and Crain, "The Impact of Regulatory Costs on Small Firms."

18. This report was written by Rebecca Strauss, associate director for Renewing America publications at the Council on Foreign Relations. Randy Becker et al., "Do Environmental Regulations Disproportionately Affect Small Businesses? Evidence from the Pollution Abatement Costs and Expenditures Survey," *Journal of Environmental Economics and Management*, 2013, pp. 523–38, http://www.sciencedirect.com/science/article/pii/S0095069613000697.

19. See Carry Coglianese and Christopher Carrigan, "The Jobs and Regulation Debate," in *Does Regulation Kill Jobs?* pp. 1–30; Tara M. Sinclair and Kathryn Vesey, "Regulation, Jobs, and Economic Growth: An Empirical Analysis," George Washington University Regulatory Studies Center Working Paper, March 2012, http://regulatorystudies.columbian.gwu.edu/files/downloads/032212_sinclair_vesey_reg_jobs_growth.pdf.

20. Mass Layoff Statistics, U.S. Department of Labor, Bureau of Labor Statistics, http://www.bls.gov/mls.

21. According to annual reports OIRA submits to Congress, available at http://www.whitehouse.gov/omb/inforeg_regpol_reports_congress. The most recent report is "Draft 2015 Report to Congress on the Benefits and Costs of Federal Regulations and Unfunded Mandates Reform Act," Office of Management and Budget, October 2015, https://www.whitehouse.gov/sites/default/files/omb/inforeg/2015_cb/draft_2015_cost_benefit_report.pdf.

22. "Highlights from the Clean Air Act 40th Anniversary Celebration," Environmental Protection Agency, September 14, 2010, http://www.epa.gov/air/caa/40th_highlights.html.

23. Gary Gastelu, "Automakers Lobbying to Replace Rearview Mirrors with Cameras," FOX News, April 2, 2014, http://www.foxnews.com/leisure/2014/04/02/automakers-lobbying-to-replace-rearview-mirrors-with-cameras.

24. Winston Harrington, "Grading Estimates of the Benefits and Costs of Federal Regulation: A Review of Reviews," Resources for the Future Discussion Paper 06-39, September 2006, http://www.rff.org/documents/RFF-DP-06-39.pdf.

25. Winston Harrington et al., "How Accurate Are Regulatory Cost Estimates?" Resources for the Future, March 5, 2010, http://grist.files.wordpress.com/2010/10/harringtonmorgensternnelson_regulatory_estimates.pdf; Winston Harrington et al., "On the Accuracy of Regulatory Cost Estimates," Resources for the Future Discussion Paper no. 99-18, January 1999, http://www.rff.org/documents/RFF-DP-99-18.pdf.

26. The most common way to portray the growth in federal regulations is the number of pages in the Code of Federal Regulations: http://www.archives.gov/federal-register/cfr. For quick reference of the growth in pages in the Code, see https://regulatorystudies.columbian.gwu.edu/sites/regulatorystudies.columbian.gwu.edu/files/downloads/pages%20in%20CFR.jpg.

27. All data on the number of economically significant regulations and their costs and benefits are compiled by OIRA and published in their annual report submitted to Congress. See https://www.whitehouse.gov/omb/inforeg_regpol_reports_congress. Annual averages are only for the first six years of each presidency.

28. There is some controversy about how benefits are being calculated, with an over-emphasis on indirect or co-benefits. For a critique of these calculations, see Susan Dudley, "OMB's Reported Benefits of Regulation: Too Good to Be True?" Regulation, Sumer 2013, http://regulatorystudies.columbian.gwu.edu/files/downloads/Dudley_OMB_BC_Regulation-v36n2-4.pdf. OMB impact totals only include those regulations for which both costs and benefits were monetized, which are only about one-quarter of all new major economic regulations.

29. Patrick McLaughlin and Oliver Sherouse, "The Accumulation of Regulatory Restrictions Across Presidential Administrations," Mercatus Center, George Mason University, August 3, 2015, http://mercatus.org/publication/accumulation-regulatory-restrictions-across-presidential-administrations.

30. Federal departments and agencies subject to OIRA oversight must submit Information Collection Budgets, which are compiled at http://www.reginfo.gov/public/. Regulatory paperwork burden is usually calculated without taking taxes into consideration. If taxes were included, they would constitute the majority of all paperwork, dominating any total count. For the purposes of this report, taxes were removed from total paperwork calculations.

31. "Dodd-Frank Progress Report: Third Quarter 2015," Davis-Polk Regulatory Tracker, October 2015, http://www.davispolk.com/Dodd-Frank-Rulemaking-Progress-Report.

32. David Luttrell et al., "Assessing the Costs and Consequences of the 2007–09 Financial Crisis and Its Aftermath," Economic Letter, Dallas Federal Reserve 8, no. 7, September 2013, http://www.dallasfed.org/assets/documents/research/eclett/2013/el1307.pdf.

33. "Will Obamacare cut costs? The growth in America's health-care spending is slowing," Economist, March 7, 2015, http://www.economist.com/news/united-states/21645855-growth-americas-health-care-spending-slowing-will-obamacare-cut-costs.

34. Juliet Eilperin and Steven Mufson, "Everything You Need to Know About the EPA's Proposed Rule on Coal Plants," Washington Post, June 2, 2014, http://www.washingtonpost.com/national/health-science/epa-will-propose-a-rule-to-cut-emissions-from-existing-coal-plants-by-up-to-30-percent/2014/06/02/f37f0a10-e81d-11e3-afc6-a1dd9407abcf_story.html.

35. "Doing Business 2015: Going Beyond Efficiency," World Bank Group, October 2014, http://www.doingbusiness.org/~/media/GIAWB/Doing%20Business/Documents/Annual-Reports/English/DB15-Full-Report.pdf.

36. Market regulation data, 2013, OECD, http://stats.oecd.org. Also see Isabell Koske et al., "The 2013 update of the OECD's database on product market regulation: Policy insights for OECD and non-OECD countries," *OECD Economics Department Working Papers* no. 1200, March 31, 2015, p. 29, http://www.oecd-ilibrary.org/docserver/download/5js3f5d3n2vl.pdf?expires=1445544413&id=id&accname=guest&checksum=CFEE08014D212EA989C61BB34C22956C.

37. See "Re-examining Regulations: Agencies Often Made Regulatory Changes, But Could Strengthen Linkages to Performance Goals," Government Accountability Office, September 2014, http://www.gao.gov/products/GAO-14-268, which found that only three of seventeen agencies reported reevaluating cost-benefit analyses after a rule was issued.

38. "Re-examining Regulations: Opportunities Exist to Improve Effectiveness and Transparency of Retrospective Reviews," Government Accountability Office, July 2007, http://www.gao.gov/products/GAO-07-791.

39. Ibid.; Randall Lutter, "The Role of Retrospective Analysis and Review in Regulatory Policy," George Mason University Mercatus Center, Working Paper no. 12-14, April 2012, http://mercatus.org/sites/default/files/publication/Role-Retrospective-Analysis-Review-Regulatory-Policy-Lutter.pdf.

40. Cass R. Sunstein, "Empirically Informed Regulation," *University of Chicago Law Review* 78, no. 1349, 2011. https://lawreview.uchicago.edu/sites/lawreview.uchicago.edu/files/uploads/78_4/Sunstein_Essay.pdf.

41. "Social and Behavioral Sciences Team: Annual Report," Executive Office of the President, National Science and Technology Council, September 2015, https://sbst.gov/assets/files/2015-annual-report.pdf.

42. This is not to say that cost-benefit analysis could not be better. Some studies have found that the quality of cost-benefit analysis varies and that perhaps only half of all impact analyses satisfy all of the official OMB requirements. See Jerry Ellig and James Broughel, "How Well Do Federal Agencies Use Regulatory Impact Analysis?" George Mason University Mercatus Center, July 2013, http://mercatus.org/sites/default/files/Ellig_FedAgenciesRIA_MOP_071513.pdf. One study found that the quality of U.S. cost-benefit analysis has been as high as the European Union (Caroline Cecot et al., "An Evaluation of the Quality of Impact Assessment in the European Union with Lessons for the U.S. and the EU," *Regulation & Governance* 3, no 4, December 2008, http://onlinelibrary.wiley.com/doi/10.1111/j.1748-5991.2008.00044.x/abstract). No studies indicate other governments are consistently conducting higher-quality analyses than the United States.

43. For evidence that an overemphasis on impact analysis leads to less consideration of alternatives, see, for example, Wendy Wagner, "The CAIR RIA: Advocacy Dressed Up as Policy Analysis," in *Reforming Regulatory Impact Analysis*, ed. Winston Harrington et al. (Washington, DC: Resources for the Future Press, 2009), pp. 56–81. For a review of how overly detailed cost-benefit analysis can impede good policy decision-making, see Christopher Carrigan and Stuart Shapiro, "What's Wrong with the Back of the Envelope? A Call for Simple (and Timely) Benefit-Cost Analysis," Georgetown University Regulatory Studies Center Working Paper, October 2014, http://regulatorystudies.columbian.gwu.edu/sites/regulatorystudies.columbian.gwu.edu/files/downloads/Carrigan_Shapiro-Back-of-the-Envelope.pdf. For an alternative more qualitative cost-benefit analysis proposal, see Amy Sinden, "Formality and Informality in Cost-Benefit Analysis," *Utah Law Review* 93, no. 2014-25, June 17, 2015, http://papers.ssrn.com/sol3/papers.cfm?abstract_id=2442357.

44. Carrigan and Shapiro, "What's Wrong with the Back of the Envelope?"
45. Jerry Ellig et al., "Continuity, Change, and Priorities: The Quality and Use of Regulatory Analysis Across U.S. Administrations," *Regulation & Governance* 7, no. 2, June 2013, http://onlinelibrary.wiley.com/doi/10.1111/j.1748-5991.2012.01149.x/abstract.
46. Jerry Ellig and Christopher J. Conover, "Presidential Priorities, Congressional Control, and the Quality of Regulatory Analysis: An Application to Health Care and Homeland Security," *Public Choice* 161, May 15, 2014, http://papers.ssrn.com/sol3/papers.cfm?abstract_id=2495459.
47. Adam Liptak and Coral Davenport, "Supreme Court Blocks Obama's Limits on Power Plants," *New York Times*, June 29, 2015, http://www.nytimes.com/2015/06/30/us/supreme-court-blocks-obamas-limits-on-power-plants.html.
48. The 99 percent figure was calculated because about 3,500 to 4,000 final rules are passed every year, of which roughly fifty have a significant economic impact. The original data can be obtained at the National Archives and Records Administration in the Office of the Federal Register, http://www.archives.gov/federal-register. For a quick reference of the number of final rules issued each year, see Clyde Wayne Crews, "Red Tapeworm 2014: Number of Proposed and Final Rules in the Federal Register," Competitive Enterprise Institute, June 27, 2014, https://cei.org/blog/red-tapeworm-2014-number-proposed-and-final-rules-federal-register.
49. Hester Peirce and Jerry Ellig, "SEC Regulatory Analysis: A Long Way to Go and a Short Time to Get There," George Mason University Mercatus Center, March 31, 2014, http://mercatus.org/publication/sec-regulatory-analysis-long-way-go-and-short-time-get-there.
50. For a good review, see Sam Batkins, "Dodd-Frank Fails at Measuring Costs and Benefits," American Action Forum, February 19, 2015, http://americanactionforum.org/insights/dodd-frank-fails-at-measuring-costs-and-benefits; Andy Winkler et al., "Dodd-Frank at 4: More Regulation, More Regulators, and a Sluggish Housing Market," American Action Forum, July 15, 2014, http://americanactionforum.org/research/dodd-frank-at-4-more-regulation-more-regulators-and-a-sluggish-housing-mark; and Business Roundtable v.SEC, No. 10-1305, 2011 BL 191644 (D.C. Cir. July 22, 2011), http://www.cadc.uscourts.gov/internet/opinions.nsf/89BE4D084BA5EBDA8 52578D5004FBBBE/$file/10-1305-1320103.pdf.
51. "Retrospective Review of Agency Rules," Administrative Conference of the United States, 2014, http://www.acus.gov/research-projects/retrospective-review-agency-rules.
52. "Re-examining Regulations," Government Accountability Office, September 2014.
53. Howard Shelanski, "Retrospective Review: July 2015 Lookback Reports," Office of Management and Budget, August 14, 2015, https://www.whitehouse.gov/blog/2015/08/14/retrospective-review-july-2015-lookback-reports-0.
54. Sam Batkins, "Administration's July 2015 'Regulatory Review' Adds $14.7 Billion in Costs," American Action Forum, August 25, 2015, http://americanactionforum.org/insights/administrations-july-2015-regulatory-review-adds-14.7-billion-in-costs.
55. National Archives and Records Administration, Office of the Federal Register, http://www.archives.gov/federal-register.
56. "Draft 2015 Report to Congress on the Benefits and Costs of Federal Regulations," OIRA, 2015.
57. Susan Dudley, et al., "Public Interest Comment on the OMB's Draft 2014 Report to Congress on the Benefits and Costs of Federal Regulations," Docket ID No. OMB-2014-0002, September 2, 2014, p. 3, http://regulatorystudies.columbian.gwu.edu/sites/regulatorystudies.columbian.gwu.edu/files/downloads/2014-OMB-Report-to-Congress.pdf.

58. Cass R. Sunstein, "The Regulatory Lookback," *Boston University Law Review* 94, 2014, p. 601, http://www.bu.edu/bulawreview/files/2014/08/SUNSTEINDYSFUNCTION. pdf.

59. Jonathan B. Wiener "The Diffusion of Regulatory Oversight," in *Globalization of Cost-Benefit Analysis in Environmental Policy*, ed. Michael A. Livermore and Richard L. Revesz (New York: Oxford University Press, 2013).

60. Jason A. Schwartz, "52 Experiments with Regulatory Review: The Political and Economic Inputs into State Rulemakings," Institute for Policy Integrity, Report no. 6, New York University School of Law, November 2010, http://policyintegrity.org/files/ publications/52_Experiments_with_Regulatory_Review.pdf.

61. Shapiro and Borie-Holtz, *The Politics of Regulatory Reform*.

62. Jason Webb Yackee and Susan Webb Yackee, "Administrative Procedures and Bureaucratic Performance: Is Federal Rule-making 'Ossified'?" *Journal of Public Administration Research and Theory* 20, no. 2, June 2009, http://jpart.oxfordjournals. org/content/ 20/2/261.abstract.

63. Sam Batkins, "Can a Regulatory Budget Trim Red Tape?" American Action Forum blog, August 19, 2013, http://americanactionforum.org/research/can-a-regulatory-budget-trim-red-tape.

64. Official correspondence from David M. Walker, comptroller-general of the United States, to Tom Davis, chairman of the Committee on Government Reform, June 7, 2006, B-302705, http://www.gao.gov/assets/380/377239.pdf.

BALANCE OWED

1. For a review of the literature, see "On Reinhart and Rogoff," Committee for a Responsible Federal Budget, May 3, 2013, http://crfb.org/blogs/reinhart-and-rogoff.

2. Andrea Pescatori et al., "Debt and Growth: Is There a Magic Threshold," IMF Working Paper no. 1434, February 2014, http://www.imf.org/external/pubs/ft/wp/2014/ wp1434.pdf.

3. "Changes in CBO's Baseline Projections Since 2001," Congressional Budget Office, June 7, 2012, http://www.cbo.gov/sites/default/files/cbofiles/attachments/06-07-ChangesSince2001Baseline.pdf.

4. "Summary of Receipts, Outlays, Surpluses, or Deficits as Percentages of GDP: 1930-2020," Office of Management and Budget, table 1.2, http://www.whitehouse.gov/omb/ budget/historicals.

5. For report, debt figures defined as debt held by the public or net public debt. World Economic Outlook Database (October 2015 dataset), International Monetary Fund, https://www.imf.org/external/pubs/ft/weo/2015/02/weodata/index.aspx.

6. World Economic Outlook Database (October 2015 dataset), International Monetary Fund, https://www.imf.org/external/pubs/ft/weo/2015/02/weodata/index.aspx. Simple (not weighted) average used for the "rest of G7" calculations. Note that the U.S. net public debt figures provided by the IMF are slightly different from those provided by the CBO. We use the IMF figures in the accompanying infographic to allow for international comparisons. The CBO does not provide figures for countries other than the United States.

7. "The 2015 Long-Term Budget Outlook," CBO, June 2015, http://www.cbo.gov/sites/ default/files/114th-congress-2015-2016/reports/50250-LongTermBudgetOutlook-3.pdf.

8. "The 2015 Long-Term Budget Outlook," CBO. We use the projection that assumes economic feedback loops of debt; and Richard Jackson et al, "The Global Aging

Preparedness Index, Second Edition," Center for Strategic and International Studies, October 2013, http://csis.org/publication/global-aging-preparedness-index-second-edition.

9. Richard Jackson et al., "The Global Aging Preparedness Index, Second Edition," Center for Strategic and International Studies, October, 2013, http://csis.org/publication/global-aging-preparedness-index-second-edition. These projections assume deficits will be financed with debt. Note that the CSIS U.S. net public debt projections are closer to the CBO's alternative scenario, which many experts believe is more realistic, than the CBO's baseline scenario.

10. Ibid.

11. *OECD Economic Outlook* 2014, no. 1, table 4.4, http://www.oecd-ilibrary.org/economics/oecd-economic-outlook-volume-2014-issue-1_eco_outlook-v2014-1-en. Note that the OECD projections are of net financial liabilities and only go to 2030, whereas the CSIS projections go to 2040.

12. "Monthly Statement of the Public Debt," U.S. Department of Treasury, https://www.treasurydirect.gov/govt/reports/pd/mspd/mspd.htm; and "Major Foreign Holders of Treasury Securities," U.S. Department of Treasury, http://ticdata.treasury.gov/Publish/mfh.txt. Foreign-owned share calculated by dividing the total amount of U.S. marketable debt by the total amount of marketable debt owned by foreigners.

13. "Major Foreign Holders of Treasury Securities," U.S. Department of Treasury.

14. Bill Conerly, "Future of the Dollar as World Reserve Currency," *Forbes*, October 25, 2013, http://www.forbes.com/sites/billconerly/2013/10/25/future-of-the-dollar-as-world-reserve-currency.

15. "Currency Composition of Official Foreign Exchange Reserves (COFER) (in millions of U.S. dollars)," IMF Statistics Department COFER database and International Financial Statistics, http://www.imf.org/external/np/sta/cofer/eng/index.htm.

16. "Market yield on U.S. Treasury securities at 10-year constant maturity, quoted on investment basis," Board of Governors of the Federal Reserve, http://www.federalreserve.gov/datadownload/Chart.aspx?rel=H15&series=0809abf197c17f1ffob2180fe7015cc3&lastObs=&from=04/01/1953&to=04/30/2014&filetype=spreadsheetml&label=include&layout=seriescolumn&pp=.

17. "Outlays by Budget Enforcement Act Category as Percentages of GDP: 1962–2020," Office of Management and Budget, table 8.4, http://www.whitehouse.gov/omb/budget/historicals.

18. "The 2015 Long-Term Budget Outlook," CBO, p. 74.

19. William D. Cohan, "Erskine Bowles: 'We Face the Most Predictable Economic Crisis in History'," *Huffington Post*, April 30, 2012, http://www.huffingtonpost.com/2012/04/30/erskine-bowles-economic-crisis_n_1464999.html.

20. Some legal scholars believe the president could technically bypass Congress, ignore the debt limit, and order the Treasury to keep printing checks, but no president has to date.

21. "Debt Limit," U.S. Department of Treasury, http://www.treasury.gov/initiatives/pages/debtlimit.aspx.

22. "The Cost of Crisis-Driven Fiscal Policy," Peter G. Peterson Foundation, October 2013, p. 6, http://pgpf.org/sites/default/files/10112013_crisis_driven_report_fullreport.pdf. The fiscal policy uncertainty index has four main components: "(a) news mentions of economic policy uncertainty; (b) the value of tax provisions expiring within two years; (c) forecasters' disagreement about government spending one year ahead; (d) forecasters' disagreement about inflation one year ahead."

23. Ibid.

24. Calculations by the CRFB on October 30, 2015. Calculations are for 2011 to 2025, comparing current law from 2011 against deficit reduction legislative changes and no other legislative changes.

25. Doug Elmendorf, "Comments About CBO's Projections for Federal Healthcare Spending," Congressional Budget Office, March 10, 2014, http://www.cbo.gov/publication/45175.
26. "2015 Long-Term Budget Outlook," CBO.
27. Calculations by CRFB on October 30, 2015, using the CBO's June 2015 long-term projection.
28. Andrew Kohut, "Debt and Deficit: A Public Opinion Dilemma," Pew Research Center, June 14, 2012, http://www.people-press.org/2012/06/14/debt-and-deficit-a-public-opinion-dilemma.
29. "In Deficit Debate, Public Resists Cuts in Entitlements and Aid to Poor," Pew Research Center, December, 19, 2013, http://www.people-press.org/2013/12/19/in-deficit-debate-public-resists-cuts-in-entitlements-and-aid-to-poor.
30. Stephen Ohlemacher and Emily Swanson, "AP-GfK Poll: Most back Obama plan to raise investment taxes," Associated Press, February 22, 2015, http://ap-gfkpoll.com/featured/findings-from-our-lastest-poll-2; see also Paul Steinhauser, "Trio of Polls: Support for raising taxes on the wealthy," CNN, December 6, 2012, http://politicalticker.blogs.cnn.com/2012/12/06/trio-of-polls-support-for-raising-taxes-on-wealthy.
31. See, for example, Paul Krugman, "Addicted to the Apocalypse," New York Times, October 24, 2013, http://www.nytimes.com/2013/10/25/opinion/krugman-addicted-to-the-apocalypse.html.
32. Sinichi Nishiyama, "Fiscal Policy Effects in a Heterogeneous-Agent Overlapping-Generations Economy with an Aging Population," CBO Working Paper no. 2013-07, December 2013, http://www.cbo.gov/sites/default/files/cbofiles/attachments/44941-Nishiyama.pdf.
33. Richard Jackson, "What world can teach U.S. about entitlements," CNN, April 25, 2014, http://globalpublicsquare.blogs.cnn.com/2014/04/25/what-world-can-teach-u-s-about-entitlements.
34. Richard Jackson, "Lessons from Abroad for the U.S. Entitlement Debate," Center for Strategic and International Studies, 2014, http://csis.org/files/publication/140324_Jackson_LessonsFromAbroad_Web.pdf.
35. "Fiscal Monitor: Taxing Times," IMF, World Economic and Financial Survey, October 2013, p. 52, http://www.imf.org/external/pubs/ft/fm/2013/02/pdf/fm1302.pdf.
36. Jackson, "Lessons from Abroad."
37. "CBO's Analysis of the President's FY 2015 Budget," Committee for a Responsible Federal Budget (CRFB), April 17, 2014, http://crfb.org/sites/default/files/cbo_analysis_presidents_fy_2015_budget.pdf.
38. "Discretionary Spending in Ryan's FY2015 Budget," CRFB, April 3, 2014, http://crfb.org/blogs/discretionary-spending-ryans-fy-2015-budget.

KEEPING THE EDGE

1. Zoltan J. Acs and David B. Audretsch, "Entrepreneurship, Innovation and Technological Change," Foundations and Trends in Entrepreneurship 1, no. 4, June 2010, http://papers.ssrn.com/sol3/papers.cfm?abstract_id=1629271. Young firms account for a smaller number of patents, but they are significantly more likely to file a radical patent than older firms. See Dan Andrews, Chiara Criscuolo, and Carlo Menon, "Do Resources Flow to Patenting Firms? Cross-Country Evidence from Firm Level Data," OECD Economics Department Working Paper no. 1127, 2014, http://www.

law.northwestern.edu/research-faculty/searlecenter/events/innovation/documents/
AndrewsCriscuoloMenon_SEARLE_jun14.pdf.

2. *OECD Science, Technology and Industry Outlook 2014* (Paris: Organization for Economic Cooperation and Development, 2014), p. 58, http://www.oecd.org/sti/oecd-science-technology-and-industry-outlook-19991428.htm.

3. Internationally comparable data on basic research is poor. Governments often do not distinguish between basic and applied research in national statistics. But according to data collected at the OECD, France is the only G7 country to apportion more money to basic research as a percentage of its GDP (0.59 percent) than the United States (0.55 percent). See figure 6, "Basic research expenditures as a percentage of GDP," Main Science and Technology Indicators, no. 1, OECD, 2012, http://www.oecd-ilibrary.org/science-and-technology/main-science-and-technology-indicators-volume-2012-issue-1/basic-research-expenditure-as-a-percentage-of-gdp_msti-v2012-1-table6-en.

4. "Global Top 100 Companies by Market Capitalisation, March 31, 2015 Update," PricewaterhouseCoopers, http://www.pwc.com/gx/en/audit-services/capital-market/publications/assets/document/pwc-global-top-100-march-update.pdf.

5. Science and Engineering Indicators 2014, figure O-1, "KTI share of GDP, by selected country/economy: 1999, 2005, and 2012," National Science Foundation, http://www.nsf.gov/statistics/seind14/index.cfm/etc/figures.htm.

6. Nicholas Bloom et al., "Management Practices Across Firms and Countries," Harvard Business School Working Paper no. 12-052, December 2011, http://www.hbs.edu/faculty/Publication%20Files/12-052.pdf; Nicholas Bloom, Raffaella Sadun, and John Van Reenen, "Americans Do IT Better: US Multinationals and the Productivity Miracle," *American Economic Review* 102, no. 1, 2012, http://web.stanford.edu/~nbloom/ADIB.pdf.

7. Calculated by PricewaterhouseCoopers, April 2015, based on data from the report "Global Top 100 Companies by Market Capitalisation." This does not include state-owned enterprises (SOEs). Several of the world's largest and most profitable companies are oil and gas SOEs like Saudi Arabia's Saudi Aramco or Mexico's Pemex.

8. Tom Gara, "Boosting R&D Spending: U.S. Companies Lead, But Volkswagen Is King," *Wall Street Journal,* June 11, 2014, http://blogs.wsj.com/corporate-intelligence/2014/06/11/boosting-rd-spending-u-s-companies-lead-but-volkswagen-is-king.

9. "Doing Business 2015: Going Beyond Efficiency," World Bank Group, 2014, http://www.doingbusiness.org/~/media/GIAWB/Doing%20Business/Documents/Annual-Reports/English/DB15-Chapters/DB15-Report-Overview.pdf.

10. Dan Andrews and Chiara Criscuolo, "Knowledge Based Capital, Innovation and Resource Allocation," OECD Economics Department Working Papers no. 1046, May 2013, p. 23, http://www.oecd.org/officialdocuments/publicdisplaydocumentpdf/?cote=ECO/WKP%282013%2938&docLanguage=En.

11. For entrepreneurship rates, see Chiara Criscuolo, Peter N. Gal, and Carlo Menon, "The Dynamics of Employment Growth: New Evidence from 18 Countries," OECD Science, Technology and Industry Policy Papers no. 14, 2014, http://www.oecd-ilibrary.org/science-and-technology/the-dynamics-of-employment-growth_5jz417hj6hg6-en. For firm pace of growth and death, see Albert Bravo Biosca, "Growth Dynamics: Exploring Business Growth and Contraction in Europe and the US," NESTA Research Report, November 2010, http://www.nesta.org.uk/sites/default/files/growth_dynamics.pdf.

12. Dan Andrews and Federico Cingano, "Public Policy and Resource Allocation: Evidence from Firms in OECD Countries," *Economic Policy* 29, no. 78, April 2014, http://papers.ssrn.com/sol3/papers.cfm?abstract_id=2443991.

13. Josh Lerner, *Boulevard of Broken Dreams: Why Public Efforts to Boost Entrepreneurship and Venture Capital Have Failed—and What to Do About It* (Princeton, NJ: Princeton University Press, 2009).

14. Edmund S. Phelps, "Entrepreneurial Culture," *Wall Street Journal*, February 12, 2007, http://www.wsj.com/articles/SB117124449952605357; Amar Bhidé, *The Venturesome Economy: How Innovation Sustains Prosperity in a More Connected World* (Princeton, NJ: Princeton University Press, 2008).

15. "Global Entrepreneurship Monitor 2014 Global Report," Global Entrepreneurship Research Association, 2014, http://www.gemconsortium.org/report.

16. Richard M. Locke and Rachel L. Wellhausen, eds, *Production in the Innovation Economy* (Cambridge, MA: MIT Press, 2014).

17. Bronwyn H. Hall, "The Stock Market's Valuation of R&D Investment during the 1980's," *American Economic Review: Papers and Proceedings* 83, no. 2, May 1993, https://ideas.repec.org/a/aea/aecrev/v83y1993i2p259-64.html.

18. Ashish Arora, Sharon Belenzon, and Andrea Patacconi, "Killing the Golden Goose? The Decline of Science in Corporate R&D," NBER Working Paper no. 20902, January 2015, http://www.nber.org/papers/w20902.pdf.

19. Ibid.

20. Dennis Patrick Leyden and Albert N. Link, *Public Sector Entrepreneurship: U.S. Technology and Innovation Policy* (New York: Oxford University Press, 2015); William J. Baumol, Robert Litan, and Carl Schramm, "Capitalism: Growth Miracle Maker, Growth Saboteur," in Zoltan Acs, David Audretsch, and Robert Strom, eds., *Entrepreneurship, Growth, and Public Policy* (New York: Cambridge University Press, 2009), p. 28.

21. Science and Engineering Indicators 2010, "Exports of high-technology manufactured goods, by country/economy: 1995–2008," National Science Foundation, http://www.nsf.gov/statistics/digest10/globalization.cfm#5.

22. Arora, Belenzon, and Patacconi, "Killing the Golden Goose?"

23. Science and Engineering Indicators 2012, figure 5-28, "Share of U.S., EU, and China S&E articles that are in the world's top 1% of cited articles: 2000–10," National Science Foundation, http://www.nsf.gov/statistics/seind12/c5/c5s4.htm.

24. CWTS Leiden Ranking 2015, http://www.leidenranking.com.

25. OECD Science, Technology and Industry Outlook 2014, figure 6.6, "Licensing income from public research, 2004–11," p. 212, http://www.oecd-ilibrary.org/docserver/download/9214011e.pdf?expires=1444401886&id=id&accname=ocid195235&checksum=F83C207AEFDFD03D205CD32F602FFF92.

26. Many countries are adopting legislation similar to the U.S. Bayh-Dole Act, which gave universities patenting rights to research funded by public money.

27. Philippe Aghion et al., "The Governance and Performance of Research Universities: Evidence from Europe and the U.S.," NBER Working Paper no. 14851, April 2009, http://www.nber.org/papers/w14851.pdf.

28. Richard F. Celeste, Ann Girswold, and Miron L. Straf, eds., *Furthering America's Research Enterprise* (Washington, DC: National Academies Press, 2014).

29. Pierre Azoulay, Joshua S. Gradd Zivin, and Gustavo Manso, "Incentives and Creativity: Evidence from the Academic Life Sciences," NBER Working Paper no. 15466, October 2009, http://www.nber.org/papers/w15466.pdf.

30. The NIH is trying to combat this problem through programs like the Pathway to Independence Award for younger researchers.

31. OECD Education at a Glance 2014, table B1.4, "Annual expenditure per student by educational institutions for all services, relative to GDP per capita (2011)," p. 218, http://www.oecd-ilibrary.org/docserver/download/9614011e.pdf?expires=1444402255 &id=id&accname=guest&checksum=53ED9BB503A2BE6C85D487CD1625F46E.

32. Science and Engineering Indicators 2014, table 4-2, "Annual Rates of Growth in U.S. R&D Expenditures, total and by performing sectors: 1991–2011," National Science Foundation, http://www.nsf.gov/statistics/seind14/index.cfm/chapter-4/tt04-02.htm.

33. Claudia Goldin and Lawrence F. Katz, *The Race Between Education and Technology* (Cambridge, MA: Harvard University Press, 2008), pp. 11–43.

34. Science and Engineering Indicators 2014, "Figure O-9: Researchers as a share of total employment in selected countries/regions: 1995–2011," National Science Foundation, http://www.nsf.gov/statistics/seind14/index.cfm/etc/figures.htm.

35. Jyoti Madhusoodanan, "2014 Life Sciences Salary Survey," *Scientist*, November 1, 2014, http://www.the-scientist.com/?articles.view/articleNo/41316/title/2014-Life-Sciences-Salary-Survey; "Remuneration of Researchers in the Public and Private Sectors," European Commission, 2007, http://ec.europa.eu/euraxess/pdf/research_policies/final_report.pdf.

36. OECD Science, Technology and Industry Scoreboard 2013, "Impact of Scientific Authors, by Category of Mobility, 1996–2011," p. 133, http://www.oecd-ilibrary.org/science-and-technology/oecd-science-technology-and-industry-scoreboard-2013/impact-of-scientific-authors-by-category-of-mobility-1996-2011_sti_scoreboard-2013-graph120-en.

37. Michael G. Finn, "Stay Rates of Foreign Doctorate Recipients from U.S. Universities, 2011," National Center for Science and Engineering Statistics of the National Science Foundation, January 2014, http://orise.orau.gov/files/sep/stay-rates-foreign-doctorate-recipients-2011.pdf.

38. Paula E. Stephan and Sharon G. Levin, "Exceptional Contributions to U.S. Science by the Foreign-born and Foreign-educated," *Population Research and Policy Review* 20, 2001, pp. 59–79, http://www.umsl.edu/~levins/Files/Exceptional%20contributions%20to%20US%20science%20by%20the%20foreign-born%20and%20foreign-educated.pdf.

39. OECD Science, Technology and Industry Scoreboard 2013, "Impact of Scientific Authors," http://www.oecd-ilibrary.org/science-and-technology/oecd-science-technology-and-industry-scoreboard-2013/impact-of-scientific-authors-by-category-of-mobility-1996-2011_sti_scoreboard-2013-graph120-en.

40. Cornelia Lawson et al., "International Careers of Researchers in Biomedical Sciences: A Comparison of the U.S. and the UK," Science Policy Research Unit Working Paper Series no. 2015-09, March 2015, http://papers.ssrn.com/sol3/papers.cfm?abstract_id=2609014.

41. "Researchers on the Move: The Impact of Brain Circulation," OECD Directorate for Science, Technology and Industry, 2013, http://www.oecd.org/sti/researchers-on-the-move-the-impact-of-brain-circulation.pdf.

42. Paula Stephan, Giuseppe Scellato, and Chiara Franzoni, "International Competition for PhDs and Postdoctoral Scholars: What Does (and Does Not) Matter," *Innovation Policy and the Economy* 15, no. 1, August 2015, pp.73–113, http://www.nber.org/chapters/c13403.pdf; and Bogdan State et al., "Where Does the U.S. Stand in the International Competition for Talent? Evidence from LinkedIn Data," April 2, 2014, http://paa2014.princeton.edu/papers/141226.

43. For a good review of trends in student migration, see "Open Doors 2014: Report on International Educational Exchange," Institute of International Education, Washington, DC, November, 2014, http://www.iie.org/Research-and-Publications/Open-Doors.

44. Carol Hymowitz, "Foreign-Born CEOs Are Increasing in the U.S., Rarer Overseas," *Wall Street Journal*, May 25, 2004, http://www.wsj.com/articles/SB108543349255419931.

45. Stephen Martin and John T. Scott, "The Nature of Innovation Market Failure and the Design of Public Support for Private Innovation," *Research Policy* 29, 2000, pp. 437–47, http://citeseerx.ist.psu.edu/viewdoc/download?doi=10.1.1.196.7452& rep= rep1&type=pdf.

46. Main Science and Technology Indicators 2013, no. 1, table 53, "Government intramural expenditure on R&D (GOVERD) as a percentage of GDP," http://www.oecd-ilibrary. org/docserver/download/9420130111eit053.pdf?expires=1435333569&id=id&accn ame=ocid195235&checksum=9A58902C17CD390858D6F79AA4F16BE7. Of G7 countries, only Germany spends more public funds on R&D as a percentage of GDP and the United States is close behind.

47. For government support for business R&D, see OECD R&D Tax Incentive Indicators, "Direct funding of business R&D and tax incentives for R&D, 2012 and 2006," December 2014, OECD National Accounts and Main Science and Technology Indicators, http://www.oecd.org/sti/outlook/e-outlook/stipolicyprofiles/ competencestoinnovate/financingbusinessrdandinnovation.htm; for basic research spending, see figure 6, "Basic research expenditures as a percentage of GDP," OECD's Main Science and Technology Indicators 2012.

48. Matt Hourihan, "The Federal Life Sciences Budget: Update and Outlook," presented at the San Antonio Life Sciences Institute Academy Innovation Forum, March 25, 2015.

49. There is little basis for R&D benchmarks in empirical research. At the firm level, an extra dollar spent on R&D does lead to an extra dollar's worth of productivity. See Bronwyn H. Hall, "Effectiveness of Research and Experimentation Tax Credits: Critical Literature Review and Research Design," Office of Technology Assessment, U.S. Congress, June 15, 1995, http://eml.berkeley.edu/~bhhall/papers/BHH95%20 OTArtax.pdf; *Measuring the Impacts of Federal Investments in Research: A Workshop Summary* (Washington, DC: National Academies Press, 2011), http://www.nap. edu/catalog/13208/measuring-the-impacts-of-federal-investments-in-research-a-workshop. But at the macroeconomic or national level, economists know extremely little about optimal public R&D investment levels. It is especially hard with basic research, which can have diffuse effects and take decades to percolate through the economy. There is no federal office that coordinates and assesses the overall performance of R&D expenditures. Fortunately, there has been a big push in the last few years with Science of Science Policy and STARMETRICS initiatives, which collect better data and think through the best way to measure impact. For background, see Bruce A. Weinberg et al., "Science Funding and Short-Term Economic Activity," *Science* 344, no. 6179, April 4, 2014, http://www.sciencemag.org/content/344/6179/41. summary; Julia Lane and Stefano Bertuzzi, "Measuring the Results of Science Investments," *Science* 331, no. 6018, February 11, 2011, http://www.sciencemag.org/ content/331/6018/678.summary.

50. Fred Block and Matthew R. Keller, eds., *State of Innovation: The U.S. Government's Role in Technology Development* (Boulder, CO: Paradigm, 2011), pp. 154–72.

51. Bronwyn H. Hall, "Effectiveness of Research and Experimentation Tax Credits," 1995.

52. The bulk of empirical evidence points to ratios that are not far away from one. See, for example, Bronwyn Hall and John Van Reenan, "How Effective are Fiscal Incentives for R&D? A Review of the Evidence," NBER Working Paper no. 7098, April 1999, http:// www.nber.org/papers/w7098.pdf.

53. Xulia Gonzalez, Jordi Jaumandreu, and Consuelo Pazo, "Barriers to Innovation and Subsidy Effectiveness," *Rand Journal of Economics* 36, no. 4, 2005, http://people. bu.edu/jordij/papers/glez,jaumandreu,pazo.pdf.

54. Bronwyn H. Hall and Alessandro Maffioli, "Evaluating the Impact of Technology Development Funds in Emerging Economies: Evidence from Latin-America," Inter-American Development Bank Working Paper no. OVE/WP-01/08, January 2008, http://idbdocs.iadb.org/WSDocs/getdocument.aspx?docnum=1404775.

55. Ben Westmore, "R&D, Patenting and Growth: The Role of Public Policy," OECD Economics Department Working Papers no. 1047, 2013, http://www.oecd-ilibrary.org/economics/r-d-patenting-and-growth_5k46h2rfb4f3-en.

56. Isabel Busom, "Tax Incentives or Subsidies for R&D?" UNU-MERIT Working Paper no. 2012-056, July 1, 2012, http://papers.ssrn.com/sol3/papers.cfm?abstract_id=2330222.

57. Alberto Bravo-Biosca et al., "What Drives the Dynamics of Business Growth?" OECD Science, Technology and Industry Papers No. 1, 2013, http://www.oecd-ilibrary.org/science-and-technology/what-drives-the-dynamics-of-business-growth_5k486qtttq46-en; Andrews and Criscuolo, "Knowledge Based Capital, Innovation and Resource Allocation."

58. Dirk Czarnitzki and Bernd Ebersberger, "Do Direct R&D Subsidies Lead to the Monopolization of R&D in the Economy," ZEW Discussion Paper no. 10-078, Mannheim, 2010, http://ftp.zew.de/pub/zew-docs/dp/dp10078.pdf.

59. Isabel Busom, "Tax Incentives or Subsidies for R&D?"; Massimo G. Colombo et al., "R&D Subsidies and the Performance of High-Tech Start-Ups," *Economics Letters* 112, no. 1, 2011, pp. 97–99, http://papers.ssrn.com/sol3/papers.cfm?abstract_id=1679064.

60. Others include the Small Business Technology Transfer program, Advanced Technology Program, and the Manufacturing Extension Partnership program. The 1980 Bayh-Dole Act shifted intellectual property rights to universities that use public research funding, which made it easier for universities to commercialize their research. The 1980 Stevenson-Wydler Technology Innovation Act allowed national laboratories to look for commercialization opportunities of publicly funded research.

61. Lewis M. Branscomb and Philip E. Auerswald, "Between Invention and Innovation: An Analysis of Funding for Early-Stage Technology Development," NIST GCR no. 02–841, National Institute of Standards and Technology, November 2002, http://belfercenter.hks.harvard.edu/files/betweeninnovation.pdf.

62. Block and Keller, *State of Innovation.*

63. Joshua Lerner, "The Government as Venture Capitalist: The Long-Run Impact of the SBIR Program," *Journal of Business* 72, no. 3, July 1999, http://www.jstor.org/stable/10.1086/209616; Sabrina T. Howell, "Financing Constraints as Barriers to Innovation: Evidence from R&D Grants to Energy Startups," Job Market Paper, January 7, 2015, http://economics.yale.edu/sites/default/files/howell_innovation_finance_jmp_jan7.pdf.

64. Sabrina Howell, "Financing Constraints."

65. Albert N. Link and John T. Scott, *Bending the Arc of Innovation: Public Support of R&D in Small, Entrepreneurial Firms* (New York: Palgrave Pivot, 2013), http://www.palgrave.com/page/detail/bending-the-arc-of-innovation-albert-n-link/?K=9781137371584.

66. Some new programs include the NIH's National Center for Advancing Translational Sciences, the NSF's I-Corps, and the Office of Innovation and Entrepreneurship's i6 Challenge.

67. For example, ARPA-E helps energy companies break into energy markets, which involves more product development than pure research. Also see "Federal Policies and Innovation," Congressional Budget Office, November 2014, https://www.cbo.gov/sites/default/files/113th-congress-2013-2014/reports/49487-Innovation.pdf.

68. For further discussion of innovation prizes, see Erik Brynjolfsson and Andrew McAfee, *The Second Machine Age: Work, Progress, and Prosperity in a Time of Brilliant Technologies* (New York: W. W. Norton, 2014).

69. For more information, see http://www.challenge.gov/list.

70. Sridhar Kota, "Revitalizing American Manufacturing: Putting '&' Back in R&D," presentation at Nanocellulose Nanomaterials—A Path Toward Commercialization, Washington, DC, May 20, 2014, http://www.nano.gov/sites/default/files/nanocellulose-kota.pdf.

71. Charles W. Wessner and Alan Wm. Wolff, eds., *Rising to the Challenge: U.S. Innovation Policy for the Global Economy* (Washington, DC: National Academies Press, 2012), pp. 74–75.

72. Hourihan, "The Federal Life Sciences Budget."

73. "The Future of Solar Energy: An Interdisciplinary MIT Study," Energy Initiative at the Massachusetts Institute of Technology, May 2015, https://mitei.mit.edu/system/files/MIT%20Future%20of%20Solar%20Energy%20Study_compressed.pdf.

74. For U.S. dominance in patents, see International Energy Agency, "Energy Technology RD&D and Innovation," figure 5.6, "Clean energy patents filed by inventor's country of origin," http://www.iea.org/etp/tracking/figures/rdd_innovation.

75. Fraunhofer Institute for Solar Energy Systems, "Photovoltaics Report," presented in Freiburg, Germany, August 10, 2015, slide 11, https://www.ise.fraunhofer.de/de/downloads/pdf-files/aktuelles/photovoltaics-report-in-englischer-sprache.pdf.

76. "Renewables 2015 Global Status Report," Renewable Energy Policy Network for the 21st Century (REN21), 2015, pp. 8–10. http://www.ren21.net/status-of-renewables/global-status-report.

77. Ibid, p. 20.

78. NIH funding doubled in just four years, leading to a surge in graduate fellowship and lab construction. But after the increase flattened out, there was an uncomfortable adjustment for young scientists and construction projects.

79. The 2007 America COMPETES Act had pledged to double the budget over seven years for research accounts at the National Science Foundation, the Department of Energy's Office of Science, and the National Institutes of Standards and Technology.

80. Celeste, Girswald, and Straf, *Furthering America's Research Enterprise.*

81. OECD Science, Technology and Industry Scoreboard 2013, figure 4.3.1, "Government funding of health-related R&D, 2012," http://www.oecd-ilibrary.org/sites/sti_scoreboard-2013-en/04/03/index.html?contentType=&itemId=%2Fcontent%2Fchapter%2Fsti_scoreboard-2013-31-en&mimeType=text%2Fhtml&containerItemId=%2Fcontent%2Fserial%2F20725345&access ItemIds=%2Fcontent%2Fbook%2Fst_scoreboard-2013-en.

82. Matthew Herper, "The Decline of Pharmaceutical Research, Measured in New Drugs and Dollars," *Forbes,* June 27, 2011, http://www.forbes.com/sites/matthewherper/2011/06/27/the-decline-of-pharmaceutical-researchmeasured-in-new-drugs-and-dollars.

83. See, for example, Michael A. Heller, "The Boundaries of Private Property," *Yale Law Journal* 108, no. 5, 1999, http://papers.ssrn.com/sol3/papers.cfm?abstract_id=146230; Simon Johnson, John McMillan, and Christopher Woodruff, "Property Rights and Finance," NBER Working Paper no. 8852, March 2002, http://www.nber.org/papers/w8852.

84. Michele Boldrin and David K. Levine, "The Case Against Patents," Federal Reserve Bank of St. Louis Working Paper no. 2012-035A, September 2012, https://research.stlouisfed.org/wp/2012/2012-035.pdf.

85. James Bessen and Michael J. Meurer, *Patent Failure: How Judges, Bureaucrats, and Lawyers Put Innovators at Risk* (Princeton, NJ: Princeton University Press, 2008).

86. "Intellectual Property: Assessing Factors That Affect Patent Infringement Litigation Could Help Improve Patent Quality," U.S. Government Accountability Office, August 2013, http://www.gao.gov/assets/660/657103.pdf.

87. James Bessen and Michael J. Meurer, "The Patent Litigation Explosion," *Loyola University Chicago Law Journal* 45, no. 2, 2013, http://lawecommons.luc.edu/cgi/viewcontent.cgi?article=1421&context=luclj.

88. Iain M. Cockburn and Megan J. MacGarvie, "Patents, Thickets and the Financing of Early-Stage Firms: Evidence from the Software Industry," *Journal of Economics & Management Strategy* 18, no. 3, 2009, http://onlinelibrary.wiley.com/doi/10.1111/j.1530-9134.2009.00228.x/full.

89. Data compiled by Patent Freedom, http://www.patentfreedom.com.

90. For reform ideas, see "Federal Policies and Innovation," CBO, pp. 36–40.

91. James Bessen and Michael J. Meurer, "The Private Costs of Patent Litigation," *Journal of Law, Economics and Policy* 9, no.1, 2012, http://jlep.net/home/wp-content/uploads/2013/02/JLEP-Issue-9.1.pdf.

92. See H.R. 3309 Innovation Act, sponsored by Rep. Bob Goodlatte (R-VA), https://www.congress.gov/bill/113th-congress/house-bill/3309.

93. Demetrios G. Papademetriou and Madeleine Sumption, "The Role of Immigration in Fostering Competitiveness in the United States," Migration Policy Institute, May 2011, p. 14, http://www.migrationpolicy.org/research/role-immigration-fostering-competitiveness-united-states.

94. Nonprofits like universities and public research labs, however, are exempt from the H-1B cap.

95. For share of permanent visas work-related, see International Migration Outlook 2014, figure 1.4, "Permanent immigration by category of entry or of status change into selected OECD countries, 2012," OECD, 2014, http://ekke.gr/ocd/wp-content/uploads/2014/12/SOPEMI-2014-E.pdf; for share of immigrants with a tertiary degree, see International Migration Outlook 2014, figure 2.2, "Share of the highly educated among the foreign- and native-born of working age (fifteen- to sixty-four-year-olds), 2013"; for index comparing restrictiveness of immigration systems for the high skilled, see Lucie Cerna, *Immigration Policy and the Global Competition for Talent* (London: Palgrave, 2015).

Acknowledgments

This collection is the product of several years of work undertaken as part of the Council on Foreign Relations' (CFR) Renewing America initiative, a special project launched in connection with CFR's ninetieth anniversary. The initiative was premised on the understanding that the United States' ability to influence world events rests on a robust, competitive economy, and that successfully addressing economic challenges is therefore vitally important for the success of U.S. foreign policy.

In order to delve into the various policy areas that support U.S. economic competitiveness, we have depended greatly on assistance from experts in each of these fields, and we are extremely grateful for their input into this project. We would like to thank several people in particular: on education policy, Joshua S. Goodman, Sean Reardon, Anthony P. Carnevale, and the entire education team at the New America Foundation, especially Jason Delisle and Laura Bornfreund; on transportation infrastructure, Jonathan L. Gifford, Joung Lee, Robert Poole, and Scott Thomasson; on trade and investment policy, Chad P. Bown, Edward Gresser, and Matthew Slaughter; on corporate tax policy, Martin A. Sullivan, Jane G. Gravelle, and Stephen E. Shay; on worker retraining, Thomas Bailey, Christopher T. King, and Carolyn Heinrich; on regulation, Curtis W. Copeland, Sam Batkins, Nikolai Malyshev, and Susan E. Dudley; on debt and deficits, Marc Goldwein and his team at the Committee for a Responsible Budget; and on innovation, Andrew W. Wyckoff, Paula E. Stephan, Varun Sivaram, Matt Hourihan, and James Bessen.

In addition, each of the reports that make up this collection was also reviewed by CFR's Senior Vice President, Director of Studies, and Maurice R. Greenberg Chair James M. Lindsay and Vice President, Global Communications and Media Relations, Lisa Shields, and we thank them for their helpful comments and feedback. Michael A. Levi, CFR's David M. Rubenstein senior fellow for energy and the environment and director of the Maurice R. Greenberg Center for Geoeconomic Studies, also provided valuable feedback on the innovation report.

This work is the product of a team effort. The CFR Publications team played an essential role throughout the publication of the individual progress reports and scorecards, and in the production of this book. We would like to thank Patricia Dorff, Eli Dvorkin, Elizabeth Dana, Ashley Bregman, and Lia Norton. The superb graphics team at Objective Subject was responsible for the infographics, and we would like to thank especially Blake Olmstead, John Lunn, and Jessica Wilson. CFR's Communications team was deeply involved in promoting this work through the media and social media. We would like to thank Lisa Shields, Iva Zoric, Anya Schmemann, Melinda Wuellner, Tricia Kaphleke, Jenny Mallamo, Megan Daley, Courtney Doggart, and Samantha Tartas. We would also like to thank the CFR.org team, especially Robert McMahon, Jonathan Masters, and contributor Steven Markovich. Patrick Costello played a vital role in bringing this work to the attention of members of Congress and their staff, Thomas Bowman led the outreach to administration officials, and Irina Faskianos and her team circulated the reports widely to state and local government officials. We thank several research associates and interns, including Robert Maxim (who authored the worker retraining chapter), Jane McMurrey (who assisted on the trade chapter), Michael Ng, Frederik Claessens, and Janine L'Heureux.

We would like to thank CFR President Richard N. Haass for his vision in launching the Renewing America initiative and for his constant support of this work. His own book, *Foreign Policy Begins at Home*, underscores why these issues matter so much for America's role in the world. And finally, none of this work would have been possible without the ongoing, generous support of Bernard L. Schwartz and the Bernard and Irene Schwartz Foundation.

Edward Alden and Rebecca Strauss
January 2016

About the Authors

Edward Alden is the Bernard L. Schwartz senior fellow at the Council on Foreign Relations and director of the Renewing America publication series.

Rebecca Strauss is associate director of the Renewing America publication series.

CPSIA information can be obtained at www.ICGtesting.com
Printed in the USA
BVOW11s0008270116

434369BV00002B/3/P